Luther and His Progeny

500 Years of Protestantism and Its Consequences for Church, State, and Society

LUTHER
AND HIS PROGENY

*500 Years of Protestantism
and Its Consequences for
Church, State, and Society*

A ROMAN FORUM BOOK

Edited by
John C. Rao

Angelico Press

First published in the USA
© Angelico Press 2017

For information, address:
Angelico Press
4709 Briar Knoll Dr.
Kettering, OH 45429
www.angelicopress.com
info@angelicopress.com

978-1-62138-254-6 pbk
978-1-62138-255-3 cloth
978-1-62138-253-9 ebook

Cover image: Ferdinand Pauwels,
Luther Posting the 95 Theses (detail), 1872
Cover design: Michael Schrauzer

CONTENTS

*To All the Saints of the Catholic Reform and the Fathers of the
Council of Trent: Defenders of the Faith, of Human Reason,
and of the True Liberty of the Christian Man*

Introduction

Half a Millennium of
Total Depravity (1517–2017)

A Critique of Luther's Impact
in the Year of His "Catholic" Apotheosis

O UR CIVILIZATION is so sick that even the best efforts to prop up its tottering remains manifest the same illness that is step by step bringing the entire structure crumbling down. The disease in question is a willful, prideful, irrational, and ignorant obsession with "freedom." And it is a malady that gained its initial effective entry into Christendom in union with the concept of the natural world as the realm of "total depravity."

It is crucially important that we both diagnose this malady and identify its historical connection with Martin Luther and the Protestant Revolution, popularly but erroneously styled a "Reformation." It is crucially important that we do so *now* because of the efforts being made this year to use the occasion of the five hundredth anniversary of Luther's declaration of war on Christendom in 1517 as an opportunity radically to rewrite and reinterpret that event and misrepresent its true nature.

1517 was not the source of our woe—any more, for that matter, than was 1962 and the opening of Second Vatican Council. Already long before 1517, all of the spiritual, intellectual, political, and social diseases that had menaced for centuries the Camp of the Saints had gathered together, ready for injection into the lymphatic system of Catholic Christendom as one "mega-malady." The common element of these various errors was a rejection of the need, or capacity, for the individual and his entire environment to be corrected, perfected, and transformed under the Kingship of Christ with the aid of faith, grace, and reason on the one hand, and social authority, both supernatural and natural, on the other.

Anyone in 1517 looking for an excuse to shake off the yoke of external authorities and declare his independence had available an embarrassment of arguments from a myriad of sources indicating that his own individual reason and conscience were a reliable and sufficient guide along the pathway to God. Nevertheless, the Christian man of the Late Middle Ages was too aware of the reality of sin to leap *directly* into an adulation of his individual willfulness. In one of history's more bizarre ironies, a pious entry was provided by the concept, propounded by Luther and Calvin, of the "total depravity" of the individual and the world in which he lived after Original Sin. Luther and Calvin argued for each believer's need to rely solely on God's grace to save him and taught the hopelessness of man's efforts to transform himself and the communities of which he was a member in a way that would conform to the commands of Christ and be pleasing to God.

This ostensibly humble renunciation of the call to "be perfect as your Heavenly Father is perfect" was offered by Luther as a means of escape from the existential despair that tormented him in his failed efforts to live up to the ideal of the Christian life (as he interpreted it), and that he then projected onto Christendom. The remedy he offered was freedom from a Law that man, in his depraved, post-lapsarian state, could not possibly aspire to keeping. From there, it proved to be very easy over the course of a couple of generations for this *negative* definition of "liberty"—a "freedom" *from* the Law—to be transformed, in the Enlightenment, into the foundation for a *positive* new and redemptive order of things. It did not take long for the Christian who had humbly declined the offer of a remedy for sin and a pathway to sanctity to begin to exult in his sins and imperfections; to see the chasm that existed between himself and God—according to Luther's teaching—not as something tragic, but as a rather desirable breathing space, the elbow room he needed to explore and develop his uniquely human capacities, without reference to God. From there, of course, it was an even shorter step to dispensing with God altogether. "Total depravity" became a self-fulfilling doctrine and the individual who could never hope to be reconciled with God made of himself a god instead.

Convinced that many of our ecclesiastical leaders would turn 2017 into a year-long celebration of the accomplishments of Luther & Company—and that Catholics need to be aware of what an historical, theological, and socio-political travesty such a celebration would be—the international faculty of the Roman Forum dedicated its twenty-fourth annual Summer Symposium at Gardone Riviera in northern Italy in 2016 to "Half a Millennium of Total Depravity (1517–2017): A Critique of Luther's Impact on the Eve of His "Catholic" Apotheosis." The lectures delivered at that event are collected in the book that the reader has before him.

Neither the symposium nor the text emerging from it was conceived of and planned as a unified, systematic history and analysis of Luther's teachings and their impact—such studies can be found elsewhere. Instead, each speaker chose his own subject, from within his own particular area of expertise. Consequently, the reader will notice nuances of emphasis and even disagreements of interpretation. Nevertheless, the fact that speakers representing a variety of disciplines had something to say about the impact of Protestantism in those different fields is an indication of the extent to which Protestantism has shaped the world in which we live.

One comment needs to be made regarding citations from Luther used by the various contributors. The accuracy and meaning of citations from Luther are often subjects of vigorous debate—both between and within the camps of his supporters and opponents. Such differences of opinion are partly due to the fact that many references come from notes taken by Johannes Mathesius and others during Luther's relaxed (and therefore possibly misleading) chats among friends, published in 1566 as his *Table Talk*. But debate is also engendered by Luther's own perplexing and often seemingly contradictory attempts to respond to the consequences of his central themes. Debated citations that are used in this text are quoted because of the authors' firm conviction that consideration of the whole of Luther's position justifies their inclusion as part of the evidence to be reviewed by them.

Luther and His Progeny is rather loosely organized in three parts, the first of which serves as a theological-philosophical-historical introduction (John Rao, "*A Necessary Reform, Depraved From Birth*"; Thomas Stark, "*Man as Victim of a Divine Tyrant: Luther's Theology of a Self-Contradicting God*"; Sebastian Morello, "*The Northern Renaissance and the Protestant Revolt*") that lays out the complex context for the Protestant Reformation and discusses some prescient appreciations of where it would lead from contemporaries such as St Thomas More. This continues with two chapters developing the tragic consequences of Protestantism over the course of the centuries to come (Miguel Ayuso, "*The Protestant Matrix*" and John Rao, "*From Man's Total Depravity to the Triumph of the Human Will: Religious Disunity and the Birth of Pragmatic Christianity*").

A second section handles specific developments of the Protestant ethos concerning the socio-political order (Christopher Ferrara, "*Luther's Disembodied Grace and the Graceless Body Politic*"), economics (Rev. Richard Munkelt, "*Religious Evolution and Revolution in the Triumph of Homo Economicus*"), law (Brian McCall, "*The New Protestant Bargain: The Influence of Protestant Theology on Contract and Property*"

3

Law"), and various sciences (Rev. Brian Muzas, "*STEM and the Reformation: Astronomy, Metallurgy, and Economics*").

Finally, *Luther and His Progeny* concludes with three chapters that bring our story down to the present and its unrepentant eagerness to carry the logic of Protestantism to its final conclusions, whatever the horrific consequences for the human person and the world in which he lives. One of these (Msgr. Ignacio Barreiro-Carámbula, "*Negative Liberty, Protestantism, and the War on Nature*") picks up on the theme of "negative liberty" and its most recent aberrant applications. Another (Fr. John Hunwicke, "*Multiple Anti-Semitisms in Luther, Lutheranism, and Bergoglio*") discusses the first Reformer's virulent language concerning the Jews and its continuing theological impact in 2017. The last entry in the text is a tragic "looking back" to a country that once was Catholic and has now been Protestant for almost five hundred years; a chapter that asks poignant questions regarding how believers can recapture a willfully distorted tradition (Clemens Cavallin, "*Sweden and the Five Hundred Year Reformation Anamnesis: A Catholic Perspective*").

It is fitting that this book ends with Cavallin's chapter on Sweden, because it was to Lund that Pope Francis went at the end of October 2016 in order to indicate his pontificate's commitment to celebrating the Protestant Reformation. The faculty of the Roman Forum hopes that a reading of *Luther and His Progeny* will indicate what a betrayal of the Catholic Tradition such a "celebration" entails.

Still, we have to admit that the pope's positive appraisal is not particularly surprising. For it was through a similarly willful picking and choosing among totally contradictory elements in Luther's thought—according to what it was that each man arbitrarily wished to find in his arguments—that the influence of the heresiarch made its first tragic steps five hundred years ago along its devastating path to the present. It is our hope that the readers of this book will come to understand the profound assault on the reason, the freedom, and the dignity of man that continuing along this path to "liberation" from the law of God entails; and that in grasping its message they will join in awakening their fellow Catholics to zealous outrage over celebration of half a millennium of contempt for the command to transform all things in Christ.

1

A Necessary Reform, Depraved From Birth

John C. Rao

DESIDERIUS ERASMUS (1466–1536), in a well-known letter to Pope Leo X in 1517, suggested that Christendom was entering into an "age of gold." And, indeed, there was much in that year—in which the Protestant Reformation began—to justify the great Rotterdam humanist's hopes for the future. Nevertheless, instead of an "age of gold," what developed from the sixteenth century onwards involved not only the destruction of the unity of western Christianity, but also the devastation of a civilization integrally connected with the Catholic religion. The culture that has taken its place is that of the triumph of arbitrary willfulness; the triumph, as the historian Richard Gawthorp notes, "of the promethean thirst for material power that serves as the most profound stimulus behind all modern western cultures."[1]

Christendom of the year 1517 was a complex sacred order—an international order full of diverse national, local, religious, state, economic, and cultural societies. An enlightened theologian could explain that all these societies were in one way or another intended to aid men to draw from nature all the possibilities for living well that the good Creator God had placed within it; that, freed from sin and enlivened by grace, they were all designed to help their members to perfect themselves and attain eternal life. He might point out that this Christian "society of

---

1. Richard Gawthorp, *Pietism and the Making of Eighteenth Century Prussia* (New York: Cambridge University Press, 1993), 284; Léon Halkin, *Erasmus: A Critical Biography* (Cambridge: Blackwell, 1994), 98.

diverse societies" reflected the "multiplicity in unity" of Christ that was the fruit of the Incarnation and obedience to the Redeemer. Drawing on the work of historians, he perhaps would also boast that such a world was kept on the right intellectual and spiritual path by a network of universities, academies, and confraternities, as well as through the work of religious and secular preachers using devotional practices both traditional and innovative. And, finally, he might argue that, having recovered from a myriad of enormous problems deeply troubling the last two hundred years—the Great Western Schism being but one example—and now invigorated by voyages of discovery in Africa, Asia, and the Americas, Christendom, for the first time in its history, appeared to be on the edge of an expansion that was truly global in character.

But marring this unity and these prospects were several profound defects—defects that the right man at the right time in the right place could exploit to overturn the whole existing Catholic order. Let us consider three of these defects profoundly menacing to the promise of an age of gold.[2]

First of all, recuperation from the disasters of recent centuries was by no means complete. The Ottomans, occupied for a time with the conquest of the Middle East and clashes with the Persian Empire, were about to attack Europe once again, with Hungary, on the border of the Hapsburg lands in Germany, as their first target.

Secondly, not all social groups had benefited from economic recovery, at least not in an equal manner. The bourgeoisie in the great textile cities, themselves divided into richer and poorer guilds, had, as a group, impeded workers from reaping the economic benefits that they might have expected to gain due to the scarcity of labor following repeated outbursts of the plague, thus stimulating serious class hatreds. In contrast to workers, peasants in many areas of Europe had indeed benefitted from the enormous mortality caused by the Black Death—and at

---

2. For a description of the problems, general and particular, of the High to Late Middle Ages, as discussed below, see John Rao, *Black Legends and the Light of the World* (Forest Lake: Remnant Press, 2011), 171–284; Also, Euan Cameron, *The European Reformation* (New York: Oxford University Press, 1991), 1–93; Jean-Marie Mayeur, ed., *Histoire du Christianisme* (Paris: Desclée, Thirteen Volumes, 1990–2002), VII, 136–137, 172, 215–308, 257, 460, *passim*; Ludwig von Pastor, *The History of the Popes* (London: K. Paul, Trench, Trübner, Forty Volumes, 1906–1913), II, 104–37; Francis Oakley, *The Western Church in the Late Middle Ages* (Ithaca: Cornell University Press, 1985), 113–14, 122, 239–43; Philip Hughes, *A History of the Church* (New York: Sheed & Ward, Three Volumes, 1949), III, 340–42. Very important to an understanding of the intellectual problems of the whole pre-Reformation era is Georges de Lagarde, *La naissance de l'esprit laique au declin du moyen age* (Louvain & Paris: Nauwelaerts, Five Volumes, 1958).

the expense of the lesser local nobility, who were impoverished and envious of the gains made by both the peasantry and the bourgeoisie. These barons were also angry with the higher nobility, which, despite having weathered the storm and grown ever more powerful, was nevertheless itself always on the alert against its possible enemies from below—and from above.

The enemies from above were those families that had succeeded in gaining control of the central power of the state in certain parts of Europe, creating the so-called "new monarchies" of France, England, and Spain. These dynasties knew that other segments of the higher nobility (the same class to which their own families belonged) looked askance upon their victory, hoping one day to replace them. Hence, they constructed regal alliances with all of the lower groups of society that had quarrels with this ambitious mass of princes, prince-bishops, and dukes.

In consequence, the enlightened observer of the year 1517 would have to admit that all of the diverse societies composing this sacred order did not always act in a manner that was truly Christian, leaving a just space for liberty and movement to their fellow corporations. Many critics of the last hundred years before the Reformation—men like Cardinals Nicholas of Cusa (1401–1464) and Giles of Viterbo (1472–1532)—complained bitterly of the destructive parochialism not only of nations, provinces, cities, guilds, and religious orders, but also of specific local confraternities.

In one sense, this negative parochial spirit emerged from a consciousness on the part of all of the corporations of Christendom of their own innate dignity; a positive awareness in and of itself, and one that was owed to the recognition of the nobility of all of nature rendered palpable by the message of the Incarnation. Nevertheless, corporate defenses against the arrogance born of the abuse of the recognition of their particular dignity were weak. And this weakness was rendered more dangerous by an understanding of Catholic piety that was generally not concentrated on sacramental regeneration, but on "sacramentals" incorporating acts of ritual devotion—"doing things" good in and of themselves, but not necessarily productive of real moral progress of individual and social value.

Finally, the Catholic sovereigns—Pope Leo X among them—in whom Erasmus placed his chief hope for the establishment of an "age of gold" were almost uninterruptedly at war with one another. The two "new monarchies" of France and Castile-Aragon/Spain became enemies due to the French invasions of Italy beginning in 1494 and their consequences for Milan and Naples. The menace of French domination and the need for a military response concerned the papacy, the other Italian states, the Empire, and the new monarchy of England, eager to place obstacles in the path of its importunate Gallic neighbor. France seemed to have the upper hand initially in Italy, but an enormous peril threatened this: the menace of the new Hapsburg king of Spain, Charles I (1516–1556), who stood on the edge of becoming Charles V (1519–1556) of Germany and Holy Roman Emperor at the imminent death of his grandfather, Maximilian I (1493–1519). As a result, the international tension at the dawn of 1517 was not promising for the peace of Europe. Everyone was on the ready and prepared to use all means possible to promote his own cause, including alliance with the Turks and—what would soon prove to be true—with heresy.

Lamentably, the recognized guides of the mind and heart of Christendom—the wise men and the spiritual directors who might have been called upon to navigate men and society through these problems—themselves suffered from a myriad of ailments, bitter warfare with one another among them.

The intellectual luminaries included, first of all, the systematic philosophers: the followers of St Thomas Aquinas, St Bonaventure, and, despite some questions of profound nature, those of Duns Scotus as well. All these thinkers were, in one way or another, convinced of the necessity of using reason, logic, and Aristotle to arrive both at a true and substantively real knowledge of nature as well as a speculative theological development of the message rooted in the sources of Revelation.

But such proponents of the so-called *via antiqua* in philosophy were opposed by a front of enemies who, despite being badly divided among themselves, were united in *not* giving to speculative reason the same value. Supporters of the extreme nominalism of the *via moderna* of William of Ockham (c.1287–1347) thought that the *via antiqua* expressed an arrogant overestimation of human abilities, and that philosophy—which, contrary to its pretensions, was incapable of arriving at real, substantive truths—had to give way to a theology founded purely on faith. Behind them stood a myriad of allies, witting or unwitting: legalists interested solely in the logic of Roman law and its consequences; anti-speculative mystics concerned with the lessons taught either by the heart or by a life of poverty; humanists following in the path of Petrarch and exalting the messages learned from Greek and Latin rhetoric or philosophers who knew how to utilize their words in a beautiful aesthetic manner, like Plato; and, finally, a bourgeoisie—already suspect to men like John of Salisbury (1120–1180) in the twelfth century—obsessed with the guidance obtained through the practical life. And all these groups, from the fifteenth century onwards, could utilize the new printing press, whose proprietors smelled gain in stimulating their intellectual, political, and pragmatic battles.

Combatting against the *via antiqua*, but also among themselves, the supporters of the *via moderna* gained the advantage in the universities, putting an end, for the moment, to the great systematic work of the philosopher-theologians of the thirteenth century, and using Aristotelian logic primarily for the purpose of either ridiculing its pretensions or engaging in often strange speculations regarding what God might or might not do through his arbitrary will. In contrast, the humanists, who experienced difficulties being accepted in the old centers of higher study, and the legalists (sometimes with the help of mystics on the hunt for a purer Christian life under the scepter of a redeemer-emperor or -king) were able to gain the edge in the courts of popes, sovereigns, lesser princes, and the Italian republics.

This meant that theology and systematic philosophy on the eve of the Protestant Reform were neglected and even trod under foot. Logical games, law, rhetoric, and an anti-intellectual mysticism held pride of place. But in practice, the winners—all of whom claimed to humble human pride and work together for the exaltation of the will of God— ended by divinizing human will instead.

Why? Because the enemies of the *via antiqua* did not leave men any theological, philosophical, or logical means to present "the will of God" other than a bald assertion of the will of a particular group or individual. The only means left for these men to give practical reality to the "will of God"—that is to say, their own will—was force. And from the very outset, in the alliance of William of Ockham, Marsilius of Padua, and the Holy Roman Emperor Louis IV (1314–1347)—whom they both served—one could see that the force in question was a mixture of physical and rhetorical power, the two always depending upon each other— the first requiring a justification by means of Catholic-sounding words in a society still committed to Catholicism; the second in need of manpower to arrive practically at the triumph of its will. A useful explanation of the endless changes that we have experienced in the modern world is the difficulties encountered by these two forces in coexisting, and their continuous hunt for better allies to achieve their specific and often colliding goals.

The clergy, the other guide of our sacred Christian society, was equally incapable of resolving its problems. Divided into particular societies just like all of the other members of a complex Christendom, the ecclesiastical estate was marred by parochialism. Bishops and seculars were engaged in "cold" and sometimes "hot" wars with religious, and religious orders were disturbed by internal battles as well as external conflicts, one against another. When clerics undertook higher studies and then taught or held important administrative positions, these wars became particularly harsh, because they also reflected the intellectual divisions discussed above.

Let us note, once again, that although there were some members of the clergy still passionate for the study of theology and philosophy, the large majority of educated ecclesiastics who became bishops or diocesan officials of significance were students of canon law or humanist rhetoric. They knew almost nothing of theology and philosophy and would have been incapable of responding to heretical attacks should these arise. The only arguments they had at their disposal were "arguments from the will"—namely, that one *must* believe and do what one was *obliged* to do because it was demanded by *the will of God*, as interpreted by the *will* of pope or council or bishop. Since the greater part of the ecclesiastics who studied theology and philosophy were nominalists, there were not lacking counselors of popes who assured them that their power to interpret "the will of God" was absolute, and that they might even eliminate the dogmatic and physical structure of the Church should they desire to do so.[3]

But the biggest obstacle to the clergy's ability effectively to guide Christendom was its own material preoccupations. Obtaining a benefice—a living—was the chief goal of the vast majority of the clergy, and, indeed, not procuring one brought with it daily problems of maintenance that buried a cleric under a mountain of material burdens.[4]

One goal of the papacy from the eleventh century onwards was to bring all of the episcopal—and perhaps of the great abbatial—benefices under its control. Although it did gain control of many of these, especially during the Avignon period, it never succeeded completely in doing so. In practice, control of episcopal, abbatial, parochial, and the many specific chapel benefices was shared by popes, bishops, religious orders, princes high and low, republics, communal governments, diverse corporate entities (including business enterprises), private families, and individuals. The real proprietors of these benefices were tempted to use them not for the adequate maintenance of priests serving the communities for which they were created, but for the particular necessities of the actual possessor.

The result was a heap of preoccupations and abuses that grew ever more complex and destructive. The proprietors of benefices deviated

---

3. See Oakley, 165, for one example.
4. Cameron, 27, 31, 36, 39, 45, 47, 53–55; Mayeur, VII, 177–207.

the use of funds towards the sustaining of their own functionaries for their own purposes, often giving the actual name of bishop or pastor to someone who was not even a member of the clergy, and frequently rewarding him with an accumulation of dioceses and parishes. Obviously, it was impossible for these men to live where they had a "cure" or to attend to their spiritual vocations even if they wanted to, although, in truth, this was rarely an object of concern. Those who gave a thought to this responsibility sent off substitutes who were consecrated as auxiliary bishops or ordained as assistant priests. Such substitutes were often ignorant, and, as a consequence of being badly paid, always on the hunt for an increase of their stipend or a benefice of their own. The entire system lent itself to misunderstandings, quarrels over who, in fact, justly owned a particular benefice, appeals to the Roman Curia, unceasing legal battles, heavy bribery, and rancor nurtured by defeated parties who remained on the alert for opportunities to avenge themselves. As Euan Cameron notes, "The institution [i.e., the Church] as a whole managed to appear simultaneously impoverished, grasping, and extravagant."[5]

Nonetheless, this was a Christendom that was conscious of its problems, with the call for a "reform of head and members" on the lips of the representatives of all groups in the century following the Council of Constance (1414–1418). Without focusing our attention here upon the success of these calls for reform, let us at least note the work of cleansing done in Spain through the cooperation of Queen Isabella and Cardinal Ximenez (1436–1517); that of bishops such as Matteo Giberti (1495–1543) of Verona and Gian Pietro Carafa (Pope Paul IV)(1476–1559) of Chieti; that of the various "observant" orders; that of "Oratories of Divine Love" stimulated by the spirituality of St Catherine of Genoa (1447–1510); that of the *devotio moderna*; that of many, many preachers thundering regularly from the pulpit, such as Geiler von Kaysersberg (1445–1510) in Strasburg and Giles of Viterbo in his harangues to the fathers of the Fifth Lateran Council from 1513–1517; that of humanists like Erasmus with his *Praise of Folly* and Sebastian Brandt (1457–1521) in the *Ship of Fools*; and, finally, that of those innumerable faithful whose names escape the historian, but about whom we nevertheless know something from the archives of the immense network of corporations, congregations, and sodalities that seemed to grow ever more influential every day and everywhere in Christendom.

Unfortunately, the obstacles to this reform of head and members were

---

5. Cameron, 27.

innumerable. Vested interests of every type and at every level put the efforts of Catholic reformers under extreme duress, giving to Protestantism its opening in places ranging from Switzerland to Holland. In good nominalist fashion, the supporters of these vested interests often appealed to the "will" of the heads of their societies and their particular "traditions" as justification for leaving abuses uncorrected, even defending these corruptions as essential to the life of the pious Christian.

Beginning with the papacy and the Roman Curia, both preoccupied with finances, Italian and international politics, and the fortunes of their extended families, Cameron underlines the downward trajectory of efforts for positive change: "The pattern usually followed was that an abuse was identified; its abolition was declared desirable; vested interests intervened; the abolition was watered down, and in most cases forgotten about even before a bull was issued."[6] Geiler von Kaysersberg complained that the Council of Basel, which for more than a decade had trumpeted its dedication to the renewal of the Church, was not sufficiently powerful to reform a convent of nuns when the city sided against it. This being the case, how could a council reform the whole of Christendom?[7] And Cameron, speaking of local interests and their power, notes that the momentarily victorious Francis I of France, who had extorted innumerable concessions to royal power from Leo X, "had a far harder battle with the Parlement of Paris over the Concordat of Bologna than he ever had with the popes."[8]

Despite the fact that there was some useful progress made, this seemed to be pathetic in comparison with the deadly blow that many reformers thought they could give to abuses with one sole monumental effort changing everything from one day to the next. "Certainly," Cameron notes, "they talked down the modest achievements of fifteenth-century reform by comparing their own day to an ideal golden age which had never existed."[9] This hunt for an "age of gold" similar to what was conceived of as existing in an apostolic utopia was represented, to give but one example thereof, in the sending of precisely twelve Franciscan missionaries to Mexico to do "well" in the New World what had been done badly in the Old.[10] Taking stock of the failure of reform in the context of this utopian vision, it seemed as though everything

---

6. Cameron, 41.

7. Pastor, II, 49.

8. Cameron, 54.

9. Ibid., 48.

10. Mayeur, VIII, 693–770; Lluís Nicolau d'Olwer, *Fray Bernardino de Sahagun, 1499–1590* (Salt Lake City: University of Utah Press, 1987).

depended upon the work of patently impotent individuals. "Because they were pious," Cameron explains, they wanted a better, purer Church; but "because they were loyal Catholics, they could not *practically* achieve it."[11] For only the legitimate authorities had the right to achieve their ultimately rather exaggerated goals.

The conclusions drawn from the "failure" of reform were very diverse. For Gian Pietro Carafa, what was needed was a flight from vain babbling to the actual wielding of a fiery sword—the method he would indeed apply vigorously upon becoming Pope Paul IV (1555–1559).[12] Geiler von Kaysersberg was more resigned. "The best that one can do," he said, "is to remain in one's corner, with his head buried in the sand, dedicating oneself to the commandments of God and doing well to gain eternal life. . . . There is no more hope. Christendom exists no longer."[13] And for Giovanni dalle Celle the measure was even more full: "They say that the world has to be renewed; I say that it should be destroyed."[14]

At this point we must concentrate our attention upon the situation in the Holy Roman Empire, which offered much tinder for the fire about to destroy Christendom, and where all men of good sense understood the necessity of a reform both of the state as well as of the Church in the century before Luther. Besides strengthened central institutions, all reformers thought that what was needed was a much more secure system of imperial finance. "Without money," as the Emperor Frederick III (1452–1493) told the future Pope Pius II, "I cannot do anything."[15]

The most immediate problem of the empire was the fact that the immense number of local princes, municipal councils, and societies both spiritual and secular, all jealous of their prerogatives, blocked the possibility of a unified and efficacious imperial political policy. What the Hapsburg emperors tried to do to strengthen the central power was to mobilize and augment their personal dynastic resources in order to construct and maintain state organs adequate to such a task. Their efforts began to have a serious effect under Maximilian I (1493–1519). The result was that those corporate powers that were more frightened by the growth of the influence of the emperor than by internal anarchy became ever more alarmed. A hunt for allies began from both sides—either to favor the growth of imperial institutions and the Hapsburg power that

11. Cameron, 92.
12. John Rao, "The Theatines and the Question of Catholic Renewal," http://jcrao.fr eeshell.org/Theatines.html.
13. Mayeur, VII, 144.
14. Pastor, I, 145.
15. Francis Rapp, *Le Saint Empire romain germanique* (Paris: Tallandier, 2000), 317.

lay behind this, or to impede it. Both sides—imperialists and their enemies—sought to foment and exploit the anger and resentment of competing groups, which Germany nurtured in abundance.[16]

One thing that stirred the rage of educated Germans—of whom there were many, given the high level of literacy in the country—was a widespread sense of ethnic offense. Educated men, foreign as well as native, knew just how strong Catholic identity in Germany was. Affection for the Church ran very deep, with German cities boasting innumerable confraternities, sodalities, and pilgrimage sites. But Germans were also conscious that foreigners derided them and their country. Italians repeated the jibes of Pius II that, "The worst mule is more sharp than a German," and that, "It was industrious Italians who gave birth to the empire," while, "negligent Germans are its gravediggers."[17] These insults were rendered more irksome because they came from Italians, lay and clerical, whom the Germans considered both corrupt and arrogant in their perversity.

The answer to foreign derision was a growth of national ethnic pride, nurtured by a mass of legends regarding the supposedly imminent and miraculous renewal of the Empire and the special character of the German people. The so called "Revolutionary of the Upper Rhine," and his pamphlet entitled "The Hundred Chapters" claimed that the first men spoke German; that the evangelization of the Germans came directly from Palestine; and even that the Redemption was only needed for non-Germans, given that Germans were already pleasing to God without it.[18]

German social anger was also deep, and for the same general reasons indicated above. Lay and ecclesiastical princes were annoyed not only with an imperial government considered too ambitious in its designs, but also with the urban bourgeoisie in cities that officially belonged to them as well as the free commercial towns that did not. The impoverished knights, of whom there were many, were angered by their need to seek positions with the great princes, a service they wanted to escape, perhaps by forcibly regaining the "rights" they lost to the peasants during the economic disturbances of recent centuries. Potential knightly belligerence added to the many other menaces and existing outrages felt by the peasantry. Peasant risings were not unknown in fifteenth-century Germany, connected with a millenarianism gathering up all the hopes

---

16. On Germany and anger, see Mayeur, VII, 309–28; Gerald Strauss, *Manifestations of Discontent in Germany on the Eve of the Reformation* (Bloomington: Indiana University Press, 1971).

17. Rapp, 300.

18. Ibid., 301, also, 290–354; Mayeur, VII, 309–28, Strauss, *passim.*

for a quasi-magical reform of church and state that would finally establish a truly Christian society.[19]

Finally, the last years preceding the arrival of Luther on the scene witnessed the bitter *Reuchlinstreit* or Reuchlin Controversy.[20] This battle erupted in 1509 with the attack launched by Johannes Pfefferkorn (1469–1523), a German Jewish convert and theologian, and the Flemish Dominican, Jacob Hoogstraten (1460–1527) on Jewish books, especially those of the Talmud, which they considered violently anti-Christian and also favorable to unacceptable magical practices. After clashes on the local and imperial level, the books, which at first were indeed confiscated, were returned to their owners until an official commission, working in the years 1509–1510, could study the question more profoundly.

One member of this commission was the humanist, Johannes Reuchlin (1455–1522), who had studied in Italy with Marsilio Ficino (1433–1499) and Giovanni Pico della Mirandola (1463–1494). Reuchlin had learned Hebrew and become interested in the Cabbala, which he studied not only to improve his knowledge of the language, but also because such a study entered into the Neoplatonic vision of the Florentine Academy that he shared. Florentine Neoplatonic thought promoted the utilization of all sources of knowledge, magical and gnostic included, in a hunt for a *prisca teologia,* both pre-Christian and external to contemporary Christianity, which would work together with Revelation for the union of man with God. One sees this clearly in Reuchlin's book, *De verbo mirifico* of 1494, in which the typical humanist disdain for Scholastic philosophical wisdom is also obvious.

Reuchlin gave a judgment almost completely favorable to the Jewish books under attack, especially those of the Talmud, accompanying this with derision of the Scholastic ignorance of Pfefferkorn, whom he dismissed as "a baptized Jew,"[21] who did not understand that cabbalistic studies were necessary for the scholar even so as properly to interpret sacred scriptures. Despite the fact that all the other members of the commission supported Pfefferkorn, the emperor accepted Reuchlin's judgment in 1511. Hoogstraten was cited before the Inquisition in Mainz in 1513 to explain himself.

Thus began a battle that in one way or another continued until 1520.

19. Norman Cohn, *The Pursuit of the Millennium: Revolutionary Millenarians and Mystical Anarchists of the Middle Ages* (New York: Oxford University Press, 1970), 118–26, 223–34.

20. Mayeur, VII, 619–20; Cameron, 104–06; E. Michael Jones, *The Revolutionary Jewish Spirit* (South Bend: Fidelity, 2008), 230–55.

21. Jones, 235.

Here, many of the intellectual tendencies already at war for centuries combatted one another. On the one side were Reuchlin and an army of humanists who vehemently attacked the ignorance of Scholastics bereft of a knowledge of Hebrew, their head himself merely "that Jew sprinkled with water" (i.e., baptized) which could not really make him a Christian![22] The most offensive—and the most efficacious—attacks came from the humanist knight, Ulrich von Hutten (1488–1523), in his *Letters of Obscure Men* of 1517, wherein he ridiculed the ignorance and corruption of the ecclesiastical institutions and authorities in general.

The opposing camp included the derided supporters of the Scholasticism of Thomas Aquinas from the Universities of Cologne and Louvain, but obviously also Pfefferkorn and Hoogstraten, who were particularly indignant. Reuchlin, Pfefferkorn said, despite his humanist arrogance, had clearly never read the Talmud. He was a Judaizer without even realizing it. "Learning is no defense against the accusation of Depravity," Pfefforkorn insisted, and biology—the fact of being born a Jew—could not impede the effects of grace.[23]

The tribunal decided in favor of Reuchlin twice, in 1513 and in 1516. He celebrated his victory by publishing another work, *De arte cabbalistica*, in which he openly sustained once again all the propositions that Pfefferkorn and Hoogstraten attacked—the use of Jewish ideas and symbols, and magical incantations included. Pope Leo X seemed to confirm Reuchlin's triumph when he sanctioned the publication of the Babylonian Talmud in Rome in 1518.

Nonetheless, in 1520 a papal tribunal overturned the first judgments, ordering Reuchlin to pay all the legal costs of the conflict. Unfortunately, this very long and bitter dispute was not actually resolved, but only swallowed up by the nuclear war unleashed by Martin Luther (1483–1546)—a war that friends of Rome, little by little, understood the *Reuchlinstreit* had contributed to preparing. Sadly, everywhere that this new and greater war resulted in a Lutheran victory, the possibility of a truly Christian reform was totally excluded.

There is no doubt that such a truly Christian reform required all the obvious changes that reformers for centuries had demanded, most importantly, an end to the corruption within the *curia* of Rome and the compelling of German bishops to reside in their own dioceses. And we have seen that there were models of successful battles against such abuses in countries like Spain already available to imitate.

Nevertheless, in hindsight, it is clear that what was even more neces-

---

22. Ibid., 243–44.
23. Ibid., 243.

sary was an underlying change of mentality that could only come from a more complete ecclesiology—one centered on the Incarnation and on the Mystical Body of Christ. There appeared the beginnings, great and small, of an appreciation for this more Christocentric ecclesiology in a variety of sources: the systematic work of the Scholastics of the thirteenth century (interrupted because of political problems and the disastrous nominalist critique of the time, but now emerging once again from out of the shadows); the Christian humanism that would take flight in the future under the wings of St Ignatius of Loyola (1491–1556) and St Francis de Sales (1567–1622); the Eucharistic fervor of the *devotio moderna* of the Low Countries and the Rhineland; and the spirituality of St Catherine of Genoa alluded to above.

St Catherine, who had experienced a vibrant sense of the suffering of the souls in Purgatory, approached reform with reference to a personal confrontation of the individual with Christ through which he could judge whether or not he were living his particular vocation in the Mystical Body as he must live it. A bishop, a priest, or a monk who experienced this confrontation would never ask for purely legal solutions to the problems of the Church, of which there were already enough on the books anyway. He would never place his hope for an improvement in the life of the Church in formal regulations specifying, for example, just how many days per year a bishop had to stay in his diocese or a priest say Mass. He would never think of his position as a cleric as being that primarily of a "proprietor of a benefice." Looking directly at the face of Christ, he would consider what his duty was as a member of the Mystical Body of Christ, according to his particular vocation, the sanctity that the fulfillment of that duty demanded, and the extent of his suffering in Purgatory necessitated by his neglect of that duty—despite the fact that his negligence was "legally" permitted by a Church run by flawed human beings. And a Christocentric clergy, aware of its duty, would, in turn, act most efficaciously upon kings, other political powers, and the members of all of the corporations of Christendom to reinforce their lay vocations and the moral tone of all of society.[24]

Luther was himself Christocentric, but his Christocentric ethos was heretical—in part with roots already old, incorporating all of the intellectual and spiritual tendencies discussed above; in part still more revolutionary in character. The reform emerging from his work utterly destroyed the Mystical Body of Christ, rendering a reformation in the

---

24. Pierre Pourrat, *Christian Spirituality*, translated by William Henry Mitchell and S.P. Jacques (London: Burns, Oates, & Washbourne, Four Volumes, 1922–1927), II, 286–90.

manner of St Catherine impossible. As the great church historian Philip Hughes says:[25]

> All those anti-intellectualist, anti-institutional forces that had plagued and hindered the medieval Church for centuries, whose chronic maleficent activity had, in fact, been the main cause why—as we are often tempted to say—so little was done effectively to maintain a generally higher standard of Christian life; all the forces that were the chronic distraction of the medieval papacy, were now stabilized, institutionalized in the new reformed Christian church. Enthronement of the will as the supreme human faculty; hostility to the activity of the intelligence in spiritual matters and in doctrine; the ideal of a Christian perfection that is independent of sacraments and independent of the authoritative teaching of clerics; of sanctity attainable through one's own self-sufficing spiritual activities; denial of the truth that Christianity, like man, is a social thing;—all the crude, backwoods, obscurantist theories bred of the degrading pride that comes with chosen ignorance, the pride of men ignorant because unable to be wise except through the wisdom of others, now have their fling. Luther's own special contribution—over and above the key doctrines that set all this mischief loose—is the notion of life as radically evil.

Luther's own training is an instance of one contemporary abuse: he only began to study theology—the reigning nominalist theology obsessed with the "inscrutable will of God"—after his ordination to the priesthood in 1507. He took his first steps towards his particular heretical position in the years 1512–1517, at the beginning of his career at the University of Wittenberg. It was in those years that he changed his intellectual and pedagogical direction from that of a nominalist still utilizing some Scholastic tools to that of a humanist. This meant emphasizing "the living word of God" instead of a nominalist logic that already worked to eliminate philosophy as a path to the truth; an emphasis, that is to say, upon sacred scripture and the Fathers of the Church—especially St Augustine—these latter considered as preachers bound to the "word" and not as systematic and speculative thinkers.[26]

Under such stimuli, Luther reacted against the "Pelagian" theological position of Gabriel Biel (c.1420–1495), inclining towards the much harsher approach of Gregory of Rimini (d. 1358). Both of these men were philosophical nominalists. But while Biel insisted that man's good deeds

---

25. Hughes, III, 529.

26. On Luther's development, see Cameron, 99–103; Hubert Jedin & John Dolan, eds., *History of the Church* (New York: Crossroad Publishing Company, Ten Volumes, 1981–1985), V, 11–156; Mayeur, VII, 681–769.

and penance, even though imperfect, were accepted by God as efficacious for salvation, Gregory of Rimini maintained that the pure will of God demanded a perfect contrition on the part of the "successful" penitent.

According to Luther's later account, his move towards the harsher position of Gregory—one that gradually contemplated the idea that such a perfect contrition was impossible—was stimulated by what is referred to as his "Tower Experience." This experience made him feel that justification and salvation came only from the outside, from God alone, from faith in God's saving power; and that this justification and salvation took place even while he remained a sinner, conscious of the thoroughness of his own sinfulness and that of the world as a whole. The individual had no free will, and even committed sin in what otherwise seemed to be good works. God alone could save him, accepting him as he was: a being whom Calvin later defined as "totally depraved."

The second stage of his development, from 1517–1520, concerned the application to the Indulgence Controversy of his ideas regarding the salvation through faith alone of totally depraved men. This began in Wittenberg with the attack on Johann Tetzel (1465–1519), continued in Leipzig at the dispute with Johannes Eck (1486–1543), and finished with the condemnation of Luther's teaching by the universities of Louvain, Liège, and Cologne, along with that of Pope Leo X in the bull *Exsurge Domine* (June 15, 1520). It was only then that Luther realized the fact that his central concept did not correspond to the real Catholic Tradition.

A third stage in the development of Luther's reform lasted from about the time of *Exsurge Domine* until the beginning of 1522 and his return to Wittenberg from the castle of the Wartburg, where he lived under the protection of the elector of Saxony after his condemnation by the new Emperor Charles V at the Diet of Worms. His intensive labor in these years commenced with three works announcing some of the enormous consequences of his perilous vision: *To the Christian Nobility of the German Nation*; *On the Babylonian Captivity of the Church*; and *On the Liberty of the Christian Man*.

From the total depravity of men, Luther deduced the necessity of viewing the church not as the visible Body of Christ, hierarchically organized, with a teaching and a sacramental life guided by the clergy in aid of a people seeking sanctity. The church, for him, was only a simple collection of baptized individuals—an argument already made by some nominalists—who had to place all of their hope in an extrinsic and unmerited justification, offered from the pure will and grace of God, without the participation of men, who remained sinners even in Heaven itself. As a result, the international Mystical Body of Christ, with its cycle of penances, indulgences, and good works, became for him an enormous hoax of the devil—and especially of the diabolical Italians. But he insisted that believers—derided and oppressed German believers in particular—were now finally able to liberate themselves from this monster by turning their attention to the "living words" of the printed Bible, the real font of Truth, which Luther insisted supported his position. It was the Word Incarnate who was to lose their attention in the process.

Luther wrote in a very popular manner, with the intention of being provocative. All his readers found in his writings what they *wanted* to find therein, as they are doing once again in 2017. Germans seized Luther's condemnation of indulgences as a weapon with which to attack Rome, and, by extension, Italians. Humanists contemptuous of Scholasticism, and still fighting for Reuchlin, picked up a mass of new arguments for destroying the systematic theologians from both Rome and Germany who now were opposing Luther. The higher German princes found in him an unexpected arm to utilize against the new emperor, Charles V, exaggeratedly powerful due his worldwide lands, and openly supporting the pope against the Wittenberg scholar. Impoverished knights and peasants on the alert to defend themselves from a sea of enemies recognized in the man from Wittenberg a spokesman who used the Bible to assert their liberties. Bishops, priests, and monks who had no true vocation, were irritated with their way of life, and ignorant of theology, gained, by means of his teaching, a justification for escaping their ecclesiastical obligations. Theologians setting to work from various centers in Germany and Switzerland during Luther's period of protective custody in the Wartburg, drew their own logical deductions from the central "evangelical" idea of total depravity and extrinsic justification; deductions regarding the significance of the Eucharist, baptism, the validity of ceremonies and devotions that seemed to relish the tools of a sinful Creation, politics, and social life in general. And, finally, publishing houses, thrilled that everyone was ready to buy Luther's texts, promoted him as an enormous and unexpected source of profit.

But what did "the true Catholics" do to defend themselves as this carnival of confusion proceeded? First of all, we must remember that bishops in German lands were often absent from their dioceses. Once again, even if they were present, the average bishop (as well as the average priest or the average layman) was ill equipped to respond to a theological argument such as that offered by Luther and his fellow Protestants. If the heretics rejected "the will" of popes and councils, and insisted that their deductions regarding total depravity were supported by the Bible—which everyone accepted as a necessary font of the Faith—Catholic nominalists, legalists, and humanists were all without intellectual resources for countering them. Besides, the Catholic emperor and the pope were far away from Germany in the 1520s, occupied with political instead of religious questions, and engaged in war with one another *pour comble de misère.*

Even more important to the explanation of the swift collapse of possible religious opposition, the arguments of Luther and Company simplified the complicated relations between princes, municipal councils, and Catholic corporations on the one hand and, on the other, a "diabolical" Church which—according to the Protestants—did not even have the right to exist. The victory of Luther meant that the "illegal" property of the old deceptive Church was there for the taking—an offer accepted by all social authorities, including Catholic prince bishops. Stolen church property provided both easy enrichment and a means of reinforcing a given local authority's strength against the pretensions of the imperial government, ever more menacing under the Catholic Charles V.

The consequence was that many local authorities chose to become supporters of "the Gospel position" until the situation of Christendom in general was "better clarified." The large majority of these choices endured, even if some of the parties involved—such as the knights and the peasants—failed in their goals due to their intrinsic weakness vis-à-vis cities and the higher nobility. And it must be stressed that these choices were made without the participation of the public in general. It was the municipal council of Zurich, to take but one example, that announced the date of the last Mass, which was heard by the whole of the population of the city before this sacred act, still alive in the hearts of the people, was abolished forever.[27]

The evidence indicates that the more that the population came to understand what the reform of Luther and Company actually meant, the less content it was. This was true also of scholars like Erasmus and Reuchlin, once they grasped the fact that the concept of total depravity robbed men of the free will that humanism cherished. But it was too late for the average man where the choice for Protestantism was made for them. They were in the hands of an *idée fixe*. Let us hear, once again, the judgment of Cameron:

> The unique quality of the Protestant reformation consists in that it took a single core idea; it presented that idea to everyone, and encouraged public discussion; it then deduced the rest of the changes to teaching and worship from that idea; and, finally, it tore down the entire fabric of the institutional Church and built again from scratch, including only what was consistent with, and required by, the basic religious message. That is to say: 1) doctrine was subjected to public

27. Jedin and Dolan, V, 166–68.

debate; 2) the test of the value and "rightness" of any religious act (whether "popular" or "elite") was its conformity to one fundamental dogma; 3) religion was simplified by a complete rebuilding of the structures of western Christianity.[28]

Still, these supporters of an *idée fixe* were a divided force, and would become ever more divided in the future. All were convinced that they understood the living word of God, found solely in the Bible. As heirs of a long and profound attack against every intellectual means of judging whether one were correct or not, they were all constrained either simply to insist upon the truth of their positions ever more intensely or to invent new arguments, sometimes strangely traditional in their Scholastic format, sometimes purely rhetorically charged. They thereby unleashed a battle to the death of different Protestant wills, a "war of all reformers against all," with no supreme court of appeal to end the conflict. Yet Cameron reminds us once again that all this theoretical battling demanded the aid of political powers that had their own motives for supporting one group of Protestants as opposed to another; powers capable of changing the *idée fixe* of the moment the better to achieve their own secular goals:

> The Reformation gave large groups of people across Europe their first lessons in political commitment to a universal ideology. In the sixteenth century, religion became mass politics. Other ideologies, ultimately more secular in tone, would take its place. The Reformation was the first.[29]

The sole effective tool for avoiding a "depraved reform" was a strong Church that was conscious of herself and of her vocation as the Mystical Body of Christ; a Church that recognized that her mission was not merely to accompany nature on its journey, but also to correct its sins and guide it to its perfection in the grand plan of the Creator God. Little by little—with the aid of some of the disciples of St Catherine, like Gian Pietro Carafa, one of the authors of the *Consilium de emendenda ecclesia*, the first papal-ordered and painfully self-critical study of the causes of the Reformation; with the assistance of St Ignatius Loyola, St Francis de Sales, and their recourse to both the *via antiqua* as well as to humanism; with the collaboration of many renewed and innovative religious orders; and through the work of the Council of Trent—this happy result began to take shape.[30]

---

28. Cameron, 422; Also, 389–421.
29. Ibid., 422.
30. See Mayeur, VIII, 223–80; Jedin & Dolan, V, 433–574.

If only it had been more complete. But it can never be as complete as many utopian reformers before 1517 thought to be possible. In practice, the Catholic Reform of the sixteenth century continued to be impeded by many of the same problems that existed beforehand. Some of these problems have still not been resolved today. Some are much worse in 2017 than they were in 1517. And they are much worse because the pre-Reformation forces leading to secularization and the divinization of the human will, "incarnated" in the Christian world through Luther's teaching, have now had five long centuries to wreak their havoc inside the Camp of the Saints. The mayhem that the logical development of that depraved teaching has caused in our own day now requires a Catholic Reform perhaps even more thoroughgoing than that of the sixteenth century. Let we, the living, think back to the long deceased Giovanni dalle Celle, accepting the first part of his lament, but modifying the second: When "they say that the world must be renewed," let us say "that Luther and his teaching must be destroyed."

2

Man as Victim of a Divine Tyrant

Luther's "Theology" of a Self-Contradicting God

Thomas H. Stark

W HAT IS THE REFORMATION all about? Is it about the papacy, Purgatory, or the indulgence trade? No, this is not what the Reformation is all about, at least not according to Martin Luther, the founder of the revolutionary movement called Protestantism. In a letter to Erasmus of Rotterdam, Luther praises Erasmus for not afflicting him "with those strange things about the papacy, Purgatory, indulgences, and the like," but instead "detecting the cardinal point," and "attacking the main thing itself."[1] What is the "main thing" that Luther is talking about? It is Luther's opinion "that free will is a pure lie."[2]

In his paper, *De servo arbitrio* (*On the Bondage of the Will*), Luther considered that "the dogma of free will" has no foundation in scripture and, therefore, has to be "completely abandoned and counted amongst fairy tales, which Paul rejects." Besides that, he saw the doctrine of free will as being inconsistent with historical experience. Erasmus of Rotterdam contradicted Luther and himself wrote a paper *De libero arbitrio*

---

1. Martin Luther, *Werke: Kritische Gesamtausgabe* (Weimar: Hermann Böhlau, 1883–2009), henceforth referred to as WA (Weimar Ausgabe), 18, 786. I am orienting myself with respect to the choice of citations on Theobald Beer, *Der fröhliche Wechsel und Streit. Grundzüge der Theologie Martin Luthers* (Einsiedeln: Johannes, 1980). In that text, Beer develops theologically the full work of Martin Luther. In most cases I adopt Beer's translation from the Latin unchanged. I am indebted for numerous stimuli to interpretation of Luther's text to Alma von Stockhausen, *Der Geist im Widerspruch. Von Luther zu Hegel* (Weilheim-Bierbronnen: Gustav-Siewerth-Akademie, Third Edition, 2003).

2. WA 18, 603.

(*On the Freedom of the Will*), in which—as the title indicates—he defends free will. In the letter with which he replied to Erasmus, Luther showed his appreciation of the fact that Erasmus had recognized the main point of his own thought.[3]

What, then, is the very foundation of Luther's thought? The whole theology of Martin Luther centres on sin and the possibility of justification of the sinner before God. However, an analysis of Luther's concept of sin leads to the recognition that Luther—in contrast to the entire ecclesial teaching of tradition—does not base sin on an *abuse* of human freedom, because Luther denies freedom of the human will *as such*. The denial of human freedom is at the very heart of Luther's anthropology.

The denial of free will has its basis in Luther's conception of God and in the relationship between God and man resulting from it. Luther follows the tradition of nominalism, the philosophy of late Scholasticism of the fourteenth century, which, in many respects, breaks with the classical Scholastic philosophy of the High Middle Ages, especially that of St Thomas Aquinas. The nominalist doctrine of God is focused on God's will and freedom.

God's free will (and its relationship to reason) has always been an important topic within the doctrine of God. St Thomas Aquinas established the principle: "The very root of all freedom is rationality."[4] This principle also applies to God. The way in which God makes use of His freedom is reasonable and therefore free of contradictions. Since the rational at the same time is the good, Thomas can state, "[A]s man necessarily demands to be happy, and it is impossible for him to intend unhappiness, so also God necessarily intends His goodness, and it is impossible for Him to intend something that cannot subsist together with His goodness."[5] The free will of God is, therefore, not be separated from His rationality and goodness. But that intrinsic, inseparable connection between freedom, rationality, and goodness in God increasingly begins to dissolve during the late Middle Ages.

John Duns Scotus established the principle, "Nothing other than the will itself is the complete determining cause of what is chosen by the will."[6] In this conception, unlike that of Aquinas, nothing that is outside of the pure will or that is distinguished from the will can have any influ-

---

3. Martin Luther, *The Bondage of the Will*, translated by J.I. Packer and O.R. Johnston (Westwood, NJ: Revell Publishers, 1957), 319.

4. Thomas Aquinas, *De veritate*, q. 24 a. 2.

5. Thomas Aquinas, *De pot.* Q. 5 a. 3.

6. Duns Scotus, "Nihil aliud a voluntate est causa totalis voluntationis in voluntate." "Opus Oxoniense," II, 25. Nr. 22, in *Opera Omnia*, XIII, 221.

ence on the orientation of the will. The absolute will, springing purely from itself—that is, from the initial impulse of its own motion—is capable of intending anything whatsoever. The direction of its intention requires no orientation by the standard of truth or the good, because there are no such measures available to focus the will—which is purely based on itself—on certain goals. It is rather the case that its goals are legitimized by the fact that the will is directing itself to them. This will does not spring from a reasonable judgment that qualifies a certain goal as a good to strive for and thus initiates a movement by which the will strives towards this goal. Rather something arbitrary can be a good to be pursued, just because the will actually focuses on it and moves in its direction. Although it is true that the will is only capable of wanting something that has previously been grasped by the intellect and presented to it, it is not intellectual cognition, and thus the orientation of the truth, that guides the will and binds it. Rather the will is autonomous in relation to the intellect by arbitrarily selecting from what the intellect is presenting to it.

This view of the will applies to the will of God as well as to the will of man. God's arbitrary will (*liberum arbitrium*) is the very essence of God; consequently, we can only realize *de facto* what God has once willed. But we cannot exclude that God could also have willed something completely different; indeed, that He even could have willed the exact opposite of what He actually did, or that in the future He might will something different from what He has willed in the past and that is in opposition to what He has willed so far. God does not want something because it is good, but something is only good because God wills it to be so. Only the first three commandments of the Decalogue, which address the relationship between God and man, possess absolute validity. All the other commandments that govern the relationships among men possess an absolute validity only as long as God gives them that validity. But He could also change these commandments—such as the prohibition of theft, the ban on polygamy, and even on murder—at any time. Thus, these commandments become a pure matter of convertible divine will. Scotus says explicitly, "[I]f God would revoke the commandment 'thou shall not kill' murder would no longer be a sin."[7]

William of Ockham goes still further in the voluntarist approach of Scotus. For example, he defines faith as "consent without evidence due

---

7. Dun Scotus, *Opera Scoti* (Paris: Vivès, 1891–1895), XIX, 148 and XXI, 537. Citation translated from R. Garrigou-Lagrange, *Mystik und christliche Vollkommenheit* (Bonn: Nova et Vetera, 2012), 308.

to the command of will."[8] With respect to God he states, "As God creates every creature just because He wants it, He can do with every creature whatever pleases Him." God could even "destroy" a man who lives according to the will of God "without any injustice."[9] Since the arbitrary destruction of a human being is murder, one is forced to think of Ockham's God as a potential murderer. The God of Duns Scotus and William of Ockham is completely unpredictable. He is—if you will—the "God of surprises."

Luther follows the nominalist approach, and especially the nominalist concept of God. He said, "I belong to the Ockhamite party, (whose teachings) I have absorbed completely."[10] Therefore, the predominant center of Luther's conception of God is God's omnipotence. However, Luther increases this omnipotence in a way that transforms it into an autocracy in the sense of a universal and sole efficacy that, consequently and ultimately, makes human freedom impossible. Even natural reason can, according to Luther, realize that a God whose providence would not empower Him not only to predict accurately all the future but at the same time predetermine it actively would be a "ridiculous God," or an "idol." The "omnipotence and providence [of God] entirely destroy the dogma of free will," says Luther. "Through this lightning strike, free will is struck down and destroyed."[11]

But how is Luther's anthropology compatible with the fact that man is made in the image of God, and that God gave him the task to mould Creation? That God created man in His own image, he states, implies "nothing about free will and the commandments." Rather, God thereby authorizes man only that "he should rule over the fish of the sea." Only in those spheres "which are below man," does man move "according to his own will and counsel," but not "in the other realms of the laws and commandments of God." In these realms "a man is not left in the hands of his own counsel, but he rather is set in motion and guided by the will and counsel of God, so that he, in the realm of God, is set into motion by the command of an other, apart from his own will."[12] He can, indeed, "build houses and maintain an office," but his freedom is limited to such activities. Man is free only with respect to "things below him."[13] Such human freedom, as expressed in classical terminology,

---

8. William of Ockham, *In* 1. *Sent. prol.* Q. 7 OT 1, 186.
9. William of Ockham, *Commentary on the Sentences*, 4 q. 9 E.
10. WA, 6, 195.
11. Ibid., 18, 615.
12. Ibid., 18, 671 f.
13. Ibid., 9, 23.

covers only the realm of *poiesis*, not the sphere of *praxis*. This is due to the fact that in the field of action that is morally relevant in a strict sense, it is not the will of the man that causes his actions. In this realm, man is not moved by himself, but is subject to the determination of God, who moves him from without. Luther states that, "free will is an entirely divine name that can apply to no one else but God's majesty alone. . . . When it is applied to man it is not applied rightfully, because it is as if also divinity would be applied to man—a blasphemy, that couldn't be greater."[14]

Luther holds, "God causes all in everything."[15] And he is well aware of the consequences of that tenet. Thus he makes the following statement: "Because God achieves and causes all in everything He necessarily also acts in Satan and in the godless wicked," so that "if we do something, it is God who acts in us."[16] The will of man is only a "beast of burden," which in its movements is completely dependent on the rider who directs and steers it:

> Man is like a horse. Does God leap into the saddle? The horse is obedient and accommodates itself to every movement of the rider and goes whither he wills it. Does God throw down the reins? Then Satan leaps upon the back of the animal, which bends, goes and submits to the spurs and caprices of its new ride. And it is not in his free choice to run to one of the two riders and to seek him, but rather the rider himself is fighting to detain him [man] and to take possession of him.[17]

Since the human will is not able, based on its own decisions, to follow the commandments of God, these commandments do not serve to inspire the human will for the good, but merely to demonstrate man's impotence. Already the first man (Adam) "was unable to will the good that means to obey, because the Spirit did not inspire him to do so." Thus was "made visible in this first man, through a frightening example, of what our free will is capable, if it is left to itself, and not continuously more and more directed and encouraged by God's Spirit."[18]

Luther is fully aware of the consequences of his deterministic anthropological premises and therefore frankly presents the opinion that Judas "necessarily became a traitor, and it was not in the hands of Judas or any creature to act otherwise or change the will, . . . but to want that rather was the work of God that He, by His omnipotence, set into motion, as

14. Ibid., 18, 636.
15. Ibid., 18, 732.
16. Ibid., 18, 691.
17. Ibid., 18, 635.
18. Ibid., 18, 675.

He does with everything else."[19] Here an obvious question arises, that also Luther posed, namely: Why did God abandon Adam? Why does He not at the same time transform the evil will that He moved? And Luther gives the answer: "This is one of the secrets of Majesty, where His judgments are incomprehensible." And the judgments of God must be incomprehensible, for the God of Luther is an arbitrary God, "for whom neither cause nor reason are in count."[20] Thus man is given over to the predestinational arbitrariness of God, even with regard to his eternal destiny: "If you appreciate that God crowns those who have no merit, it must not displease you that He damns those who do not deserve it."[21]

At this point, we have to take into account the second pillar of Luther's anthropology, one that complements the complete denial of the freedom of the human will: the doctrine of the total corruption of human nature. Luther sees a "deep crookedness and depravity and wickedness in our nature; yes, it is in itself a wounded nature, completely leavened by malice."[22] The real reason for the corruption and wickedness of human nature is, according to Luther, however, not founded upon the original sin of Adam. Rather, the root cause for the depravity and sinfulness of man for Luther is the physical nature of man. In his anthropology Luther identifies the physical nature of man totally with that aspect of human corporeality that allows man to be inclined to sin, which St Paul calls the "flesh" and which Luther calls "the most unsubstantial" and "least valuable part" of man.[23] For Luther, however, man is determined completely and consistently by the flesh, and thus inclined to sin. Therefore, he identifies not only human corporeality totally with the flesh inclined to sin, but beyond that also denies the classical distinction between body and soul, basic for philosophical anthropology. "But I, in my boldness," says Luther, "do not separate flesh, soul, and spirit at all, because the flesh does not desire otherwise than through the soul and the spirit, by which it is alive."[24]

That means Luther follows Aristotle in his view that the soul is the animating principle of the physical body, and thus the principle of the self-movement of the organism. Consequently, also following Aristotle, he considers the human spiritual soul as the action-driving principle of all conscious human actions. Here, though, Luther effects a reversal of

---

19. Ibid., 18, 715 f.
20. Ibid., 18, 712.
21. Ibid., 18, 731.
22. Ibid., 56, 361, 18–21.
23. Ibid., 18, 744.
24. Ibid., 2, 585, 31–32.

the Aristotelian approach. He does so in that he derives from his judgement that all human life and action is consistently determined by the sinfulness of the "flesh" the conclusion that the soul as the principle of human life and action must be determined by the sinfulness of the flesh. The soul thus doesn't have the body at its disposal as a morally neutral tool—as with Aristotle—but, rather, the sinful flesh also contaminates the human soul and directs its aspirations towards sin. "The same man, the same soul, the same spirit of man is," as Luther puts it, "mixed and tainted with the desires of the flesh."[25] And, "All is flesh, because all is carnally minded."[26]

From this reversal of the classical theory of the soul he then deduces the denial of human free will. Because if man is essentially "flesh," and if "flesh" is determined by the fact "that it cannot submit to God,"[27] then man, due to his possession of a nature depraved by sin, is also unable to decide for the good freely. "Thus, since men are flesh, as God Himself testifies, they can only be carnally minded, therefore the 'free will' is suitable for nothing else than sinning."[28] Hence, even the supposedly good works of man are in truth nothing but manifestations of human sin. Even the one who does good sins—and he *particularly* sins *in* the good he does.

At this point Luther again carries out another modification of the Aristotelian tradition. Confronting the orthodox theologians, Luther points out, "Sin possesses . . . a *perseitas* in every good work. . . . The man does good, so he sins, for the man who does good, is the subject, and the sin is his *passio*, his weakness."[29] In these explanations, the term "*perseitas*" of sin is of central importance. "*Perseitas*" means "being in itself." In the Aristotelian theory of categories this "being in itself" represents the key provision of the category of substance as opposed to the "accidentals," that have existence exclusively in another entity. When Luther attributes *perseitas* to sin, that means that for him sin is not a changeable quality of men and thus an accidental category, as previously supposed. Rather, sin for Luther is an essential *determination* of man that necessarily relates to the *substance* of man and designates man's very *nature*.

It goes without saying that Luther's concept of man entails certain consequences with respect to the concept of God, who is the Creator of man. And this is the reason why Luther can't stop at Ockham's position

25. Ibid., 2, 586, 4–5.
26. Ibid., 18, 742.
27. Ibid., 18, 736.
28. Ibid., 18, 735.
29. Ibid., 8, 77, 9–18.

of an arbitrary God, but rather has to radicalize it. Whereas Ockham had still excluded any contradiction in God and His arbitrary exercise of power, Luther's God, in His essence, is downright determined by an inner self-contradiction. Luther is therefore compelled to assume a self-contradiction in God because his anthropological premises force him to shift the origin of evil into God.

For if God created man as a corporeal being, and if the physical nature of man is to be equated with the "flesh" in the pejorative sense, which tends to sin with necessity; when, therefore, man—due to his nature—is not capable of doing anything else but sinning, then ultimately God is responsible for the sin of man. In His creation He provided man with a nature that is necessarily inclined to sin; that is constitutionally incapable of doing the good; and that even in its supposedly "good deeds" is still sinning.

Thus, human freedom appears to be an illusion. And it is all the more an illusion as the enslaved human will is, in any case, only capable of carrying out what it is driven to do by an external power, be it God or the devil, while the human being does not have the possibility to decide by which of the two antagonistic powers he wants his will to be determined. Moreover, since God "causes all in everything"[30] without exception, we are left not only to conclude that "if we do something, it is God who acts in us."[31] Rather, yet *another* conclusion results from this; namely, since God "necessarily also acts in Satan and in the wicked,"[32] then it becomes absolutely clear why Luther attributes to God the self-declaration, "I am the one who creates good and evil."[33] Because God is "so preposterously powerful"—as Luther puts it—"that He ascribes good and evil, two incompatible things, to the unity of His eternal nature."[34] Luther therefore states explicitly, "God contradicts Himself."[35] And the very root of this self-contradiction in God is that the nature of God does not consist in pure goodness, but also encompasses evil.

At this point the question arises whether the suggested self-contradiction refers to God's nature, or only to man's cognition of God. As for the human cognition of God, Luther distinguishes three forms or stages of this cognition. These he denotes with the terms "light of nature," "light of grace" and "light of glory."[36]

30. Ibid., 18, 732.
31. Ibid., 18, 691.
32. Ibid., 18, 691.
33. Ibid., 40, II, 417.
34. Ibid., 40, II, 417.
35. Ibid., 43, 202.
36. Ibid., 18, 785 (26–38).

What Luther called the "light of nature" is what is classically referred to as natural reason. This natural reason is not capable of understanding why it should be just "that the good is afflicted, and that the evil prospers."[37] To solve the problem emerging therefrom, it is first necessary to overcome natural reason, even to destroy it, in order to climb to the next level of the cognition of God, because "[r]atio adheres only to visible things. It must be killed here, so that the Word and faith have space." But how can ratio be killed in order to create room for faith? According to Luther's view, this can only happen through acts of radical unbelief: "It [ratio] cannot be killed otherwise than by despair, mistrust, hatred and grumbling against God, so that the spirit, when all external objects are removed, only clings to the word and the sacraments and only finds rest in them. For God is incomprehensible and a nothingness in all His wonders and works."[38]

Neither from God's natural nor from His supernatural actions is reason, therefore, capable of recognizing God's goodness and justice. Only faith, which Luther calls the "light of grace" is able to perceive God's justice in the fact that the good suffer and the evil prosper. Faith, according to Luther, does not arise from reason enlightened by grace, as has been traditionally assumed, since faith can only access the space wherein reason has already been "killed." Faith is therefore based solely on the "word" and the "sacrament." However, a problem emerges at this level of knowledge of God that springs from the "light of grace" as well. For even faith is unable to recognize God as just, since even for the faith (that is the "light of grace") it is not comprehensible "how God can condemn the one who [due to the anthropological premises set by Luther] by his own efforts cannot do otherwise than become sinful and guilty. At this point both the light of nature and the light of grace declare that the blame is not of the miserable man, but of the unjust god. For they [both faith and reason] cannot judge differently about God, who gratuitously crowns the wicked man without merit and who doesn't crown another one but rather damns him, who is probably less [or] at least not more wicked."[39]

That means neither natural reason nor faith arising from grace—which after overcoming reason is based solely on word and sacrament—is able to recognize God as good and just. Thus, Luther says about the "works righteous":

37. Ibid., 18, 785.
38. Ibid., 43, 395, 14–19.
39. Ibid., 18, 785.

At least in their hearts they called Him [i.e., God] a tyrant, even if they say "father" with their mouth.... All these say secretly in their heart: God acts tyrannical; no father is He, but in truth an adversary, which indeed is what He truly is.[40]

The heart does not say, Abba, Father, but rather tyrant, enemy and adversary. All of those call God a tyrant in the heart. Because it is necessary that you hate him whom you fear, therefore it is necessary that even blasphemies and curses follow this hatred.[41]

Therefore Luther frankly admits, "As others are tempted to steal, so am I to speak blasphemy."[42]

But besides the knowledge of God, or better put, besides the relationship with God enlightened by the "light of nature" and the "light of grace," Luther assumes a third knowledge or relationship of this kind, illuminated by what he calls "the light of glory." He comments on this in the following way:

But the light of glory speaks differently and will subsequently show that God's most just and obvious justice indwells in God's judgement. Until the light of glory appears, we are to believe this truth, exhorted and encouraged by the example of the light of grace, which accomplishes a similar miracle in natural light.[43]

That means the resolution of an apparent contradiction. Hence, Luther wants to say that just as faith in the form of the "light of grace" resolves a contradiction detected by natural reason, faith in the shape of the "light of glory" resolves a contradiction on which faith in the form of the "light of grace" stumbles and finds itself provoked to rebel against God.

But what is faith in the form of the "light of glory"? From the passage cited above one must conclude that that faith lies in a sort of anticipation of the vision of God in eternal glory. Only this anticipation makes it possible to recognize God as good and just and to acknowledge Him as such, because in this world and lifetime nothing provides any indication for recognizing God as being good and just, neither from the perspective of natural reason nor from the perspective of faith in the shape of the "light of grace." For to this world and lifetime applies the tenet:

40. Ibid., 56, 368, 18–29.
41. Ibid., 57 Röm 188, 25f.
42. Ibid., 40, I, 524, 9; 40, II, 90, 8.
43. Ibid., 18, 785.

As God's wisdom is hidden under the appearance of folly and the truth under the guise of a lie—in the same way God's word occurs, as often as it occurs, . . . under the appearance of a contradiction.[44]

And it is the same with God's will. It is indeed, "good, pleasing, perfect," but it is hidden under the appearance of evil, in a way so displeasing and desperate, that it appears to our will by no means as God's will, but as the devil's will.[45]

While Thomas Aquinas defines faith as "a certain participation in the divine truth in us,"[46] faith, in Luther, turns into a pure existential act of despair, a leap into the anticipation of eternal glory, founded solely upon the resolve of the will, a glory that does not find an analogous representation in this world and lifetime, neither one that can be recognized by reason, nor one that faith, solely grounded in word and sacrament, is able to grasp. The revealed God and the hidden God cannot be mediated, either by natural reason or by reason enlightened by faith. Rather, they constitute a contradictory opposition. The only thing that can help here is the sheer resolve to throw oneself into a hope for which experience and knowledge do not provide any justification. When Luther indicates that those to whom he refers as the "works righteous" are secretly saying in their hearts "tyrannically acts God; no father is He but adversary," so Luther confirms them in their judgment, saying that "He [God] really is thus." But Luther immediately objects, "But they [the works righteous] do not know that you have to agree with this adversary, and that He thus becomes a friend and father and otherwise never will be."[47]

However, this anticipatory affirmation of God, born out of desperation, has a prehistory. The "light of glory" arises only at the end of a process in which a peculiar dialectic prevails. Only in passing through this dialectic can man reaches his true being. "The nonbeing is a thing without a name, the person in sin. Development is justification. Being is justice. . . . Through the new birth [in Christ] man goes over from sin to righteousness, and thus from nonbeing through development to being. When that happens he acts rightly."[48]

However, should this *not* happen, one must add, man does not act rightly and therefore cannot reach his goal. Since the real being of man exclusively emerges as a result of a dialectical process, the entire process

44. Ibid., 56, 477, 31–33.
45. Ibid., 56, 447, 3–7.
46. Thomas Aquinas, *De pot.* Q. 6 a. 9.
47. WA, 56, 368, 18–29.
48. Ibid., 56, 442.

must be willed, including its various stages, and its starting point as well. That means also the state of sin is to be aimed at, because man is only able to achieve his true purpose through the dialectical overcoming of sin. And as the overcoming of the state of sin requires that this state must be taken up in an affirmative manner in the first place, that it might be overcome, Luther therefore claims, "Whoever wants to become just has to become a sinner; whoever wants to become good, proper, just, in short shaped godlike and a Catholic Christian, shall first become sick, evil, perverted, in short devilish, a heretic, infidel, a Turk. . . ."[49] And finally this dialectic also corresponds to God's acts, because "[it] is God's nature, first to destroy and annihilate what is in us before He gives His own."[50]

With this we have returned to our question concerning the nature of God. Here now the urgent issue arises whether the dialectic of human existence also reflects an analogous dialectic in God Himself. Or, to put the question more precisely, when Luther, as already quoted earlier, asserts that "God contradicts Himself,"[51] then the query arises whether this contradiction in God only characterizes our (always limited) understanding of God, or whether the nature of God is in itself determined by contradictions. In view of the preceding considerations, the answer becomes apparent.

When Luther, as already cited, deems that God is "so preposterously powerful" that he "attributes good and evil, two incompatible things, to the unity of His eternal nature,"[52] it should clearly follow that the contradictions in God pertain not merely to our (limited) understanding of God but also to God's very nature. And that these contradictions in the nature of God can only be resolved by means of a dialectical process—at this point by a process of divine self-constitution—is exactly what Luther suggests when he states, "God must first become the devil, before He becomes God."[53] With this sentence Luther claims two things: first, that God develops; and, second, that He can only develop to what He essentially is by passing through the opposite of Himself.

For any theology led by reason, be it of Scholastic or even nominalist origin, such contradiction in God would be simply unthinkable. But Luther doesn't appreciate reason very much. Rather, he believes that "reason is the devil's harlot, who can do nothing other than blaspheme

---

49. Ibid., 5, 195.
50. Ibid., 56, 375, 18 f.
51. Ibid., 43, 202.
52. Ibid., 40, II, 417.
53. Ibid., 31, 249.

and desecrate everything that God speaks and does."[54] Syllogisms he therefore referred to as "sheer knavery that the devil deals in."[55] Luther subsequently also rejects, together with reason, the complete tradition of rational theology. He then concludes that "the Church can not possibly be reformed unless the entire stock of doctrines, conclusions, Scholastic theology, philosophy, and logic, as they exist today, be uprooted and replaced by something else."[56]

But what could this "something else" be? It is a theology, and a philosophy inspired by it, that forms exactly that particular strand of modern thought that elevates conflict and contradiction into a position in which they become the key principle of mind and spirit; and this because the divine cause and origin of the spirit already bears this conflict and contradiction in itself and must carry it out in itself. This requires a principle of process in the Divine, in the course of which the Divine constitutes itself by negating its self-negation, arising from its inner self-contradiction, and thus—in negating the negation—overturns this contradiction, so as finally—through this double negation—to constitute itself as a unity and as Absolute.

This process of self-constitution of the Divine, in which the Divine—proceeding from the initial conflict—gradually has worked its way up to the unity of the Absolute, is carried out in the realms of the world and history. It is in these realms that the divine spirit has to objectify itself as nature and culture—that is as its other self—because only in that way can it become the object of its own self-reflection. Hence, also, the form in which the world exists is determined by those antagonisms that already prevail in its divine origin. And therefore the world is a historical world through and through, because it is in the world that the process of divine self-constitution in the shape of history takes place. Because the divine self-constitution is being driven by the "productive power of negation," the course of history, in whose inexorable progress the divine self-constitution takes place, is determined by conflict and contradiction. History is thus permanent revolution driven by negation and dialectic. And what we have here before us here—sketched very broadly—is the basic philosophical and theological concept of German Idealism, and in particular of the philosophy of Hegel.

---

54. Ibid., 18, 164.

55. Citation according to Hartmann Grisar, *Martin Luthers Leben und sein Werk* (Freiburg im Breisgau: Herder, 1926), S.228.

56. WA, *Epist.*, T. I, 64.

3

The Northern Renaissance and the Protestant Revolt

Sebastian Morello

Introduction

THE RENAISSANCE PERIOD saw not only the rise of humanist "new learning" education and its social consequences, but also that of what was arguably the most important political crisis in the history of Christendom; namely, the Reformation. It is in the response of Renaissance thinkers to this crisis that we see the true significance of Renaissance political thought, and how these men (if only we would read them) still offer some remedy to the situation in which we find ourselves today due to the Reformation.

In this chapter, we will focus our attention specifically on the thinkers of the Northern Renaissance, especially Thomas More, and on how the scholars with whom we are concerned utilized the new humanist learning to respond to the political crisis created by the Reformation. One cannot even begin to understand the present situation of the West without grasping the elements of this pivotal rupture in its history. Protestantism has, to quote Henry Sire, "formed the outlook of the modern world."[1]

We will look specifically at the Reformation doctrines of total determinism (the Protestant conception of predestination) and total corruption (the Protestant conception of the anthropological consequences of original sin, later described by John Calvin as the state of "total depravity"). Then we shall focus on the sundering of faith and reason and, in

---

1. Henry J.A. Sire, *Phoenix from the Ashes: The Making, Unmaking, and Restoration of Catholic Tradition* (Kettering, OH: Angelico Press, 2015), 55.

turn, the separation of grace and nature that follow from the two doctrines just mentioned above. Finally, we shall assess the Reformation as an attack on the principle of tradition and the very identity of Christendom.

The danger here is to present the Reformation as the sole cause of the social problems of modernity. This would be a serious exaggeration. Nevertheless, the Reformation should be seen as one major cause in a chain of causes, with all the subsequent causes being inferior in gravity. Thus, all subsequent causes are innately linked to the Reformation. Not all aspects of the complexity of the modern social matrix can be explained by some *direct* reference to a particular feature of the Reformation. However, there will be *some* relationship that can be determined, and this is partly what needs to be teased out.

The Crisis of the Mind

The anti-intellectualism of the Reformation that we shall first consider was already in part established in the academy throughout Europe. The positing of faith against reason was not original when the Reformers posed it; the claim had already been made by several Renaissance humanists and is raised repeatedly by Lorenzo Valla.[2] Humanists, including Thomas More and John Fisher, were certainly discontented with the direction in which "Thomism" was going. With the development of the late medieval manualist school, philosophy had become ever less grounded in experience and was departing into an anti-realist world of unapplied logical extrapolations. This movement was underpinned by an increasing skepticism caused by doubts about metaphysics which led philosophers to seek certainty in logical necessity.

For many, the "new learning" movement of the Renaissance was an attempt to return to realism. Unfortunately, however, many did not put away the late Scholastic manuals in favor of the primary sources of Aristotle and Thomas Aquinas, but simply became hostile to the whole classical realist tradition. They developed a curriculum almost solely devoted to the eloquence-focused *trivium* (grammar, rhetoric, and dialectic), mostly neglecting the more philosophical *quadrivium* (geometry, arithmetic, astronomy, and music), and for substance looked to the existential reflections of Cicero and the plays of Ovid. The emphasis on the *trivium* was in part inspired by skepticism. As people lost confidence in the notion that an argument might be right or wrong, they looked

2. See Paul Oskar Kristella, *Medieval Aspects of Renaissance Learning* (Durham, NC: Duke University Press, 1974), 64.

evermore to judging it by its wit, beauty, and extent and application of vocabulary. These became the measure of whether one should be persuaded or not.

Broadly speaking, then, this was the state of the academy.[3] It was in this general context of widespread skepticism that the Reformers appeared. Also, it was in this context that geniuses like More and Fisher established a path that did not fall prey to the exaggerations of many of the anti-Thomistic humanists, nor the anti-intellectualism of the Reformers, nor the anti-realism of the manualists. Rather, they sought a middle path, welcoming the "new learning" of the Renaissance, whilst seeking to be students of the realism of the High Middle Ages. They saw no reason to place rhetoric and grammar in opposition to metaphysics and logic, but rather sought to form themselves in both. It was precisely this that—as far as the Reformers were concerned—made such men a force to be reckoned with.

Total Corruption and Total Determinism

The doctrine of total corruption constitutes the view that, subsequent to the fall of the first couple, man is not merely wounded by sin, but utterly ruined by it. Grace, therefore, does not build on nature, for grace cannot redeem that which is *totally* corrupt. In turn, grace merely saves the soul from itself. Total determinism comprises the view that God arbitrarily decides who shall be saved and who shall not before they are created; therefore, there is no *cooperation* with God's grace. The choice has already been made, irrespective of one's moral character, reception of the theological virtues, and gifts of the Holy Ghost.

This dual doctrine reduces man to a brute, and two forms of government follow from its anthropology. One is that of draconian leaders, and the other that of the liberal oligarchy which maintains the impression that they are the peoples' choice. Luther preferred the former, which is illustrated by such famous sayings as:

> Peasants are no better than straw. They will not hear the word and they are without sense; therefore, they must be compelled to hear the crack of the whip and the whiz of bullets and it is only what they deserve.

---

3. It was later in reaction to such skepticism that Descartes chose to pursue absolute certainty, choosing the epistemological point of departure which ultimately gave rise to a continuing tradition of philosophical skepticism. Descartes would have been horrified to discover that this was the consequence of his writings, for he was seeking a way to do away with skepticism for good.

Like the drivers of donkeys, who have to belabor the donkeys incessantly with rods and whips, or they will not obey, so must the ruler do with the people; they must drive, beat, throttle, hang, burn, behead, and torture, so as to make themselves feared and to keep the people in check.

With this view of the "ordinary man," a certain manipulation of the masses was seen to be absolutely necessary. This was the road to tyranny that More feared so much, condemning the ruler who "thinks of his subjects as his slaves."[4] Sire notes the following:

> We fail to see any popular movement for Protestantism, or the humble labour of missionary preaching with which the Christian Faith was first planted in Europe. Professing a religion of freedom, the Protestants imposed their creed by the harsh exercise of civil power and by the proscription of what had been for centuries the religious birthright of the people.[5]

The people are treated as incapable of developing virtue, and are led to believe they can happily abandon the life of virtue. Such a people could have respect for nothing but force. From this justification for draconian rule grew an elitism that saw Protestantism as something the majority might resist but that could, nevertheless, be disseminated. For not only did it support the power of the princes and local lords, but some argument could be constructed that it was for the good of the people, whether they knew it or not. Here, then, the first European intelligentsia developed; that intelligentsia which has played a role in the manipulation of the "ordinary man" ever since. Sire notes the following about the Reformation:

> The first feature to be noted, in which it is the ancestor of modern liberalism, is Protestantism's elitist character. It can be seen that a movement which appealed to the written word of scripture in an age in which many were illiterate, and which invoked scholars' interpretations of the Greek text to challenge traditional teaching, was essentially the work of a minority.[6]

More saw clearly, as no one else really did, how Protestantism allowed for a tyranny over the "ordinary man" at the hands of a rapidly established intelligentsia. This was the kind of problem to which he—as a philosopher, lawyer, and politician with a pure notion of the polity as

---

4. Thomas More, *The History of King Richard III and Selections From the English and Latin Poems* (New Haven: Yale University Press, 1976), 140.

5. Sire, 57.

6. Ibid., 55.

existing to serve its subjects—was very sensitive. For this reason, More could accept neither Luther's view of the need for a dominating leadership of oppressors nor Tyndale's opinion that kings should rule by some tyrannical mode.[7] Both views stemmed from the same anthropology; one that conceived of man as an irrational creature without a will, who belongs more to either a herd or a pack than to a political community.

In fact, More thought that the "ordinary man" was nothing like a brute, but rather that he was perfectly capable of applying his reason and discerning the moral law, specified and summarized in the Decalogue, but in its contents, to More's mind, pertaining primarily to the natural law.[8] In his understanding of the Decalogue and the universality of the natural law, More was in agreement with Aquinas.[9] In turn, More (and Aquinas, for that matter) was about as far as a Christian can intellectually be from the Protestant view that the possibility of virtue is closed to those who belong to the arbitrarily *un*elected, and irrelevant for salvation to the arbitrarily elected. Samuel Gregg notes, "More does not accept Tyndale's claim that man's nature is totally corrupted. Rather, he affirms that there is an order of the knowledge of good and evil 'built' into human nature which man is capable of knowing through reason."[10] As we shall later aim to demonstrate, More's understanding of human dignity, which arises from man's rationality, is rooted in two main influences: Aquinas's realism and Pico's humanism.

More knew that "despite the Protestants' claim to speak for the ordinary layman, their revolt was not a popular one. There was no place in Europe where the peasantry, by far the largest part of the population, received the Reformation gladly, let alone instigated its entry."[11] The Northern humanists, who soon found their mission as defenders of Catholicism, really did have the good of the peasantry in mind, and were not blind to the fact that the "Reformation was the work of kings, of the nobility, and of the urban plutocracies. All the Reformers, notably Luther, Calvin, and Knox, relied explicitly on those elements and directed their main proselytic efforts at them."[12]

The Great Peasants' Revolt (1524–1525) had particularly disturbed

---

7. See Alistair Fox, *Thomas More* (Oxford: Basil Blackwell, 1982), 162.

8. See Thomas More, *Dialogue Concerning Heresies* (New York: Scepter Publishers, 2006), 169.

9. See Thomas Aquinas, *Summa Theologica* (Westminster, MD.: Christian Classics, 1981), I–II, 100, 1.

10. See Samuel Gregg in Travis Curtright, ed., *Thomas More: Why Patron of Statesmen?* (New York: Lexington Books, 2015), 104.

11. Sire, 55.

12. Ibid.

More because he understood this to be a direct result of Reformation ideas about man and his nature. The combination of the rejection of reason via the doctrine of *sola fideism*, and the rejection of free will via the doctrine of absolute determinism, presented man as a brute who could act in any manner and remain free of any culpability.

More was right to view these doctrines as deeply pernicious, for they have led to an understanding of human action independent of considerations concerning universal moral norms, as discussion has moved toward deliberations of "what is *right* for *me*" to determine the moral value of an act or decision. In turn, this has resulted in state law being instituted with no reference to *perennial law*. Alistair Fox notes that More, of course, "recognized that the Lutherans' view that the elect were justified by faith arbitrarily, and deterministically disposed, logically implied an irrelevancy of all temporal laws."[13]

This has, in fact, had a detrimental effect on the Western social sphere, not in that it has brought about the utter discarding of temporal law, but rather in that it has served as the genesis of a conception of temporal law as in no way reflecting perennial law. Specifically, this has led to the invention of new laws and the changing of existing laws at a pace unknown before in any human community. Of course, this in turn has brought about a certain *justifiable* contempt for the law, which has increasingly been seen as something arbitrarily imposed. Finally—and this is what the Northern humanists greatly feared—it has led to a public policy determined by what will please the masses, reflecting the latest "craze" that excites them, as if desperately seeking to cool the passions of a snarling pack of hounds. Following from Reformation anthropology, the only other alternative to arbitrary law being determined by the mob is the "Leviathan option" suggested by Hobbes, and which, in fact, found expression across Europe to differing degrees in the twentieth century.

Protestantism laid a certain foundation for the subsequent rejection of natural law, for continuous political instability, and for a "might-is-right" ethic that at times led to explicit justification of governments so draconian that we would deem them almost entirely indistinguishable from tyrannies. But, of course, all this is preceded by a vision of man as a totally determined—and in no way a *self*-determining—being. Luther himself summarized this as follows:

> Man is like a horse. Does God leap into the saddle? The horse is obedient and accommodates itself to every movement of the rider and goes whither he wills it. Does God throw down the reins? Then Satan leaps

13. Fox, 160.

upon the back of the animal, which bends, goes and submits to the spurs and caprices of its new rider.... Therefore, necessity, not free will, is the controlling principle of our conduct. God is the author of what is evil as well as of what is good, and, as He bestows happiness on those who merit it not, so also does He damn others who deserve not their fate.[14]

It is not hard to imagine the horror of More, Erasmus, Fisher, and others at such a view of human dignity, and such a blasphemous presentation of God's relationship with man. Also, one might note that such a view of God would inevitably lead to secularism, if for no other reason than that no one could worship such a God for long, since he resembles more a beast than the Creator.

Let us momentarily consider one of the major political consequences of Reformation doctrine concerning the will: the modern denial of the existence of the human will in and of itself. One of the actions of the human will is obviously to make our conduct correspond with our intellectual convictions. Those who have a weak will, through a lack of virtue, may give way to temptation and in turn act "inauthentically"— that is, in a way that is contrary to their convictions.

In itself, this is not hypocrisy. Hypocrisy is the deliberate attempt to contrive a false appearance of virtue or moral integrity by claiming to hold higher standards or more noble beliefs than is actually the case. This is utterly different from holding certain modes of behavior to be wrong while being fully aware of one's capacity to fall into such behavior. For example, the person who says gossiping is unacceptable but nevertheless falls into occasional gossiping, is not a hypocrite. In fact, such a person should be trusted far more than someone who simply denies any wrongdoing in the act of gossiping. On the other hand, a hypocrite would "virtue-signal"—talking about how he would never dream of gossiping and then gossip in the next instance, denying that such a term can be applied to his activity.

For this distinction to be held, however, there must be some belief in the existence of the will. The modern view has departed from any such belief, and tends to view the human agent merely as harboring a collection of desires. If, then, there is some discrepancy between moral beliefs and desires, this is viewed not in terms of the person's pursuit of the good and the struggle implied by the reality of concupiscence, but rather as a mere conflict between different desires. In turn, it is believed that the agent—to be authentic—should act on whichever he *feels* to be

14. Patrick F. O'Hare, *The Facts about Luther* (Charlotte, NC: TAN Books, 1994), 266–67; Luther, *De servo arbitrio*, 7, 13, seq.

the *strongest*. In this view, if a person were to gossip, he would be a hypocrite if he then said he believed gossiping to be a vice.

This explains in part the current enthusiasm for publicly vilifying any person with homosexual inclinations who claims homosexual *acts*, or the "gay lifestyle" in general, to be immoral. A disbelief in the human will coupled with the militancy of the "gay agenda" causes such persons to be condemned as "self-haters" and hypocrites, and such a condemnation does, indeed, follow from the modern anthropological vision, in its denial of the existence of the human will as explained above.

Now, this modern denial is nothing more than a slight development of the Reformation denial of free will, which obviously makes the will altogether obsolete. The Reformation denial of free will is tantamount to the denial of the will's very existence. This, in turn, has given rise to exactly what More envisaged; that is, a social structure that functions by encouraging the state's subjects to act on their basest inclinations, lest rulers be accused of preventing the people from living *authentic* lives. Due to the Reformation, the human community has an anthropological justification for reducing itself to a pack of brutes seeking the satisfaction of their strongest desires. In turn, such actions as criminalizing adultery or prohibiting pornography, far from being healthy state leadership and coercion toward the objective good, are seen to mark a positive injustice. Finally, the conclusion is that the more openly depraved one is, the less hypocritical one is. The more a society celebrates expressions of degeneracy, the freer it demonstrates itself to be.

In the face of the Reformation anthropological view, implied by the doctrine of total determinism, More was something of a prophet. He knew exactly what the consequences would be, and states the following:

> [T]he unhappy deeds of that sect must needs be imputed to the sect itself, when [the] doctrine thereof teaches and gives rise to their evil deeds. A Christian man's evil conduct cannot be imputed to his Christianity. For that conduct is contrary to the doctrine and conduct of Christ. . . . [But] what good deed will someone study or strive to do who believes Luther that he has no free will of his own by which he can, with the help of grace, either work or pray? Will he not say to himself that he can sit still and leave God alone? What evil will they care to forbear who believe Luther that God alone, without their will, works all the iniquity that they do themselves?[15]

Above anything, More and his friend Erasmus reacted against the absolute rejection of free will and saw that this was the fundamental

15. Thomas More, *Dialogue Concerning Heresies,* 424.

philosophical problem underpinning the error of the Reformation. Both More and Erasmus—the latter having attacked Luther's doctrine of total determinism as early as 1524 with his work *The Freedom of the Will*—had understood the issue clearly when the rest of Europe still thought the problem lay solely at the level of reactions against decadent clergy and a strange use of indulgences.

Here we can note the influence of the Italian Renaissance. The Florentine eccentric, Giovanni Pico della Mirandola (1463–1494), was something of a role model for More. More wrote a biography of Pico in 1504, in which he insists that Pico's "life and works will repay being studied carefully and often brought to mind."[16] Pico had presented a theological view of man utterly antithetical to the later determinist anthropology of the Reformers. In his work *On the Dignity of Man*, Pico had placed into the mouth of God the following words:

> In conformity with thy free judgement, in whose hands I have placed thee, thou art confined by no bounds; and thou wilt fix limits of nature for thyself.... Thou, like a judge appointed for being honourable, art the molder and maker of thyself; thou mayest sculpt thyself into whatever shape thou dost prefer.[17]

More did not follow Pico to the *absolute* self-determinism that Pico advocated, and an illustration of Pico's extremism is the almost total absence of grace in his account of man's relationship with God. Nevertheless, Pico believes that man *can* make real choices about his own life, and that man is not merely presented with a plethora of choices all of which have equal value, but rather, by choice, can order himself toward that which is worthy of respect, or alternatively that which is worthy of no respect. Pico describes this in the following way:

> If you see a man given over to his belly ... it is a plant not a man that you see. If you see anyone ... delivered over to the senses, it is a brute not a man that you see. If you come upon a philosopher winnowing out all things by right reason, he is a heavenly not an earthly animal. If you come upon a pure contemplator ... banished to the innermost places of the mind, he is ... a divinity clothed within human flesh.[18]

Pico, not discounting all his exaggerations, teaches here that our choices change us for better or for worse, and whether they are admirable is determined by whether they are in conformity with reason. It is

---

16. Thomas More, *The Life of Pico* (New York: Scepter Publishers, 2010), 5.

17. Giovanni Pico della Mirandola, *On the Dignity of Man* (Indianapolis: Hackett Publishing Company, 1998), 5.

18. Ibid., 6.

precisely here that we can see the impact of Italian humanism on More's thought. More understands the human person to be a creature endowed with a noble mind, characterized by his freedom, worthy of intellectual autonomy, and requiring the cultivation of virtue for his true self-determining nature to be revealed. Finally, he sees man as that creature that can reach his end only in God, which implies the actuation of the intellect in wisdom. More saw in the "new learning" of the Renaissance a clear and certain answer to the view of man presented by the Reformers. Essentially, it boiled down to a question of human dignity.

The understanding of human dignity that sees man as the image of God specifically insofar as he is a rational being capable of truly free acts expresses an anthropology that is at the heart of the Catholic tradition. It can be traced through the Fathers, is explicit in the thought of the medieval theologians, and was utilized magnificently by More and other Northern humanists in response to the explicit denial by the Reformers of the two attributes that cause man to reflect his Creator: rationality and freedom. Furthermore, the Northern humanists recognized that such a denial would lead to the absolute rejection of the entire Christian narrative. For only a nature that shares some "connaturality" (being rational) with the Eternal Logos (divine rationality) could be assumed by the Logos in the Hypostatic Union. There is nothing about a totally corrupt nature—and in turn a totally corrupt intellect—which is connatural with the Eternal Logos. In this sense, Reformation anthropology would not only mark the denial of man's intrinsic nobility, but also the denial of the intelligibility of the Christian narrative itself; the Incarnation ceases to make any sense!

Grace and Nature, Faith and Reason

The Northern humanists responded to the Protestant rejection of reason with a synthesis of medieval realism and the "new learning" of the Italian Renaissance. Maritain referred to More as a "bon disciple de saint Thomas d'Aquin."[19] Although the Thomism of More has often been neglected by scholars, Gregg points out that More was influenced by the thought of Aquinas in three key areas: faith and reason, philosophical anthropology, and political philosophy:

---

19. Jacques Maritain, *"La Philosophie du Droit,"* in Richard O'Sullivan, ed., *The King's Good Servant: Papers Read to the Thomas More Society of London* (Oxford: Basil Blackwell, 1941), 41.

Thomistic thought informs crucial elements of More's contribution to crucial debates—specifically discussions concerning the relationship between faith and reason, the character of the will (especially its place vis-à-vis reason), and the place of equity in the workings of judicial systems—that shaped the social, political, and legal landscape of sixteenth-century Europe.[20]

More was not bringing together two entirely separate traditions, for Aquinas's thought had already greatly influenced some figures of the Italian Renaissance. Pico's famous *Nine-hundred Theses* (issued in 1486) had included forty-five theses in defense of Aquinas's works.[21] It should not surprise us, then, that More saw no conflict between the thought of the medievals and that of the Italian humanists, despite Lorenzo Valla's opinion to the contrary. Clearly, as Gregg points out, "More was well-versed in Aquinas's writings,"[22] and More referred to the Angelic Doctor as "the flower of theology, and a man of that true and perfect faith."[23] More had been appalled that the word "Thomistic" had been used as a pejorative term by Luther in a rebuttal to Henry VIII,[24] and, no doubt, More's defense of Aquinas's thought was at least in part a response to the claim in Tyndale's work, *The Obedience of the Christian Man*, that bringing philosophy into theological reflection was gravely mistaken.[25] More had even used Thomistic epistemology in his apologetics, in which he suggests that the relationship between mental images—or *phantasmata*—and the immaterial intelligence be considered as an analogue of the pious Christian's use of sacred images and statues.[26]

More was not alone as both a humanist and intellectual disciple of Aquinas. Indeed, Rex notes that "Fisher's theology is marked by a . . . far from unsuccessful attempt to reinvigorate the old blood of the Scholastics with the new blood of the humanists."[27] Fisher, like More, had described Aquinas as "most learned and at the same time most holy."[28]

20. Gregg in Curtright, 95.

21. See Kristella, 72.

22. Gregg in Curtright, 99.

23. Thomas More, *Confutation of Tyndale's Answer*, in *The Complete Works of St Thomas More* (New Haven: Yale University Press, 1997), VIII, 713.

24. See More, *The Complete Works*, V, 324.

25. See William Tyndale, *The Obedience of the Christian Man* (Clermont-Ferrand: Digireads, 2012), art. 154–158.

26. See Thomas More, *Dialogue Concerning Heresies*, 60–62.

27. Richard Rex, *The Theology of John Fisher* (Cambridge: Cambridge University Press, 2003), 1.

28. Edward Sturz, S.J. *The Works and Days of John Fisher* (Cambridge: Harvard University Press, 1967), 162.

The love that the Northern humanists had for Aquinas was, however, coupled with a hatred for subsequent developments in Scholastic education, and so "in the minds of More and figures such as John Colet, Fisher, and Erasmus, there was an important distinction to be made between Aquinas and many of his Scholastic successors."[29] The dislike was mutual. The sixteenth-century Scholastics did not like the humanists' emphasis on rhetoric because they believed it to be underpinned by skepticism, and the humanists did not like the Scholastics' emphasis on unapplied logic for exactly the same reason.

It seems they were both correct. Both groups had departed from the study of *ontology* due to a growing spirit of skepticism, to which we referred earlier. It was precisely this problem, however, that More and the Northern humanists sought to address by "walking a middle path"—that is, by welcoming the "new learning" while also emphasizing the importance of the *via antiqua*[30] and applied logic of the medieval Schoolmen. Gregg points out that Fisher was instrumental in this process:

> Fisher had no hesitation in placing figures such as Aquinas and other Scholastic thinkers such as Albert the Great, Bonaventure, William of Paris, and Gregory of Rimini side-by-side with the very humanist emphasis upon learning Hebrew and Greek in the theology curriculum followed at Cambridge University.[31]

One of the grave problems with the *via moderna*—the name used by the Northern humanists for sixteenth-century Scholasticism, or at least what claimed to be Scholasticism—was the degree to which this system of thought was influenced by the nominalism prevalent throughout European universities at that time. The *via moderna*, then, became much more concerned with elements of Aristotelian logic which raised questions of "other possible worlds," unlike the *via antiqua* of Aquinas, which was not only fiercely committed to realism, but sought to place philosophy at the service of reflection upon the concrete events and truths of Christ's Redemption. This realism is precisely what the thinkers of the Northern Renaissance sought to return to in their focus on "historical realities" in the Bible and human life, influenced by their reflections on the historical writings of the Greeks and Romans.

Not discounting the Northern humanists' commitment to Aquinas, their understanding of the *end* for which one was educated belonged

---

29. Gregg in Curtright, 97.
30. See Rex, 19.
31. Gregg in Curtright, 99.

distinctly to the Renaissance. It was a classical education of sorts, developing out of the medieval cathedral schools, but now with a new focus on the cultivation of those who would go on to make good servants of the state. This, in turn, meant a heavy emphasis on rhetoric.[32]

Students needed to graduate knowing how to speak among lords. The Northern humanists were especially attentive to Ovid and Cicero and to the relationship between rhetoric and philosophy. Cicero had taught that beautiful speech is essential to the expression of truth, so that its claim to be true will be persuasive. Rhetoric was necessary because the purpose of education was no longer exclusively to prepare young men for ecclesiastical careers, but rather to form those who would go on to the noble courts of Christendom and serve the state with the power delegated to them by the Crown. This way of understanding "the educated man" was deeply established already in the courts of the Italian city-states, where scholars were employed with a view to procuring the state's proper ordering and, in turn, its proper end. The idea was supported by Plato, whose works were being greatly revived as part of the Renaissance movement, with his notion of the scholarly guardians in *The Republic*. For this reason, Lorenzo de Medici considered it imperative that he have such figures as Pico and Ficino at his Florentine court.

The change in the European conception of education is key to understanding the Northern humanists' response to the Reformation. They saw the Reformation as a political crisis, and because they believed the pursuit of knowledge to be of primary importance in securing the good of the state, they saw in the Reformers' rejection of reason the potential corruption of the entire socio-political sphere. It worked both ways; that is, insofar as the Reformation corrupted the state it was an attack on reason, for reason underwent formation to be at the service of the state, and insofar as it rejected the place of reason it also attacked the state, for the state could only be properly ordered by right reason.

Furthermore, following the Scholastic view of grace building on and perfecting nature, the Northern humanists saw the Church as capable of transforming the natural social sphere and bringing the state's subjects to Christian perfection. For this reason, as education became explicitly ordered toward the good of the state, the study of scripture and theology remained at the heart of the curriculum. For the Northern humanists, then, the conclusion was that as Reformation ideas continued to

---

32. See James McConica in George M. Logan, ed., *The Cambridge Companion to Thomas More* (Cambridge: Cambridge University Press, 2011), 23.

seduce people away from the truth, in which alone their rational nature could be perfected, the state was guaranteed to degenerate. Consequently, the state had a duty to defend itself against the dissemination of such ideas.

The Reformers repudiated philosophy and its acceptance and use in theology as mere works, opposed to the pure reception of faith. Also flowing into all their subsequent socio-theological thoughts and arrangements were admixtures of the kind of political vision which could be detected already in such figures as Marsilius of Padua and (in a different way) Machiavelli—namely, a clear departure of political thought from the framework of the *natural law*. This, in turn, led to a focus on the need for the sort of strong and even draconian leadership to which we referred earlier. Something of the development in question can be seen in Luther's response to the Great Peasants' Revolt, whose suppression without limits to violence he justified on the basis of the role of the prince as drawn from his exegesis on St Paul's Epistle to the Romans concerning obedience to civil rulers.

This view of the acceptability of a brutal exercise of civil power is exactly what the Northern humanists predicted would emerge if reason was rejected by conceptually positing it against faith. The Northern Renaissance was a highly intellectual movement, with a special focus on the study of philosophy, theology, and biblical scholarship. Northern humanists argued specifically for the consonance of faith and reason. Their foresight was extraordinary, for due to the sundering of faith and reason we have subsequently seen the rejection of both in the social sphere. The denial of reason has emptied faith of its intelligibility, and therefore the rejection of faith, too, has easily followed. Of course, it is one of the ironies of the Reformation that while the Reformers claimed to reject the philosophical pursuit altogether, many of their conclusions had fundamentally philosophical points of departure. Sire points this out clearly:

> [Luther] had the further misfortune to conduct his studies at the University of Erfurt, which was a bastion of nominalist teaching. That school rejected the rationality of the Thomist tradition, teaching that human ideas have no real relation to things but are mere labels or symbols for what the mind perceives. The nominalist teaching, with its contraposition of faith and reason, is reflected in Luther's pronouncement (made before he broke with the Church) that "there are many things in the Catholic Faith which manifestly appear contrary to reason and whose opposites are in accord with reason." Because of that persuasion, Luther found himself staring into an abyss of unbelief, in which he would be left at the mercy of his fears. He resolved the

dilemma by deciding that the crucial element in reconciling an individual to God was a spontaneous act of faith, in return for which God granted justification. . . . We may trace from this doctrine the modern misconception of faith as an essentially irrational position, a sacrifice of reason to religious duty, as if there were some virtue in the suspension of the proper faculties of the intellect for God's sake.[33]

The ultimate consequence of viewing religious assent as an irrational act has been the banishing of religion from the public square. This, for More and the Northern humanists, was of greater importance than any other issue raised by the Reformation. Sire goes on to explain the current state of affairs:

The effect of Luther's teaching is to turn faith into a personal gesture, and that is the only understanding of it to which liberal [modern] humanists are willing to attach any value. . . . Once the concept of faith is thus subjectivized, the corollary is to deny it the right to social expression. The Christian is expected to recognize his belief as a personal whim, with no connection to objective reality, and Christians in fact accept that imposition. . . . As widely used, "faith" is a euphemism for superstition, an acceptance of notions that cannot be proved and that the objective mind would reject. Thus, the legacy of the Reformation, with its attack on the supposed superstitions of Catholic Faith, is the transference of the whole of religious belief to the realm of superstition.[34]

In the socio-political sphere this has led first of all to the possession of religion by the state, and then the total banishing of religion—all purely due to a false conception of religion. It was to avoid this situation that More considered it *just* to employ civil, secular power to defend the objectivity of the Christian assent against heresy. More foresaw that sundering faith and reason would lead to the death of the intellect. He knew that sundering grace and nature would lead to secularism, though he himself would not have used such a term.

Tradition and the Identity of Christendom

The Reformation was an attack on the very principle of tradition. Ralph McInerny notes the following:

What Descartes set in motion in the world of thought, Luther a short time before had set in motion in religion: the solitary individual stand-

---

33. Sire, 61.
34. Ibid., 62.

ing in judgement on tradition, having to verify for himself each and every claim on penalty of being less than human, or less of a Christian.[35]

This is not to say that new demands were made of reason, for there is nothing reasonable about rejecting an entire tradition of collected wisdom to replace them with one's latest thoughts, or perhaps the doctrine of whoever happens to shout the loudest. Indeed, the anti-traditionalism and individualism which resulted from the Reformation are one and the same error—namely, barbarism, or the seeking of some achievement independently from the collaborative pursuit which demands reference to one's community and antecedents, and seeking such success to the point of wishing to destroy the efforts of those who are greater and wiser.

One of the major effects of the Reformation in the academy has been the obsession with originality; that one is deemed a "genius" not by becoming deeply learned within an intellectual tradition, and thereafter in gratitude contributing to that tradition, but rather by deliberately departing from a tradition, even before gaining much familiarity with it. The Reformation gave concrete theological foundation to the astonishing pride and conceit of those who wished, in one great sweep, to toss away all of Christendom's masters of the intellectual life, with the whole European educational enterprise and the civilizing tradition of the primary evangelized lands. It has been permissible—and deemed admirable—to cultivate this attitude ever since. This is of the utmost importance for understanding our political situation today, for the academy is where minds are formed, and what happens in the academy affects the future of the human community.

The Renaissance humanist approach appeared to be the perfect antithesis to this attitude. One of the principles that characterized the Renaissance thinkers was a particular reverence for the intellectual heritage of Europe. They studied the philosophers of ancient Greece and Rome, but also the sacred scriptures, the Apostolic and Church Fathers, and the medieval Scholastics. Some, like Pico and Ficino, were so keen to learn something from all the sources available to them that they failed to discriminate properly, and in turn became fascinated by Qabbalah, sorcery, and astrology. Even this, however, emerged from a sincere reverence for the western intellectual heritage, which really was understood to be a single heritage and tradition, at "the feet" of which one was encouraged to sit and learn. James McConica offers a very helpful explanation of the humanist position in the following passage:

35. Ralph McInerny, *The Very Rich Hours of Jacques Maritain* (South Bend: University of Notre Dame Press, 2003), 86.

The humanism of the European Renaissance was subtle precisely because it was not an ideology or philosophy. Its adherents could indeed be passionate in pursuit of aims that could be widely varied, but in their origins, the central texts of their enterprise were the same as those of the medieval university: the magisterial legacy of Greece and Rome, of antique grammar and rhetoric, of Aristotle and, especially in the north, of the fundamental texts of Christian antiquity, notably those of scripture and the Church Fathers. This was the bedrock of European culture, revisited from time to time in a "classical revival" marked by a fresh resort to antiquity and a new period of intellectual achievement.[36]

When this admiration and reverence for tradition is confronted with the attitude of Luther, who famously stated, "St Augustine or St Ambrose cannot be compared with me,"[37] it is not surprising that the Northern humanists were horrified at what Luther's movement might mean for the educational legacy of Christendom.

We can grasp another reason for More's admiration of Pico. In Pico's *Nine-hundred Theses*, as well as his other three main works (*On the Dignity of Man*, *On Being and the One*, and *Heptaplus*), Pico draws on all the ancient Greek thinkers, from the pre-Socratics to Aristotle; the Neoplatonists; the Roman Stoics; the Church Fathers; the Jewish metaphysicians; the Muslim commentators on Plato and Aristotle, who had so profoundly influenced the medieval Scholastics a couple of centuries before; and the medieval Schoolmen too, whose student Pico considered himself to be. Pico also worked with astrologers, with fellow humanists, as well as with anti-humanists such as Savonarola. It seems that for More the whole western canon of education that had been brought together and sanctified by the Catholic Faith could be found in the mind of Pico. More says in his biography of Pico that he was a "perfect philosopher and a perfect theologian"[38] because he was essentially a man of Christendom, since he sought to be a disciple of its whole intellectual heritage.

Pico became More's role model because More, too, wished to be a "man of Christendom." It is interesting that More was a devout Catholic and Franciscan tertiary, a humanist and philosopher, and a lawyer and politician. This is intriguing because these three facets of More's identity stem directly from the three-fold identity of Christendom—a civilization of faith, wisdom, and law. These are the legacies of Jerusalem, Ath-

36. McConica in Logan, 22.
37. Martin Luther, *Werke* (Erlangen: C. Heyder, 1826–1857), 31, 236.
38. More, *The Life of Pico*, 8.

ens, and Rome. Europe, then, was marked by a great synthesis of ideas, patronized and regulated by the Church, and with a seeming sense of continuity. The fact that such eclecticism could constitute a single tradition was attributed by More to the sanctification of this tradition by the Catholic Faith. This is the tradition that, More insisted in his letter to the Masters of Oxford University, was "required in every place of learning by the Church Universal."[39]

The Northern humanists were not departing from the medieval tradition, as Bertrand Russell claimed they were in his *History of Western Philosophy*,[40] but rather reacting against the notion that it was sufficient to learn this by the study of endless logic manuals, which reduced Scholasticism to the memorization of pithy formulae. They saw such "manualism" as a departure from Scholastic realism, and wished to work in continuity with the latter through the original texts of Aquinas and other medieval Schoolmen. It is understandable that the humanists could not see how "manualism" amounted to the pursuit and attainment of wisdom and that they wished to return not only to the original works of Aquinas and other Scholastics, but also to those whom the medievals themselves had read. It is precisely because More understood the Catholic intellectual tradition as an intrinsic unity that he taught that the Scholastic doctors "of these eight hundred years past . . . do consent and agree with the holy doctors of the other eight hundred years before."[41] The Protestant movement was, in More's eyes, a rebellion against this great tradition.

As alluded above, this tradition was for the first time playing an important role in the lives of educated laity, as cathedral schools and colleges, where those studying were doing so for futures in the clergy or some religious order, ceased to be the only places of learning. The noble courts of Europe were now centers of scholarly endeavor, and the humanists saw this as a great moment for Christian civilization. But just as philosophy, then, was becoming central in the lives of some of the laity, the new Protestant sects were teaching that the discipline of reason was directly damaging to faith.

More suggested that it was not reason that did violence to faith, but pride, and this is a theme that runs throughout the whole of the *Dia-*

---

39. Thomas More, *Letter to the Reverend Fathers, the Commissary, and others of the Guild of Masters of Oxford University*, 29th March 1518 in Stephen Smith, ed., *For All Seasons: Selected Letters of Thomas More* (New York: Scepter Publishers, 2012), 76.

40. See Bertrand Russell, *History of Western Philosophy* (New York: Routledge, 1995), 499.

41. More, "Confutation of Tyndale's Answer," in Yale, VIII, 368.

logue Concerning Heresies. For More, faith and reason together allowed one to be subject to the entirety of reality, whereas pride placed one in a state of illusion, and, ultimately, sin. The Reformation, as More saw it, was a pride-driven movement; for only pride could inspire such a rebellion as this against the intellectual tradition of Christendom. Only pride, as far as the Northern humanists were concerned, could motivate one to reject all the learning and piety of the Christian civilization. More pointed out that even the doctrine of arbitrary predestination led only to two positions: presumption or despair, both of which are manifestations of pride.

This was not, then, really "reform." This was *rebellion.* Even the new biblical translations emerging out of this movement were judged by More to be an act of rebellion against the principle of tradition. This was not because he was against the notion of the scriptures being in the vernacular—in fact he was decidedly in favor of an English biblical translation[42]—but, rather, as Eamon Duffy notes:

> More's objections to Tyndale's renderings are both linguistic and theo-logical. By rejecting the traditional terms, Tyndale deliberately drives a wedge between the text and the Church's understanding of the text, developed over fourteen hundred years of divinely guided reflection, prayer and preaching.[43]

It should be noted that More sought to avoid putting people to death, and tried to find alternatives to this measure. It is generally agreed that he sentenced no more than six people to death.[44] Nevertheless, he *did* put those people to death, and it is impossible to understand More's response to the Reformation—with his use of civil power, coercion, and the death penalty—unless we understand his concept of the European identity and its intellectual heritage.

He foresaw that the Reformation had the potential to tear Europe asunder. This is why the political consequences of the Reformation are so significant today; we no longer find ourselves in a "Christendom," but in a fragmented Europe. This fragmented Europe is undoubtedly the indirect consequence of the Reformation, for all subsequent causes can be traced back to the Reformation. And More certainly would not have held that the solution could be found in an anti-Christian secular oligarchy like the European Union.

42. See Duffy in Logan, 207.
43. Ibid., 206.
44. See Rex in Logan, 94.

For More, it was not so much that England and, say, Poland for example, had different cultures, but rather that they had different ways by which they expressed the same culture. Europe had a single culture because it had a shared *cultus*—the Catholic Faith. For this reason, More could easily feel profound attachment to Pico, a man with both a Mediterranean mind and heart, and for that matter the whole "new learning" movement. Equally, More, in his *Dialogue of Comfort against Tribulation*,[45] could just as effortlessly "get inside the heads" of Hungarians facing a people with a different *cultus*, and, therefore, a different culture—that of the Ottoman Turks.

More knew that the Reformation was not the introduction of a new expression of the *cultus* of Europe, nor a true reform of a merely decadent *cultus*, but rather a new *cultus* altogether, a false *cultus*. This had to be seen, then, as an invasion of Christendom from within, a weapon of the devil, with precisely its objective being the tearing apart of the lands of Christian charity. Indeed, there was greater reason to defend Christendom from the enemy *within* the gates than from the Ottoman enemy that was at this time *at* the gates, preparing to move more deeply into the European continent. This was especially true since Luther had taken it upon himself to preach explicitly that Christians must not resist an Islamic invasion, but welcome it as a deserved punishment from God.[46]

More saw the protection of the Catholic Faith by state coercion not only as the defense of the true religion, but also as the execution of a duty to guard the culture of the land, and, in turn, the kingdom's relationship with all of Christendom. The Reformation was a force of direct violence to the single unifying principle of Europe, and therefore the entire social fabric of Christendom. This was unavoidably a deeply political issue. It was therefore imperative for the "secular arm" to assist the Church in the suppression of the Reformation—not only to protect the Church, but also in order to protect *itself*. As far as More was concerned, a civil community of the baptized was not only to be ordered toward the natural good, but ordered toward the supernatural good. Indeed, this function belonged to the very essence of what it was to be a Christian state, and coercion, if necessary, could legitimately be part of such ordering. As a consequence of the Reformation, Europe came eventually to abandon such an understanding of the state and its pursuit and defense of the true religion. It has opted for a model of "religious pluralism" instead.

45. The last of More's "Platonic dialogues," written in 1534 whilst imprisoned in the Tower of London awaiting execution.
46. Duffy in Logan, 211.

Presenting all the problems society now faces with the privatizing of religion, the encouragement of religious pluralism, and the dependence of such novelties on lists of "positive rights," is beyond the scope of this chapter; nevertheless, we should address a few relevant points.

The privatizing of religion directly conflicts with the central principles of most confessions, which have mandates of various kinds to spread their teachings until the state is identified with the faith in question. In turn, the modern position does not resolve the problem of religious conflict, but merely puts the adherents of religions in some way in opposition to the state as well as to each other.

The experiment of "religious pluralism" demands some degree of indifferentism, or plain disbelief regarding claims to religious truth. This, in turn, has meant that those who have their voices heard are not those who appear to have a more credible claim to *truth*, but rather those whose threats of violence are more credible. The pandering of the West to Islamic views, many of which would not be tolerated of any less violent ideology, can be seen as a result of "religious pluralism." It is necessitated by the abandoning of classical politics alongside acceptance of the religiously diverse social sphere established by the Reformation, and its subsequent dissolution into very many sects, all in disagreement with one another.

Of course, via the ideology of "religious pluralism" the modern liberal state is prepared to exercise a type of religious tolerance. It should not be thought, however, that "religious pluralism" has come about merely due to necessity, so as to cope with the many religious sects now present in historic Christendom. Rather, it is part of the agenda belonging to the modern liberal state, *because* it is the intellectual and social heir of the Reformation. In order to grasp what this means we must "step back" and look at the structures of Protestantism and liberalism, to see how they have the same "template," as it were.

Protestantism was the first major corrosive force to be accepted by the social sphere in Europe. Protestantism did not enter the religious worldview of the people—that unifying principle of the social sphere—in order to effect in that worldview an authentic development or to make a contribution. Nor did Protestantism come authentically from out of the already established worldview, in order to build upon it. Rather, Protestantism took certain truths of the already existent religion and held to those truths at the expense of other religious truths. It took articles of the "papist faith" and posited them as antithetical to the ones it accepted, even though on closer scrutiny the suggested opposition was found to be false by Catholic intellectuals like More and Fisher. These false dichotomies can be listed: faith against works, grace against freedom, scripture against tradition, religious merit against reason and virtue, baptismal priesthood against ministerial priesthood, etc. Certain truths of Catholicism are here preserved, whilst others are discarded, the result being a sort of half-Christianity with nothing whatsoever actually contributed by the Reformers. Sire describes this occurrence in the following way:

> [N]o heresy has ever found Catholicism too narrow a dispensation and sought to enrich it; the efforts of heretics have always been directed at taking away, at cutting down, at impoverishing. There will always be those for whom the all-encompassing embrace of the Church, its satisfaction of every human need and longing, its catholicity in the fullest sense, is too much for their narrow understandings.[47]

This is what we mean by a "corrosive force," that which only corrodes, and contributes nothing. This is another way in which we can identify the Reformation as a type of social and religious barbarism: for it is easier to destroy than to build, and barbarism's mode of operation is that of destruction, just as that of civilization is to build. In the case of Protestantism, even those articles of the "old Faith" that are retained are preserved only in a deformed manner, for their proper intelligibility can only be rendered in the light of those articles which Protestantism rejects. There are many ways in which a movement can be corrosive, and one such way is for the movement to exist in parasitic form, attaching itself to an already established framework and then deconstructing it. Protestantism, following the parasitic methodology, deconstructed the religious framework in the areas where it was able—like a virus—to spread, and in consequence deconstructed the culture of which the religious framework was both the source and guardian. However, once that to which a parasite is attached dies, so too does the parasite die: by killing that on which it depends it kills itself.

Any corrosive force can exist insofar as there is an object to corrode. So Protestantism, as a corrosive force seeking to perpetuate itself, has merely morphed so as to continue to exist as a parasite in the political sphere, taking the form of the ideology of liberalism. It now targets no longer religion, as it has achieved the privatizing of religion, but instead merely the social values that had their origin in—or were at least supported by—the religious framework that has ceased to be. Secular liberalism, then, is the direct heir to the Protestant heritage. It is simple enough to trace liberal ideas to Enlightenment ideas, and those back to Reformation ideas; and, of course, these all, in a sense, belong to a single movement of *abandoning heritage*.

---

47. Sire, 63.

Liberalism, proceeding along the same lines of the parasitic methodology of Protestantism, corrodes and contributes nothing to the social fabric to which it attaches itself. Liberalism deconstructs the tradition of the culture and, as it deconstructs, it also rejects. Liberalism only *protests*, denies, rejects, deconstructs, and never affirms or builds. In this way liberalism, like evil, is a privation. Even that which liberalism appears to affirm is only a round-about way of denying something which has long been held, and held for good reason: the affirmation of a woman's "right to choose" is merely a denial of the unborn child's humanity, the affirmation of "animal rights" is only a denial of *innate* human rights and duties, the affirmation of "marriage equality" is just the denial that marriage is ordered toward the bearing and educating of children, and the list could go on. Liberalism, in its turn, is Luther's corrosive parasitic "Frankenstein's monster" of the polity. More may not have been able to see that this would be the exact consequence of Luther's movement, but there was something "prophetic" in his foresight that the Reformation was precisely a political crisis before anything else.

Finally, something else should be said about the Reformation concerning its consequences for the public square. All political theory (how man lives in community) is preceded by philosophical anthropology (what man is), and more immediately by ethics (how man should live). In turn, the concept of *conscience* developed and proposed during the Reformation has had enormous consequences for the political sphere, insofar as it has been the key to establishing the individualist position which is itself the personal disposition expected of those in a liberal society—that is unless the way one is disposed happens to correspond to the agenda of the political class, in which case one is expected to publicly celebrate one's position, and shame those who will *not* celebrate it.

Protestantism, reacting against the notion that one should inform one's conscience, and therefore be sensitive to the guidance of an authority (as this might imply some legitimate submission to the Church), formulated a concept of conscience as simply the "voice of God within": "Conscience is God's vicegerent in the soul," to cite a quotation generally attributed to Calvin. It is impossible, then, on Protestant terms, for the conscience to be in error, as God, who supposedly speaks within, cannot be mistaken. In the modern secularized version of this understanding, the conscience is thought to be an independent moral instinct that should be the guiding principle of our actions. The concept of an *erring* conscience, then, is incomprehensible to many. Worse still, the notion that one should inform one's conscience sounds alarmingly like a call to brainwashing, and the rejection of "authentic conscience." Neither the Protestant's "voice of God within" nor the secularist's "moral instinct" needs to be informed (through learning) or formed (through virtue and purity). For them, there is no need really to seek the truth and conform one's acts accordingly. If one then couples this with the total denial of the human will, it is impossible to see how degeneracy would not follow.

It has been suggested that More's later writings—which focus predominantly on the errors of the Reformers—mark a departure from his perceived humanist views of intellectual freedom and the religious toleration put forward in *Utopia*. In fact, More was only a humanist insofar as he saw education as ordered toward human development and social cultivation, and understood the humanist movement to be centered on a renewed fascination with "the treasures" of Western civilization, which is, indeed, precisely what he judged the Reformers to be threatening. Duffy explains this:

> [I]t is More's remarkable consistency in defense of Christian humanism that is most striking. The allegations of discrepancies between the author of *Utopia* and the author of . . . the *Dialogue* [*Concerning Heresies*] arise from a failure to grasp the force of More's urgent analysis of the special dangers threatening Catholic Christendom in the 1520s.[48]

For this reason, it pertained to Christian *charity* to prevent the spreading of heresy among the people, for it was "a matter of eternal life and unending death."[49] It also belonged to Christian *justice*, for the state rightly promised to keep internal peace for its subjects and could not both keep this promise and allow the spreading of Protestantism. More held Protestantism to be contradictory in every way, and a religious position that was so contradictory in itself could only be socially divisive. The Reformers claimed that their position was grounded in a literal understanding of scripture, and only this. More argued that this was contradictory in three ways, which Richard Rex describes as follows:

> It was self-contradictory (in that scripture does not identify itself, but is identified by the Church), contrary to scripture (which itself affirms the authority of the Church), and contradicted by experience (in that those who appealed to scripture alone soon came to differ over almost every major theological topic).[50]

Above this, however, it was Luther's core doctrines, posed as quasi-dogmas in opposition to traditional Christian doctrine that so worried

48. Duffy in Logan, 205.
49. Rex in Logan, 98.
50. Ibid., 97.

More. Even Duffy—a historian not known for his religious orthodoxy—writes the following exceptional passage on this issue:

> Protestantism was the worst of heresies, lethal to Christian society,
> because . . . [Luther's] exaltation of faith alone as the key to salvation
> makes virtue irrelevant and thereby dissolves all order and moral cohe-
> sion. From this it follows that Christian rulers have a duty to protect
> their people from this demonic teaching, and in doing so the use of
> force, including the death penalty, is legitimate and necessary.
> More . . . recognized that Luther's teaching of justification was under-
> pinned by his teaching on predestination, and was an outright repudi-
> ation of human free will. . . . [This] went to the heart of More's own
> Christian humanism. For him salvation was the crowning and purifi-
> cation by grace of man's natural inclination toward virtue.[51]

Luther's new teaching was "lethal to Christian society" because it
swept "from under the feet" of the political sphere the entire moral
framework on which it depended. More's response was not merely a
series of hateful acts against dissenters, but followed specifically from
the Church's *just war doctrine*,[52] as the state was duty-bound to defend
its citizens against that which would corrupt the civil order. Heretics,
even constitutionally, were identified as enemies of the kingdom. More
was well-versed in the thought of St Augustine, and in his early twenties
he had delivered a series of public lectures on *The City of God*.[53] More,
then, knew well that the *just war* tradition had been explicitly initiated
by Augustine not to deal with conflict between states, but rather to justify a "call for forcible repression of heretics"[54] by the civil power.

Religion was, in More's view, fundamental to social order. Religious
division, he judged, was intrinsically divisive *for society*, and as Rex
notes, "Lutheranism was a particularly potent solvent of obedience and
order."[55] In turn, as far as More was concerned, "a new doctrine meant a
new order."[56] The socio-political order that we find ourselves subject to
in the West today is the continuation of this new order. The collected
facts of More's "public career suggest that he saw heresy as the greatest
political issue facing his times,"[57] precisely because the tearing apart of

---

51. See Duffy in Logan, 209.
52. See ibid., 210.
53. See Peter Ackroyd, *The Life of Thomas More* (New York: Vintage, 1999), 100–02.
54. Duffy in Logan, 210.
55. Rex in Logan, 97.
56. Duffy in Logan, 211.
57. Ibid.

Christendom, the de-Christianization of Europe, and the replacing of the virtuous life with degeneracy is exactly what he foresaw as the consequences.

Conclusion

All together More's writings against the doctrines of the Reformers, written over five years, total around one million words.[58] Repeatedly in this chapter we have used the word "Reformation" to describe the movement with which More was engaging, but really, when thinking about More's response and why he understood Luther's movement to be so grave, it is worth remembering that "More never encountered 'the Reformation'; history had not yet bestowed this appellation on the crisis in which he lived. What More encountered, as he saw things, were heretics."[59] As far as More was concerned, heretics were people so full of pride that, on the basis of their personal opinion, they would tell all Christendom that it was wrong, and always had been wrong. The proof of their pride was the fact that they would "go willingly to death on account of a personal opinion."[60]

John Wycliffe's Lollard movement had been something of a medieval precursor to Protestantism, and this had enabled the English to have some experience of just how divisive heresy could be for the state. For this reason, since "the time of Henry V, the oath sworn by every man who took office under the Crown had included an undertaking to assist the Church in the struggle against heresy."[61] More, therefore, had taken a royal oath of fidelity before God that he would use his secular power to combat religious dissent.

Here we should recognize more explicitly something to which we alluded earlier, and which perhaps More would not have conceded: the culpability of the Renaissance movement in the cultivation of Reformation sympathizers. According to Erasmus, "Christ, who rules the hearts of the faithful, cannot be made to serve professors; neither lawyers nor logicians may dissect the living fabric of his Gospel."[62] This may sound very pure and pious, but in fact already we can see here the desire for a "simplification" of the Gospel, which includes a separation of the analytical discipline from how we think about the Faith. Such a shift removes

---

58. See Ibid., 210.
59. Rex in Logan, 97.
60. Ibid.
61. Ibid., 108.
62. Brian P. Copenhaver & Charles B. Schmitt, *Renaissance Philosophy* (Oxford: Oxford University Press, 2002), 272.

Revelation from its objectivity in the Church to the intuitions and movements of "the hearts of the faithful." It is not difficult to see how this lends itself to the support of Reformation ideas.

It cannot be denied that the Renaissance as a movement and historical event was itself one of the contributors to what led up to, and finally became, the Reformation. In the Renaissance we see a return to the Church Fathers, and with that a resistance *among some* to study medieval theology. We see an emphasis on scripture in order—among some—to oppose certain aspects of Church tradition. We see repeated ridiculing of the Scholastic method from figures such as Lorenzo Valla. We see (especially with Pico) a fascination with Islam and Jewish mysticism, with the implication being that truth can be sought not merely among those outside the Church, but among those explicitly opposed to the Church. We see (especially from Erasmus) repeated mockery of popular piety, as well as a certain contempt for the vocation of the consecrated religious. All of these points can be found, in one way or another, to be consonant with Reformation ideas.

Nevertheless, the men of the Northern Renaissance—especially the English Renaissance—did become a powerful force *against* Protestantism. Furthermore, when we study the response of the men of the Northern Renaissance we are presented with principles still of tremendous value regarding how we can respond to the socio-political situation within which we find ourselves. We would gain much from approaching the problems of today in a "Moresque" way. Indeed, the first step on such a path could be the first toward the restoration of Christendom. One thing is crystal clear: there is nothing about Luther and his Protestant rebellion that we should celebrate.

4

The Protestant Matrix
for Modern Politics and Rights

Miguel Ayuso

Introduction

It WAS ON A Saturday, October 31, 1517, that the Reverend Father Martin Luther of the Order of St Augustine, Master of Arts and Doctor of Theology, Professor of Sacred Scripture in the University of Wittenberg, left nailed on the door of the old castle of this city a statement in which were contained his Ninety-five Theses on the power and the efficacy of indulgences. The dispute that this opened with Rome nevertheless transcended the disciplinary and dogmatic order in which it subsequently developed, bringing with it important consequences in the moral, juridical, and political order. It could not have been otherwise, since Christendom, the *res publica cristiana*, with all of its limits, defects, and failings, was a hierarchical grouping of peoples, linked together in accordance with organic principles in subordination to the emperor and to the pope, the two stars of whom St Bernard of Clairvaux had spoken.

The attack on the papacy could not help but cause immediate consequences regarding the emperor. Hence, Luther could not limit his revolution to denying *in practice* the authorities of Christendom, but also had to forge a *theoretical* (or, more accurately, a pre-ideological) system with a clearly practical dimension in the Aristotelian sense of the term: that is to say, one that was moral, juridical, and political in character. The result is that an historical approach to the Lutheran Revolution, especially one read with full respect for philosophical categories and concerns, must be completed by means of another that is more formally philosophical in nature. It is this that we have sought to do, following the path of those masters of traditional Hispanic thought of the second half of the twentieth century that surmised its necessity and explained it with clarity.

In looking back at the sense of the work of Professor Álvaro d'Ors, for example, we observe that it was tightly tied together with a consideration of the effects of Protestantism in ethics, politics, law, and the economy, "against the secularization of the non-confessional 'European' spirit, against the political form of 'the (modern) state,' against 'subjective rights,' against 'capitalist consumerism.'" It indicated, at the same time, for that very reason, the necessity of a preliminary critical analysis of the consequences of the Protestant Reform and "a persevering effort to purge it by means of new and authentically Christian—that is to say, Catholic—attitudes; by means of a new confessional ethic on which would depend a new 'world order,' a new and just concept of law and right, and a dismantling of the capitalist status quo."[1]

And then Professor Francisco Elías de Tejada, the creator of the *Hispanic Seminar on Natural Law* and author of a splendid framework for understanding the ruptures of Christendom, for his part focused first and foremost on Luther—even if it is clearly true that:

> [T]he Lutheran heresy is equal to many of the medieval heresies in heretical matter, and indeed even repeats literally some of these, such as that of Wycliffe and Huss in the charismatic conception of political power, in denying Eucharistic Transubstantiation and in exalting the spirits of the peasants in the wars of the Lollards and the Peasants' War. However, Luther differed from all of them due to the gigantic diffusion and the rooting in daily life that a propitious occasion offered his work.

> While medieval Christendom previous to Luther was, despite its fissures, a political edifice founded upon the unity of the Faith, starting with Luther such unity would be impossible. After Luther, with the disappearance of the unity of Faith, the spiritual organism of Christendom died, to be substituted by that of "Europe," a mechanical equilibrium among different confessions that coexisted with one another.[2]

Europe in Comparison with *Christendom*

This Lutheran mechanism, which worked on consciences and was a direct result of the introduction of the principle of freedom of judgement, was translated by Machiavelli to behavior, by Jean Bodin—by

---

1. Cf. Álvaro d'Ors, "Retrospectiva de mis últimos XXV años," *Atlántida* (Madrid) n.13 (1990): 90–99. For a deep interpretation in English of this author's thinking, see Frederick D. Wilhelmsen, "The Political Philosophy of Álvaro d'Ors," *The Political Science Reviewer* vol. 20, n.1. (Fall, 1991): 144–85.

2. Francisco Elías de Tejada, *La monarquía tradicional* (Madrid: Rialp, 1954), 38.

means of "sovereignty"—to political power, and by Hobbes to natural law (with Locke following thereafter), thus consolidating its power over European political institutions:

> Christendom died to allow Europe to be born when this perfect organism broke down between 1517 and 1648 in five successive ruptures, five hours for its delivery and rearing, five dagger blows into the historical flesh of Christendom. These five ruptures were the religious rupture of Lutheran Protestantism, the ethical rupture with Machiavelli, the political rupture at the hands of Bodin, the juridical rupture through Grotius and Hobbes, and the definitive rupture of the Christian Mystical Body with the Treaties of Westphalia. From 1517 through 1648 Europe was born and grew, and to the degree that Europe was born and grew, Christendom failed and died.[3]

This opposition between Christendom and Europe, impressed firmly upon traditional Hispanic thought,[4] led to the sharp separation between the geography and history of Europe, with the implicit consequence of contemplating Europe as an historical concept; that is to say, "a type of civilization, a style of living, a conception of existence, which the Germans would call a *Weltanschauung*." The problem was then translated to the content of this civilization. And there began the discrepancies.

Christopher Dawson, for example, did not really admit the difference between medieval and modern civilization, so that the latter could be treated as nothing other than a prolongation of the former.[5] Others, and here I think, for example, of Augusto del Noce, insisted upon the divisibility of modernity, one part of it in continuity with and the other in contradiction to the Christian centuries.[6]

It is clear that the vision of Dawson was rooted in the English environment, where the forms of medieval life were preserved to a high

---

3. Ibid., 37.

4. Cf. Miguel Ayuso, "Spanish Carlism: An Introduction," in *A Catholic Witness in our Time: A Festschrift in Honor of Dr. Robert Hickson* (Fitzwilliam, NH: Loreto Publications, 2015), 325–48.

5. Christopher Dawson, *The Making of Europe. An Introduction to the History of European Unity* (London: Sheed and Ward, 1939), 284–90. Elías de Tejada, in the book quoted before, made some criticisms regarding Dawson's explanation. And Dawson, finally, without mentioning the dispute, published a booklet only in Spanish: *España y Europa* (Madrid: Punta Europa, 1959).

6. See Augusto Del Noce, *The Crisis of Modernity* (Montreal-Kingston-London-Ithaca, McGill: Queen's University Press, 2014). But Modernity is not divisible at all, responds Danilo Castellano. Cf. Bernard Dumont, Miguel Ayuso, and Danilo Castellano, eds., *Eglise et politique. Changer de paradigme* (Perpignan: Artège, 2013).

degree. The reason for this preservation lies in the precious gift of stability, which permits men to order their future and that of their families in accord with eternal laws. Perhaps the only force that may have possessed this stability in the contemporary age was the British Kingdom. Nothing of the sort happened in the Latin world, and in particular in the Hispanic world. It is that which explains the opposed visions regarding the medieval and the modern.

Dawson, in effect, sustains that—regarding most of the topics of current concern—Spain was not only an integral part of the European community but also one of the *creators* of modern European culture; that is to say, post-Renaissance culture. And he thinks that the real cause of modern lack of comprehension of Spain and her culture has to be sought in the failure of the mainstream of modern European thinkers to understand that so much has been said and written regarding the "two Spains" that they have fallen into a state of forgetfulness regarding the reality of the existence of two Europes; and that that Europe to which Spain belongs—the Europe of Baroque culture—possesses a greater degree of international unity than that of the culture of Nordic Europe. Nevertheless, Protestant Northern European historiography has deprecated and minimized the importance and the value of Baroque culture. And Dawson notes that that which turns out to be surprising is that the majority of Spanish historians have not paid much attention to this either.

But the story does not stop here, since the concept of Europe came to have results of a peculiar significance in Spain, such that if in the north the idea of "Europe" was associated with the tradition and especially with the idea of Christendom as a supernatural unity, in Spain, in contrast, it acquired an *anti-traditional* character, being associated with innovation and the introduction of new forms of life and revolutionary and subversive ideas:

> It is easy to understand the reason for all of this. In Spain, the innovative party has always been the patron of Europeanization, in such a way as to make it logical that those most attached to national traditions and ideals looked at Europe as an external and hostile power, as a unity that was opposed to Spanish unity, as the tool for an incorporation into a strange way of life and different and irreconcilable ideas.[7]

Traditional Spanish thought, in effect, sustains that between medieval and modern civilization lies the evil of secularization:

> Europe, then, would mean nothing other than a secularized formula for devastated Christendom.... [For this reason,] Spain, stubbornly

7. Christopher Dawson, *España y Europa*, 11–12.

rejecting the Reformation, was not able to look upon that fraudulent substitution with pleasure. . . . For the Spanish mentality there could not be a great difference between an American and a European Catholic. The American was also a part of Christendom. On the other hand, there was a great difference between a Catholic and a heretic, even if both were Europeans. The distinction was founded then on a criterion of faith, not on differences of race, geographical location, cultural climate, etc. Europeanism and Occidentalism are forms of separatism, and theologically inadmissible.[8]

This meant that Spain came to be nothing other than a "Lesser Christendom," a kind of Reserve Christendom, a frontier, rearguard Christendom that preserved in time the old spirit that was in the throes of death, a victim of a laicized Europe in almost all its parts. And "Europeanism" remained as "the ideal of incorporating Spain into modern Europe, a Europe of coexistence and religious neutrality, abandoning the sense of our past, which was always faithful to the political and religious unity of Catholicism."[9] Only recently, with the approach of Spain to the "European level," has that nuance been blurred, although it nevertheless still retains a certain significance in that the laicizing forces continue to welcome the theme of Europe and Europeanization so as to sell their cultural products, in union with this, on the national market.

Secularization

The trait that characterizes modern Europe—which, we have seen, is merely a fraudulent replacement for Christendom—is secularization, which to a good measure is also a result of Protestantism.

Christian society, in its origins, was a network of institutions that enjoyed internal autonomy in such a way as to permit men to find their freedom inside this ensemble of diverse societies. Freedom, then, was something to be developed through a complex medium of distinct societies and through the course of human events, conflicts included. And, in the end, freedom was crowned by the freedom to give oneself to God and thereby participate in divine freedom.

It is precisely here that one sees a second trait of Christian unity, one that was due to the vital medieval conviction that all of reality was the

---

8. Álvaro d'Ors, "Preface" to the Spanish edition of Romano Guardini, *Der Heilbringer in Mythos, Offenbarung und Politik* (Madrid: Rialp, 1948).

9. Rafael Gambra, "Comunidad o coexistencia," *Verbo* (Madrid) nn. 101–02 (1972): 52. I have developed the argument in "From State to Clubs (Passing through Civil Society)," in Eoin Cassidy, ed., *Community, Constitution, Ethos* (Dublin: Otoir Press, 2008).

work of God: that all things that are were created by Him from nothing and that, therefore, reality in general was nothing other than a gift—a gift of God. Reality contained its own laws, which were reflections of divine wisdom and love, and in man these were found in a special manner since he did not merely submit to the law alone but also governed himself according to his judgment.

Thirdly and finally, we can see that medieval society was arranged as a sacred world. Given that God was made man, the whole of Creation was elevated to a sacred level; there took place what might be called the divinization of reality. In such a reality it was fitting to distinguish, but not to separate, church and political community, the supernatural and natural:

> The consecration of the world made it the case that man be considered not just as any specific thing or institution and nothing more, nor as a mere block of matter without meaning, but rather as a reality always bathed in the grace of God. Yes, all of reality lived its own life, but it lived it inside the life of God. God was so close to man that man almost touched Him physically. Man saw Him in all things that existed. The most dramatic symbol of this sacralization of the cosmos was found in the rite of coronation. Although the king or the emperor did not receive any new sacrament when he was crowned (for there are only seven sacraments, not more nor less), the king received through coronation a sacramental. His oath to the laws of the land and to justice was not simply a contract between the king himself and his subjects. On the contrary, it was a contract into which figured God and His grace. The political order just as the social order belonged to the order of the sacramental. Heaven was intermingled with earth for the purpose of blessing the latter, and time was absorbed inside of eternity. All of creation found its rhythm in the Trinitarian life of God the Father, the Son, and the Holy Spirit. Sacred society, in sum, was a consequence of the Incarnation and the Redemption. A state separated from the Church, a society stripped of the divine, a religion restricted to the privacy of the individual conscience, would have been nightmares and monstrosities for a man of Christendom in the centuries that it flourished. He enjoyed a union between the divine and the natural that was the result of the very structure of existence, in the way that that existence had been transformed by the salvific work of Christ.[10]

10. Frederick D. Wilhelmsen, *El problema de Occidente y los cristianos* (Seville: ECESA, 1964), 22. This book, written by this author directly in Spanish, is a valuable handbook of philosophy and theology of history. See also, Frederick D. Wilhelmsen, *Christianity and Political Philosophy* (Athens: University of Georgia Press, 1978), 129 ff. and 174 ff. Two chapters are especially interesting for us: "Donoso Cortés and the Meaning of Political Power" and "The Natural Law Tradition and the American Political Experience."

Although one observes both some tension and even opposition between them, Renaissance Humanism to begin with, and Protestantism afterwards, both militated together to crush this sacral world and impel secularization. The first took as a point of departure a psychological foundation that produced an impact in the socio-political order and also took on a religious sense. Psychologically, man discovered the potentialities that belonged to human nature in and of itself, without any reference to the grace of God. As a result, it stripped man and natural reality of their sacred character. In addition to the political impact of such an attitude, with regard to which we will soon return, it is fitting to indicate its complex religious significance, since religion began to retreat to the personal conscience of man, just as if God had retired from the world. The Faith passed from being a corporative act to one that was purely individual.

It is clear that here one is dealing with a process in whose development time played an important role. In the religious sphere, for example, neither the majority of the most significant personalities—nor, even less, the mass of the population—professed atheism. However, many things began to point to a future that would not only reject the sacred character of the world but also the very reality of the Christian God. Perhaps one could indicate an exception in the Hispanic world, where, in contrast, the Renaissance did not have this significance of a discreet rupture, but rather that of a singular human enrichment of medieval theocentrism that ended by being estranged from any anthropocentrism potentially contained within it. It was this enrichment of theocentrism that precisely constituted the civilization of the Baroque.[11]

A brilliant writer, speaking with regard to Quixote, explained this recently:

> In the first part of the book, Don Quixote incarnated the spirit of a moribund Middle Ages that had been made vassal to the petulant youthfulness of the Renaissance, and scorned a person who still was guided by the codes of chivalry, treating him like a ridiculous and moth-eaten good-for-nothing. In the second part, there took place in the work of Cervantes the same metamorphosis that was produced in those same years in Spanish life in general: the Renaissance as a force rebellious to Don Quixote surrendered, being shown as decrepit and foundationless before the reborn pluck of the Middle Ages that was so intimate to the ideals of Quixote. Don Quixote was thus established as

---

11. Cf. Frederick D. Wilhelmsen, *The Metaphysics of Love* (New York: Sheed and Ward, 1962), for a profound interpretation of Baroque and in particular Spanish Baroque. See also Alberto Wagner De Reyna, "Barroquismo y vocación de Iberoamérica," *Reconquista* (Sao Paulo) n. 2 (1950): 97 ff.

a symbol of a Spain that battled against its epoch, that had the guts to combat the triumphal and prideful spirit of the Renaissance to the point of succeeding in dominating it, brandishing the life force of a medieval cosmic vision. Cervantes knew how to symbolize this battle through the exploits of his character, who succeeded in imposing himself on an unsociable and hostile world. And to this quixotic exploit of reimposing the ideas of the Middle Ages upon the corrupted spirit of the Renaissance we give the name of the Baroque.[12]

However, the destruction of Christian unity, weakened by the Renaissance spirit and the acceleration of the secularizing process, had to wait for the Lutheran protest and its consequences.[13] It is true that Luther, on the one hand, with his fatalistic predestination, represented a reaction against the optimism of the time. Still, by breaking the harmony between faith and works consequent upon the separation of grace and nature, he also broke all the chains upon which were forged together true social and political life. And, indeed, if human nature in general lacks value, reason has none either, and, consequently, man cannot discover the laws of politics and of moral life. Thus disappeared "the marvelous logical equilibrium of liberty with the natural law in the business of eternal salvation, . . . constructed on the dualism of the Creator who legislates with the human creature, who is free, rational, and responsible."[14]

The cultural and historical sterility implied in such a plan was turned into an aggressive secularizing agent with Calvinism, the destroyer of the unity of all that lay at the heart of traditional life. In a manner that took another road that, at least in appearance, was opposed to that of the Renaissance, it came to affirm a non-sacramental vision of existence, constituting this anti-sacramentalism as an intrinsic element of the Protestant cosmic vision: the double revelation—natural and supernatural—of God to man was a papal sophism; the world lacked a sacramental value that could conduct us to its Creator.[15] This was the "theology" with which the Puritans disembarked in Massachusetts and that was later to shape the "Americanist" ideology.[16]

12. Juan Manuel De Prada, "La victoria de Don Quijote," *XL Semanal* (Madrid), 27 March, 2016.

13. Cf. Brad S. Gregory, *The Unintended Reformation: How a Religious Revolution Secularized Society* (Cambridge, Massachusetts and London: The Belknap Press of Harvard University Press, 2012).

14. Francisco Elías De Tejada, "El derecho natural, fundamento de la civilización," *Revista Chilena de Derecho* (Santiago) n.1 (1974): 290.

15. Frederick D. Wilhelmsen, *El problema de Occidente y los cristianos*, 39 ff.

16. John Rao, *Americanism and the Collapse of the Church in the United States* (St Paul, MN: Remnant Press, 1984).

The State

The secularized product of Christendom that we call Europe was shaped *de iure* after the Peace of Westphalia as a concert of "states." Here, also, we encounter the spirit of Protestantism.

All references to the term "the state" bring with them various ambiguities that oblige us to an initial work of pruning to make their meanings clear.[17] Limiting ourselves to one of the most leafy branches in need of such pruning, it is sufficient for us now to note that beyond the timeless political community, "the state," as an historical concept, became identified with "the modern state [i.e., a time-bound entity, ed.]."[18] Thus, we are faced with the confusion created by the great German juridical writers of the nineteenth century who applied their own categories of thought (the separation of powers, the difference between society and state, etc.) to the Greek, Roman, and medieval world.[19] The state of one particular moment in historical time, substituting itself for all previous forms of political cohabitation, was now seen as having the form of a person distinct from citizens; as being an artificial entity that was the fruit of a social contract, a product of human genius, and gifted with sovereignty.[20]

The *actual* history of the state was then repeatedly attacked, and from many angles. As with so many other matters, the state's full nature was detached from the sole principle of sovereignty, whereas the two were linked together so closely beforehand.[21] Let us simply quote one recent

17. See my books ¿*Después del Leviathan? Sobre el Estado y su signo* (Madrid: Speiro, 1996); ¿*Ocaso o eclipse del Estado? Las transformaciones del derecho público en la era de la globalización* (Madrid: Marcial Pons, 2005), and *El Estado en su laberinto. Las transformaciones de la política contemporánea* (Barcelona: Scire, 2011).

18. Carl Schmitt, "Staat als ein konkreter, an eine geschichtliche Epoche gebundener Begriff" (1941), in his vol. *Verfassungsrechtliche Aufsätze aus den Jahren 1924–1954. Materialen zu einer Verfassungslehre* (Berlin: Duncker und Humblot, 1958), 375 *et seq.*; and *Der Nomos der Erde im Volkerrecht des Jus Publicum Europaeum* (Köln: Greven, 1950).

19. Cf. Ernst-Wolfgang Böckenförde, *Die deutsche verfassungsgeschichtliche Forschung im 19 Jahrhundert* (Berlin: Duncker und Humblot, 1961).

20. Cf. Bertrand de Jouvenel, *Du pouvoir. Histoire naturelle de sa croissance* (Genève: Éditions du Cheval, 1945), and Francesco Gentile, *Intelligenza politica e ragion di Stato* (Padova: CEDAM, 2000).

21. Manuel Garcia Pelayo, *Del mito y la razón en el pensamiento político* (Madrid: Revista de Occidente, 1968), and *Idea de la política y otros escritos* (Madrid: Centro de Estudios Constitucionales, 1983); Richard H. S. Crossman, "The Beginnings of the Modern State," in *Government and the Governed. A History of Political Ideas and Political Practise* (London: Christopher, 1939); Friedrich August von der Heydte, *Die Geburtsstunde des souveränen Staates* (Regensburg: Josef Abbel Verlag, 1952); Gioele Solari, *La formazione storica e filosofica dello stato moderno* (Torino: Giappichelli, 1962); José Pedro Galvão De Sousa, *O totalitarismo nas origens da moderna teoria do Estado* (São Paulo: Saraiva, 1972); Bertrand de Jouvenel, *Les débuts de l'Etat moderne* (Paris: Fayard, 1976).

effort to trace the history of the concept of government in the West from its patristic origin—where "the governmental regime" was viewed as the art of leading souls—to its petrification in the juridical-administrative language of the modern state. Here, the stages of a progressive secularization are reconstructed, as well as the mutations underlying how—towards the end of the Middle Ages—developments were leading to an inversion of the relationship between the government (the regime) and—here we are speaking of monarchical power—the kingdom. The conclusion is that, faced with the exaggerated vision that "the government" presupposed the existence of the (modern) state, for centuries it was, nevertheless, the demands of the "governing regime" that still defined the conditions of the exercise of power.[22] It took until the sixteenth century—after Machiavelli—for the state, fruit of a secular evolution and victor in this contest due to an unprecedented crisis, to impose itself as the foundation of the civil order and constitute the principle of governmental practices. Then the exercise of the governmental power of "the regime" and a certain image of the virtuous prince that went along with it, faded away before the assertion of the rights of "the sovereign."

Let us note that already quite long ago, Professor Álvaro d'Ors, starting from the well-known assertion of Carl Schmitt regarding the historicity of the state—particularly in contrast with the Hispanic experience—laid down the requirements of statehood. In a strict sense, the state has not always existed, and it is possible that it will cease to exist some day in the future. Another thing that is certain is that a society established as a relatively independent unity in a specific territory always was founded with a common system of government superior to that of the family. To designate this form of social existence that always has existed and could only with difficulty disappear—he suggests—we can use the world "republic." We can do this so long as we divest it of its reference to a concrete form of government in opposition to a kingdom, and do not claim to indicate more than that which it literally means—"the public thing," or, better, "the public management":

> The state, properly understood, appeared in the sixteenth century as a reaction to and for the overcoming of the anarchy provoked in some European nations by the religious wars. Spain, seeing herself happily free from these wars, did not truly feel the need for the state, and because of this, the theory of the state—a political construct, made by "politicians"—was badly received by our classical thinkers. And, in

22. Michel Senellart, *Les arts de gouverner. Du "regimen" medieval au concept de gouvernement* (Paris: Seuil, 1995).

fact, the state was only brought into reality in Spain very slowly and with great difficulty, and always driven by foreign influences, above all French, since it is in France that the idea of the state obtained its greatest rationalization, beginning with the work of Bodin, the first great theoretician of the state.[23]

A "state-driven" order was thus secured in the context of the Protestant pseudo-Reformation. This encouraged territorial particularism, reinforcing a retreat from the universal through its pessimistic anthropology. Such a driving force utilized distrust as a category for dealing with human life, and destroyed, in consequence, the communitarian character of collective life—since one of the bases for community existence is trust. Let us look at these factors one by one.

The Christian world was tied to the natural law, but also to an existential order at the top of which—where "Christendom" as such was concerned—stood the Sacred Empire.[24] This symbolized the unity of nations and political corporations in a union that embraced them without annihilating them as separate entities. Nascent secularization made it possible that each part could gain a consciousness of its own genius, isolated from the full community of Christendom, which was losing its sense of purpose while each nation sought to fulfill its destiny outside of the common good of all Christians in the political order. That common good was justice and charity inside Christendom and defense against the enemy of Christian civilization outside of Christendom:

> Instead of finding its mission in the life of all fatherlands together, internationally Christian, each nation (with the exception of Spain and the world Christianized by it) chose a political goal that had nothing to do with Christianity as such. For example, France—although it did not deny its Catholic Faith—made compromises with Protestant nations and fought against Catholic nations in favor of a "glory" that was purely secular and national. One can call this phase of secularization of the West the absolutizing of the state. In the final analysis, the state counted more (and still counts more) than the demands of Christianity.[25]

With the *communitas* or *universitas christiana* destroyed, the idea of the state was appropriated for the construction of a new political form. In effect, the abandonment of the natural and existential order in

---

23. Álvaro d'Ors, *Una introducción al estudio del derecho* (Madrid: Rialp, 8th edition, 1982), 118–19.

24. Cf. Francisco Elías De Tejada, *Sacrum Imperium und überstaatliche Ordnung* (Eichstätt: Abenländische Akademie, 1952).

25. Wilhelmsen, *El problema de Occidente y los cristianos*, 28–29.

which, historically, this form had been incarnated had to lead to an artificial construction emptied of communitarian substance. Politics had to be replaced by "cratologia"—that is to say, the science of the use of "force," which Machiavelli rooted in the innate origin of power, which Bodin contributed to affirming with his decisive introduction of the idea of sovereignty, and which Hobbes, most particularly, constructed into a new "science" of politics.

Let us note, to begin with, that although the state was initially nothing other than a political form, speedily, because of its doctrinal presuppositions and historical circumstances, it moved from this limited position to work for a substantial transformation of the conception of political life in general. It did so for ideological reasons; that is to say, stimulated by an unfounded rationalism. The key for understanding this lies in its abandonment of the logic of government and its substitution with that of a statist logic, which is the product of a mere contract and of its consequence, sovereignty.

The earlier vision was based on the natural sociability of man and saw the reality of government as something natural that was inherent in society along with a large number of fundamental laws suitable to a political organism. The latter, in contrast, with its eye aimed at the problem of the origin of political power, orients and explains itself from the point of view of sovereignty, and thus enters into the realm of epistemology rather than pure *praxis*. Hence, it arrives at the radical conclusion that there can be no other form of human or extra-human order, whether natural or created, that is not that of the state itself, the modern political mode, just as the Greeks could not conceive of life outside of the polis—although for very different reasons in so far as the origin of the polis was indeed natural, the product of an ordering of things, while in the modern case, the organization is purely mechanical in character. And therefore, in presupposing a situation of disorder in which one lives in a manner that is anti-political rather than non-political, whether this situation be one of struggle or of indifference, until for utilitarian reasons they institute a political order, it is men who definitely generate that order: artificially, and by means of a pact.

This comes about thanks to the concept that legitimates the statist form of civil order, making it absolutely sovereign, politically and juridically. In effect, Bodin's concept of sovereignty, overturning as it does the organic concept of authority, gave to the state, in its monopolization of the political order, the ability to legislate, and with that power the monopoly of law. Therefore, the order of the state was organized through laws that constituted the public space in which that state rules. The political and the juridical were mixed and confused. At first the political prevailed, but—with time—the juridical came to prevail, and juridicality—in reality legislation—did so to the detriment of the political and politics:

> This change, prepared by Bodin and the contractualist doctrine, took place after the French Revolution under the influence of Rousseau and his doctrine of popular sovereignty. Sovereignty from the very outset had begun to oppose the predominance of custom as a means of knowing the right, since it proclaimed law and legality justified by the will of the state alone, whose force and life depended upon the effectiveness of the state apparatus. For this reason compulsion constitutes an essential requisite of state law in contrast to the traditional idea characteristic of law. In sum, modern sovereignty made men conceive of the political form of the government not as an historical form of putting "the public thing," in whose life all men essentially participate, in order, but rather, as an organization existing through a right and laws and a life of its own, determining its own order as well as that of society at large. The result is that the practical politics of the modern political state is perceived as being the sole order possible and the sole means of living in a human and secure manner. While the ordering of life presupposes political liberty, the modern organizing force creates security to the detriment of this liberty. The government of the modern state is really not "political" in the sense of having a capacity to decide. In contrast, it is a state institution that limits itself to develop the consequences of the original decision setting up the social contract and submission to the state: it is a mere executor, an executive power.[26]

The consequences implicit in social contractualism then developed progressively on the historical plane, thanks to the political-juridical doctrine of sovereignty. And these can be summarized—according to the author whom we have been following in this last discussion—by noting that to the degree that the sovereign state's level of monopoly of political and social activity grew, the identity of the state and the government also grew, the latter losing its political character—its power to make practical decisions—in exchange for acquiring a bureaucratic, administrative tone. The extensive and undistinguished use of both terms together—state and government—indicates this clearly.

Behold, therefore, the two faces of the modern state: from the moment that it broke the old unity of Christendom apart, it fed a tendency towards the universalization of the state model while seeming to promote a twofold structure of society. But this is only an apparent paradox, analogous to the apparent paradox of pluralism. For pluralism

---

26. Dalmacio Negro, *Gobierno y Estado* (Madrid: Marcial Pons, 2002), 23.

seems to promote a uniqueness within a very different kind of unity. But plurality and pluralism, unity and unitarianism actually develop on two different levels, with no room for their actual encounter. They proceed on the level of reality and ideology, similar to the question we are discussing here. Thus, on the one side, we find the tendency to a universal order based upon the plurality of natural political realities, while on the other we see a homogenized particularism, and in our own time a homogenized globalism. In this sense, the modern state was the protagonist of the first globalization.

What we have just seen obliges us to return to our presuppositions. The Lutheran *gnosis* consisted essentially in the refusal to recognize the real being of created things. Created things had to be constructed. This takes place as soon as the political consequences of Lutheranism—the reduction of the political to naked power and its juridical consequences—the reduction of "justice" (in parentheses) first to "law" and then to subjective pretensions considered as "rights"—developed. It is worthwhile to spend some time to dwell upon each of these aspects of the question.

Modern Liberty and its Political Sequel

We have spoken of the Lutheran *gnosis*, and we must refine the meaning of this *gnosis* in order to understand what has been said as well as what is to follow. Although to begin with its meaning may only have been evident to those capable of divining the logical consequences derived from its basic affirmations, time unveiled the gnostic essence of the Protestant Reformation. In effect, one really had to wait for the Lutheran Hegel to divine in all of their fullness the fundamental choices made by the Reformation—its rationalist matrix; choices that are not justified by reality, but rather only affirmed and imposed above and against reality.[27]

This is true, for example, for Lutheran "liberty," understood as "negative liberty," which, in turn, leads coherently to the primacy of conscience over the objective order (conscience as the sole font of good and of evil; subjective conscience that does not *receive* order, but rather *claims to be order in itself*) and freedom of judgment (whether it be absolutely individual or communitarian, such as when it is exercised by a body calling itself "the People of God") regarding scripture. The "pri-

---

27. Danilo Castellano, "Prime considerazioni a propósito della 'riabilitazione' di Lutero," *Instaurare* (Udine) vol. XLIV, n. 2 (2015): 9.

mary decisions" of the Reformation mark the affirmation of the will over reason and are, therefore, the renewed manifestation of the pride that characterizes Original Sin: the desire that the order of Creation bend itself to human will.[28]

Such gnostic liberty—whose roots are very deep and distant in time, Luciferian and Adamic to begin with, and built upon the principles of not serving God and of giving the law to oneself—found a cultural climate particularly favorable for proposing and developing itself anew with the Protestant doctrine that signaled a strong and decided choice in favor of rationalism. And it is the case that the Lutheran idea of "Christian Liberty," subsequently secularized, came to give birth to modern ideology:

> It is a liberty that is always understood as an autonomy in the strict sense of the word, an independence of man with respect to whatever class of obligations or norms that are imposed from sources alien to his subjectivity. It is a liberty that can only be understood as indeed being a first or absolute principle, since if anything conditions or limits it, it ceases to be what it is. . . . And it carries the mark, in all of the history subsequent to Luther, of the negation of free will in man, which is an essential premise for it.[29]

On the political plane, the doctrine of Luther is, as already noted, at the origin of the modern state, which is conceived of as an instrument of punishment for human wickedness, absolutely required because of this but only as a "necessary evil." Moreover, the modern state, above all starting with the Peace of Augsburg (1555), became "intolerant":

> [S]o intolerant as to oblige many Protestants to abandon Europe to be able to preserve their own (although erroneous) convictions regarding conscience, liberty, and religion. The Lutheran doctrine reinforced absolutism in virtue of a gradual and articulated process, an absolutism that did not delay in "twisting itself" into modern democracy, in particular by invoking popular sovereignty, which is the other route of the strong modern state for affirming negative liberty, irrational will, and the absolute primacy of the individual in all orders, including that of Creation.[30]

---

28. Juan Antonio Widow, *La libertad y sus servidumbres* (Santiago de Chile: RIL, 2014), cit., 239 ff.

29. Ibid., 237.

30. Danilo Castellano, "Prime considerazioni a propósito della 'riabilitazione' di Lutero," 11.

What is at question here is a utopia, upon which have been constructed distinct moral doctrines and political theories that have produced a heterogeneity of ends, since none, in fact, has succeeded in reaching liberty as "liberation" (as most openly promoted by liberal "liberty") without encountering contradictions or rhetorical impasses:

> Locke did not succeed. His doctrine has led, on the politico-juridical level, to pure positivism through the hermeneutic of rationalist natural law offered—on his judgment—through the sovereign. Neither did Rousseau obtain it; Rousseau, whose political theory was supported by and concludes in totalitarianism. Kant could not reach it, constrained to make of the autonomy of the will the instrument of republicanism, and thereby not distancing himself in practice from the conclusions of Rousseau, for whom he nourished and manifested an irrational enthusiasm. Not even Hegel was able to do so; Hegel who made of the state the highest moment of subjectivity, by definition free in its self-determination. Finally, the "new" liberal doctrines of our time do not obtain it, obliged, as they are, to invoke a theoretical nihilism (already a contradiction) in order both to impose "neutral" juridical orders to confront reality and the good as well as to impose vital practices that are inspired by relativism. The difficulties and the contradictions of our time are a sign and at times a proof of the absurdity of liberal liberty as liberty. Liberal liberty, properly speaking, is "negative liberty," that is to say liberty exercised with respect to the sole criterion of liberty, that is to say, without any criterion at all. It matters little, from the theoretical angle, although the question becomes relevant in the practical realm, whether this liberty is exercised by the individual or by the state. What stands out is the fact that it postulates that liberty is liberation: liberation from the finite condition, liberation from one's own nature, liberation from authority, liberation from necessities, etc.[31]

Liberal liberty is, then, essentially a demand for independence from the order of things; that is to say, from the ontological datum of Creation and, in the final analysis, independence even from oneself:

> Liberal liberty, therefore, demands coherently, although absurdly, the sovereignty of the will, whether that of the individual, of society, or of the state. It claims always to affirm liberty with respect to God and liberation from His law with the intention of affirming the will/power without criteria and, at most, admitting those criteria and only those that derive from it, and that—in depending on it—are not properly

---

31. Danilo Castellano, "Qué es el liberalismo," *Verbo* (Madrid) n. 489–90 (2014): 730–31.

criteria. Hence, the demand for so called "concrete" liberties: freedom of thought as opposed to freedom for thought; freedom of religion as opposed to freedom for religion; freedom of conscience rather than freedom for conscience, etc.[32]

In sum, liberalism is the child of Protestantism, and particularly of Calvinism, and both—one author has concluded—are the perpetual enemies of the Catholic city. It is crucially important to understand this, because "a man incapable of realizing the role of Protestantism, and above all of Calvinism, in history, cannot obtain any vision of the crisis of our times."[33]

Subjective Right and Human Rights

Also of great importance is the juridical consequence of the Protestant conception of liberty, that which concerns subjective rights and, *a fortiori*, those that are called "human rights."

Classical wisdom, more perennial than merely ancient, observed the equation of right and justice by identifying "right" with "the just," both in Greek (*to dikaion*) and in Latin (*id quod justum est*). Right was the primary object of justice, although its definition quickly had to be developed by discussing the art of discerning it, the "sentence" proclaiming a judgement with regard to it, the law itself (in so far as it may be "just" only when the facts of the universal type coincide exactly with the facts of the particular case), and even the moral faculty that each one of us possesses regarding what belongs to him and what is owed to him.[34]

The first two developments we find in St Thomas himself, while the two last belong to the second Scholastic era, respectively to Francisco de Vitoria of the Order of Preachers and Francisco Suárez of the Jesuits. Aquinas indicates it by utilizing the same word "right" to identify the art by means of which we reach the knowledge of the just (*ars artem quam qua cognoscitur quid sit iustum*) as well as also the judgment given by the person administering justice (*quod redditur ab eo ad cuius officium pertinet iustitiam facere*).[35]

32. Ibid., 731. See Julio Alvear, *La libertad moderna de conciencia y religión. El problema de su fundamento* (Madrid: Marcial Pons, 2013).

33. Wilhelmsen, *El problema de Occidente y los cristianos*, 51.

34. Cf. Alain Sériaux, *Le droit natural* (Paris: PUF, 1993); Juan Vallet De Goytisolo, "Introducción al derecho y a los denominados derechos humanos," *Verbo* (Madrid) n. 259–60 (1987): 1017 ff.

35. St Thomas Aquinas, *S. Th.* II-II, 57, 1, ad 1.

The third, in contrast, is not accepted by St Thomas, although he does not exclude it. It is a question of perspective.[36] For him, as for the Roman jurists, right is not primarily an ensemble of rules; hence, he affirms expressly that the law is not "right," but rather a certain rationale of "right" (*lex non est ipsum ius proprie loquendo sed aliqualis ratio iuris*), since:

> [J]ust as with external works that are realized artistically there preexists in the mind of the artist a certain idea that is the "rule" of the art, thus also reason determines the justice of an act in conformance with a pre-existing idea in the understanding, as a certain idea of prudence, and, if it is formulated in writing, this receives the name of law, inasmuch as the law—according to St Isidore—is "a written constitution," and hence that the law is not right itself, properly speaking, but rather a certain rationale of right.[37]

Nevertheless, the Spanish Dominican of the sixteenth century, although he does not reject his predecessor's thinking, indeed looks at it from the angle of a law whose relevance is growing: for him the law *is* also right (*alio modo capitur ius pro lege ipsa*), although naturally "in so far as it is just."[38] And with the Jesuit, subjective right appears among the things that are analogous to right, extending this to the faculty of what is seen as one's own or indeed what (justly) is owed to him (*facultas quaedam moralis quam unusquisque habet vel circa rem suam vel ad rem sibi debita*).[39]

Although debate has also focused upon the idea of the law as a thing that is analogous to right, it has been more intense with respect to the question of subjective right. Some authors have criticized the very concept of "subjective right" as harmful to objective justice, indicating that the subjective-objective distinction is the product of a rationalist analysis unnecessary for the grasping of juridical reality.[40] And although the understanding of right also as a faculty or power has precedents in Catholic thought, "the effort to distinguish the faculty from the rule, the subjective from the objective, is very particular to the Protestant rationalist doctrine, which tends to reinforce individualism and to relativize

---

36. Cf. Miguel Ayuso, *De la ley a la ley. Cinco lecciones sobre legalidad y legitimidad* (Madrid: Marcial Pons, 2001); Michel Bastit, *Naissance de la loi moderne* (Paris: PUF, 1990).

37. St Thomas, *S. Th.*, II–II, 57, 1, ad 2.

38. Francisco de Vitoria, *De iustitia*, 57, 1, 7.

39. Francisco Suárez, *De legibus*, I, 2, 5.

40. Cf. Michel Villey, *Leçons d'histoire de philosophie de droit* (Paris, Dalloz, 1957), and *Seize essais de philosophie de droit* (Paris, Dalloz, 1969).

the objectivity of the criteria of justice."[41] Other authors, in contrast, have modulated their judgment, rejecting not so much the concept of subjective right as its tendency to slip into mere presumption. Their analysis starts with the definition of right offered by Gaius as *obligatio iuris vinculum quo necessitate adstringimur alicuius solvendae rei, secundum nostrae civitatis iura.*[42] And this serves not only for contracts, but also for all natural obligations, in such as a way that even when right is a *facultas* or power, it cannot slide away from an *obligatio*, at times from an *obligatio iuris*, at others an *obligatio moralis*, since the duty that demands to be completed gives birth to right as its complement:

> Subjective right is not for that very reason created through the positive norm. It is "gathered" from the positive norm that recognizes in the subject also the action to assert it. Subjective right is not a *facultas agendi* based on the norm for acting, as the doctrine of juridical positivism continues to sustain. The *norma agendi* cannot either posit or remove the *obligatio iuris*.

Subjective right is the *facultas moralis*, as Suarez,[43] for example, sustains, in the sense that the satisfaction of a natural inclination or the response to a natural vocation are at times required in order to fulfill a necessity or a duty.

"Human rights" have to be understood in this context, that of modernity, which is tightly linked together with subjectivism:

> In effect, the tendency that was universally manifested since the Renaissance took the form of a regression from the objective toward the subjective. Thus, in the religious sphere, the objective data concerning supernatural realities were seen to be supplanted by the subjective principle of "free judgment"; that the moral and juridical order, the notions of end and of common good and of objective order instituted with aims of their realization were substituted with the "idea of duty" and by the "harmonization of the liberty of each and everyone with that of all." On the political plane, one ceased to look at institutions as products of laws previous to and higher in their foundation to individual wills and considered them instead as the result of a "social contract," as the fruit of a harmonization of individual liberties. In consequence, one could not assign them more ends than that of safeguarding the prerogatives and the original rights of individualism. And in the economic realm, the idea of the satisfaction of material necessi-

---

41. Álvaro d'Ors, *Una introducción al estudio del derecho*, 33.
42. Gaius, *Instituta*, I, 3, 13 pr.; and *D*, 44. 7. 3 pr.
43. Francisco Suarez, *De legibus*, I, 2, 2.

ties found itself subordinated to the law of "free competition," when it was not entirely eclipsed by it.[44]

With respect to that which interests us here, what stands out from the previous vision is the consideration of liberty as a *prius*, as an absolute value, absenting all bonds and limitations, and secondly, with even more direct meaning for the concept of right, the beginning of an assertion of right as subjective right. In this sense, and arriving at the last stages of the development, we can say that:

> The vice of liberalism ... consisted in the inversion of the order of values. Instead of considering the manifestations of liberty as material that one had to regulate ... it converted liberty itself into the ultimate and supreme rule. And as a consequence, it stripped reason of its practical supremacy; it only saw the human act, when it escaped from its own governance, as lacking in integrity. These two errors provoked a third, which consisted in looking at the power of man as the expression of his right.[45]

It is thus that liberalism made "the slipping away of the objective to the subjective" a general phenomenon, confusing what is right with the prerogatives of the person; with the power—that emanated from his character as a free being—to exploit these prerogatives and to ordain their consideration. And this power is what has been called subjective right.

To split the notion of "the rights of man" from the category of "subjective right" turns out to be an impossible task. And precisely because of the complex assumptions of individualism, subjectivism, rationalist natural law theory, and liberalism by means of which the idea of subjective right—and, therefore, the rights of man—was bred, developed, and consolidated, these categories do not possess only a technical-juridical meaning. They also possess an ethical or moral, political, ideological, and even mythical and symbolic scope. Furthermore, it is to these last ideological and symbolical meanings that our principle attention must be given, since, in the final analysis, they are the ones that show themselves to be truly relevant in the contemporary conceptual universe and in the juridical orders that consecrate them.

The concept of human rights was born—at least virtually—open to the concept of the transcendence of right (even though they were secured on rationalist bases). Human rights have now been transformed into mere "claims," secured at first *against* the order of things, and codified

44. Louis Lachance, *Le droit et les droits de l'homme* (Paris: PUF, 1959), 146 ff.
45. Ibid., 160 and 148.

afterwards in a new kind of order as "civil rights": which, even as it limits them, affirms them indiscriminately with the aid of the new order.[46]

Capitalism

Capitalism began to develop in the Low Countries and England before the Protestant Reformation, owing to the economic transformation that ended in becoming the Industrial Revolution. It also began with the decline of the corporations and their ancient liberties due to state centralization and the emergence of the bourgeoisie as a new social class. But nascent capitalism received its spirit from Calvinism.

It is known that both Luther and Calvin denied free will to men at the same time that they affirmed the total depravity of human nature and therefore the uselessness of works for salvation. We spoke earlier of the potential historical and cultural sterility of Lutheranism, since it made all development of Christian doctrine impossible by basing faith exclusively in scripture and refusing authority to the Tradition of the Fathers. This fossilized religion, lacking in all dynamism, received a new spur through the spirit of revolt of Calvin, who added to the common elements of Protestantism a fresh component: that the blessing of God, administered through the blessings of this world, is a sign of predestination.

Hence, the Protestant and especially Calvinist origin—according to the affirmation of Max Weber[47]—of the capitalist ethic, which was precisely that which, for example, converted the Anglican schism into Protestantism. Without Calvinism, the new industrial means would have been able to be channeled by Catholic morality to the service of the common good instead of that of a purely particular good, and the world would have been different. However, Calvinism deviated the new economic and industrial progress towards a mentality and a psychology of internal insecurity, insisting that the individual, as such, enrich himself and in this manner symbolize his salvation for the entire world and for himself as well.

Liberalism, in its economic form, derived from the Calvinist spirit. In Scotland, England, Holland, and the United States, the Calvinists have always been great capitalists. In France, moreover, a country with a Catholic majority, a very important part of the riches (above all financial

46. Danilo Castellano, "El derecho y los derechos en las Constituciones y Declaraciones contemporáneas," *Verbo* (Madrid) núm. 533–34 (2015): 326.

47. Max Weber, *Die protestantische Ethik und der Geist des Kapitalismus*, first appearing in 1904–1905.

and industrial) has always been in Protestant hands. And it is a fact that, although Calvinism lost its energy doctrinally, it kept its force as an ethic (the Protestant ethic); an ethic that placed work in the position of honor while it reduced contemplation and leisure to the rank of epiphenomena. History shows this abundantly in the aftermath of the English Revolution of the sixteenth century, in the position of the Low Countries during the same period, in the French Revolution, and in the confiscation of the goods of the Church in Spain in the nineteenth century.

A panoramic vision of distinct European countries during the seventeenth century permits us to make some important observations.[48] In the France of Louis XIV, for example, the politics of sumptuary enrichment favored by the Crown served as a tool for the total and definitive submission of the nobility to the royal power, which turned out in the final analysis to be itself bought, by the power of money at the service of the Crown. And if in France the monarchy possessed a fictitious aristocratic representation, in the countries that fought France a parallel fact occurred.

Thus, in Holland, a purely mercantile bourgeoisie lacking an aristocracy and hostile to the (apparently) aristocratic French monarchy supported the leaders of a Liberal Protestantism that sustained Spinoza.

And particularly in England, where—beginning with the Revolution of 1688 and the social transformations that followed it—a situation developed that was almost the reverse of that of France, since power ended up in a Calvinist oligarchy of Whig merchants that displaced the Tory landowners and ended by dressing up the power of money in a monarchical garb. The liberal oligarchy was represented in a monarchical form with its established church, as "defender of the faith." England, at the end of the seventeenth century, was a definitively Protestant country that had as its leaders rich traders of noble-like appearance who were conducting merchant affairs throughout the world. Hence, one could affirm that England was not so much a monarchy as an oligarchy represented in a monarchic fashion. As a result, it had to turn into the model for all constitutional monarchies (and parliamentary systems afterwards): this is the thesis of Sombart, a thesis that all economic histories confirm by showing the importance of international luxury commerce in the initial financing of capitalism and the initial support that colonialism gave to the Industrial Revolution in England, that would not have been possible without this previous financing.

48. I follow Francisco Canals, *Mundo de Dios y Reino histórico* (Barcelona: Scire, 2005), 72 ff.

At the end of the eighteenth century came the Great Revolution in France, the work of a rich bourgeoisie divorced from the Catholic religion and profoundly influenced by the Protestant and capitalist spirit that was establishing itself over time. The symbol of this can be found in the famous slogan of Guizot, "Enrichissez-vous!" There is no phrase that symbolizes more cynically the liberal spirit married with the Calvinist. The highest good is placed in the material things of this world. Later, the liberal and Calvinist doctrine would open the path to atheism in the Marxist reaction against it.

In nineteenth century, Spain also experienced a Calvinist influence, although an indirect one. Calvinism, which did not enter Spain with theological rigor, made its impact through masonic culture. The confiscation of the goods of the Church repeated that which happened in England three centuries earlier. It was what has been called an "immense thievery" that served to create a propertied class at the service of the Revolution, swiftly baptized for its approach as "moderate," and finally confirmed in its path as "conservative." The key to the Carlist Wars is the enormous support that Spanish liberalism found in European capitalism, a support that made it possible for a handful of Masons and bourgeois, who totally lacked support in the population, to take control of the destiny of country.[49]

Towards a Conclusion

Let us return to the two authors that helped us to introduce the current theme.

The first of these permits us to summarize the perplexity of the present situation:

> The modern age is essentially Protestant and its beginning must be fixed not in the appearance of the printing press (1440), nor with the fall of Constantinople (1453), nor with the discovery of America (1492), but only with the Lutheran rising against the Church (1517). What we do not know is when the modern age ended—the "contemporary" world being nothing other than its prolongation—since the declarations of "post-modernity" that circulate through the world today do not seem to correspond really to a new era in the course of history. Similarly, those "futurist" movements of seventy years ago were not followed by a real and general historical change. Yes, there are symptoms of the breakdown of the non-confessional ethic, of the state, and of pacifism. One can also sense the profound dissatisfaction with the

---

49. See again my "Spanish Carlism: An Introduction," cited above.

results of juridical individualism and legal positivism, and a certain alarm in the face of the madness of capitalist immorality. Still, we do not know how these phenomena of general exhaustion will end, crystallizing a new form of existence that may permit men of the future to speak of a new historical era. I do not know. The signs of the times seem to me to be inexplicably contradictory. . . .[50]

The other author permits us to rid ourselves of a certain scruple. He does so by evoking the legend of Supay from the old Inca mythology. It was said that the immense chain of mountains where the Bolivian peoples today live was in remote times a plain covered with trees in which nested birds of diverse plumage. The father Sun God looked down from the heavens with pleasure at his own greatness, and the Moon Goddess only looked at mortals out of the corner of her eye at the moments that she rose in the sky.

One day, an Indian just like any other made a flute and began to play it, and in doing so nature gained a more vigorous life: the trees grew, the rivers ran with more water, the birds sang with more spirit through the music conjured up by the little flute. And another day came in which the same Indian, knowing his strength, wanted to test it further. He played his flute with such vigor that in his frenzy nature gained life to such a point as to lose its rhythm. And then the mountains fell upon the valleys, the rivers overflowed, the trees sank into the abyss, and humanity was at the point of perishing.

The father God, looking down from his heights, saw what the little Supay had done, descended to the earth and tried to redo his work, but without success because of the great extent of the havoc that had been caused. However, taking the flute in his hands, he smashed it against a rock. The little Supay from that time onwards went from town to town, like a soul without fire, weighed down with a shoulder bag in which were found all the illnesses and all the calamities imaginable, death along with them. Thus things continued throughout centuries, until bearded men dressed in iron arrived in those lands and Supay, changing into a defender of the land that he had destroyed, began to protect the Indians from them.

This legend reflects exactly the situation of Protestantism with respect to the western world. Some Protestant churches were able to fight communism yesterday as—let us add—others today defend the natural law with respect to marriage and life. However, these actions lack their own proper content:

50. Álvaro d'Ors, "Retrospectiva de mis últimos XXV años," 99.

The West was medieval Christendom, and it was this that the Supay named Luther destroyed. He may now want to protect this same work the he contributed to destroying against the men who arrive from the East. He stirred up the disease and now wants to cure it. From the standpoint of pure logic the work of Supay is the most nonsensical work of all—not the Supay that was born in Bolivia, but the Supay who wore a hood of an Augustinian friar and was born in a German city named Eisleben.[51]

51. Francisco Elias De Tejada, *Consecuencias del protestantismo* (Salamanca: Congregación Mariana Universitaria, 1949), 8–9.

5

From Man's Total Depravity to the Triumph of the Human Will

Religious Disunity and the
Birth of Pragmatic Christianity

John C. Rao

Luther's central teaching asserted the complete dependence of the individual—incapable of avoiding evil even in the best of his actions—on God's arbitrary grant of the personal grace permitting his otherwise unwarranted eternal salvation. This teaching logically destroyed the role of the Church in the attainment of a man's final end. One immediate, practical consequence of that destruction was that even those political rulers, secular corporations, and private persons who gave support to Luther's doctrine for primarily spiritual reasons could gain palpable material benefits through their confiscation of the property of a now-illicit ecclesiastical institution. But given that Protestantism's core teaching logically undermines the sacral role of all natural societies, the existence and property of every corporation in Christendom was ultimately at risk of possible condemnation and expropriation at the hands of those tempted to pull off such a profitable heist.

I would argue that, in the long run, the chief effect of a spiritual teaching that began by trumpeting even the best man's nothingness in the face of God's omnipotent will has been the triumph of purely human willful forces highly skilled in justifying whatever temporal gains their physical power permits them to secure. Moreover, the strategies developed over time for dealing with the consequences of the doctrine of total depravity have allowed such purely human willfulness to protect itself from being identified as the materialist, self-interested force that it

93

really is. These strategies, rather ironically—given their starting point—baptize the triumph of successful wills as something "godly" rather than all too human, and even as the sole protection against the "truly" sinister dangers that threaten society. Moreover, they block revelation of the fraud thus perpetrated, discrediting all of the natural and supernatural tools that men might otherwise mobilize to lead them back to philosophical sanity, theological orthodoxy, and social justice.

Everyone in the modern world has suffered from the destructive impact of the doctrine of total depravity. Nevertheless, it was only gradually that the full implications of this dangerous doctrine became apparent. This is owing, first, to the logical force of Luther's argument, but also to the illogical but temporarily useful approaches adopted by many of Luther's loyal disciples in order to fend off the most horrible implications of his teaching—lest they lose the positive benefits they believed that had gained therefrom.

A desire for acceptable as opposed to unacceptable change led various "reformed" communities to maintain bulwarks against radicalism based on older, still powerful, but actually quite contradictory principles of orthodox Christianity. Ironically, a similar eagerness to obtain certain benefits perceived to have been gained in Protestant lands while fending off that same unwanted radicalism had the greatest significance in gaining access for Luther's destructive logic to wreak its havoc within the Catholic world. The reality of both of these developments together confirms the conviction of some nineteenth-century counter-revolutionaries that Protestants are only bad when they are rigorously Protestant, and Catholics, on the contrary, only when they are not rigorously Catholic.[1] Our task, in this chapter, is to identity the tactics that segments of the Protestant world adopted to avoid the logic of their guiding principle, how it was that many Catholics accepted such strategies, and why the actions of both groups baptize that triumph of the human will inescapably accompanying Luther's core teaching.

Ironically, Protestant push-back against the most radical implications of Protestant doctrine began with Luther himself. Luther—who rigorously applied his fundamental principle to a critique of the Mass as a sacrificial thank-offering pleasing to God—proved to possess many conservative instincts. He reacted violently against those of his followers who logically related his central teaching to customary practices and the existing social order in ways of which he disapproved. Such "logicians" included the "Enthusiasts" who imposed radical liturgical and icono-

---

1. See, for example, John Rao, *Removing the Blindfold* (Kansas City: Angelus Press, 2013), 63–70.

94

clastic policies in Wittenberg during Luther's protective custody at the Wartburg; knights and peasants defending their armed uprisings by appeal to his arguments regarding the duties of the German nobility and Christian freedom; and followers of Ulrich Zwingli (1484–1531) who supported an understanding of the Eucharist precluding that Real Presence which Luther still firmly maintained. The fury of Luther's reaction against his more radical offspring grew as he aged and the divergences within Protestantism solidified and increased. Mark Edwards suggests that "perhaps some of this fury was born of an almost unconscious awareness that his message lent itself to misunderstanding, or, even worse, that his message, at least on one level, was just what his opponents said it was."[2]

Whatever the case may be, Luther's response was undeniably vigorous. Aided politically by evangelical princes and city councils, and armed theologically with an appeal to "Gospel paradoxes" to block the unwanted logic of the doctrine of total depravity from developing, Luther sought to impose his personal vision of the meaning of scripture and the kind of Christian order that he insisted was harmonious with it. In doing so, he could not avoid demonstrating that his basic, nominalist-inspired emphasis on the need to obey the omnipotent divine will could only be given flesh—could only be "incarnated"—by demanding acceptance of *his* will, rather than that of Zwingli or any of the other of his Protestant opponents. In other words, the exaltation of God over man required the victory of at least one man's will over that of his competitors. As Paul Hacker notes, critiquing Luther's general willfulness and its consequences:

In his last lectures, he taught: "Faith snatches the merit of Christ and asserts that we have been liberated by His death." Now a man who wants to "snatch" or claim or arrogate a gift is no longer recognizing it as a pure gift. The part of man in salvation is here overstrained and overemphasized. Luther did not notice this. However, the new concept of faith inescapably initiated a development in which religion becomes at first man-oriented and eventually man-centered. The reflexivity, apprehensivity, and assertiveness of this sort of faith constituted the seed of an anthropocentrism in religion and of idealism in philosophy. The seed has grown exuberantly.[3]

2. Mark Edwards, *Luther's Last Battles* (Ithaca: Cornell University Press, 1983), 37; Euan Cameron, *The European Reformation* (New York: Oxford University Press, 1991), 207–09.

3. Cited in Michael Davies, *Cranmer's Godly Order* (Fort Collins: Roman Catholic Books, 1976), 32.

Despite Luther's prestige as the founder of the Reformation, disputes regarding the interpretation of his central teaching continued to shake the Protestant world after his death. Even inside the restricted Evangelical camp itself, battles were fought over everything from efforts to reconcile faith and good works with the doctrine of total depravity to a more intense insistence on separating them. Some believers moved ever closer to Jean Calvin's Reformed Christianity, while others reacted vigorously against it. These disputes among Adiaphorists, Antinomians, Synergists, Maiorists, Osianderans, Gnieso-Lutherans, and Philippists forced many Evangelicals to organize their thinking more rigorously in ways that even entailed a serious return to the Aristotelian and Scholastic methodology initially rejected by the nominalist and humanist Luther.

Hence, the "word of God" in scripture, with a little push first from Luther and then from Aristotle, was turned against "the depravity principle" that the founder of Protestantism had also rooted in Holy Writ. For those eager to fight movement down the crypto-Calvinist path with every tool at their disposal, doctrinal protection even involved a return to much Catholic liturgical dress and ceremonial, as well as orthodox devotional practices and even the revival of individual confession. A Formula of Concord, presented at the fiftieth anniversary of the Augsburg Confession on June 25, 1580, and signed by fifty-one princes, thirty-five cities, and 8,000 pastors, was designed to end these extensive controversies. Calmed they undoubtedly somewhat were; ended they definitely were not.[4]

Already in the 1520s, non-Evangelical theologians had begun to secure the help of political authorities for *their* particular adaptations of the central Protestant doctrine, and just as vigorously as Luther had done. Zwingli depended upon the support of his own municipal council in Zurich, as did reformers in other cities of Switzerland and the Rhineland region. Calvin's Reformed Christianity had to cultivate the good will of forces ranging from the Geneva city authorities to French noblemen, the electors of the Palatine and of Brandenburg, and the Dutch stadtholders. All of these forces, both the successful and the unsuccessful ones, also elaborated their doctrinal convictions, quickly producing a diversity of national and local confessions of faith paralleling that of the supporters of Luther and the final statement of Anglican beliefs under Elizabeth. Moreover, these varied Protestant forces also had to address and defend themselves against the doctrinal pronouncements of

---

4. Cameron, 361–69; Jean-Marie Mayeur, ed., *Histoire du Christianisme* (Paris: Desclée, Thirteen Volumes, 1990–2002), VIII, 15–54.

the Council of Trent, which had given to Catholicism a new and militant confessional character.[5]

The consequence of such militant developments was religious warfare. This began with the conflicts between Protestant and Catholic cantons in Switzerland in the 1520s and continued on a major scale down to the Thirty Years' War which devastated the Holy Roman Empire (1618–1648) and the Civil War which badly disrupted British life (1642–1651). The aftermath of the Thirty Years' War witnessed new and in many respects even greater efforts rigorously to reinforce specific confessional demands upon the large number of individual German states with a clear majority of one or the other of the contending religious forces. But Prussia eventually forsook the clear confessional path, as did post-Civil War Britain, each in its own distinct manner. An examination of the situation of both countries is essential to understanding the subsequent dismantling of the remaining substantive elements of what still passed for a Christian society, Catholic as well as Protestant, and the accompanying triumph of the human will.

Although the subjects of the elector of Brandenburg—styled "king" in Prussia after 1701—were by a large majority Evangelical, the ruling House of Hohenzollern was, as indicated above, Reformed Christian by confession. The dynasty's attempts to strengthen the unity of the population through conversion to Calvinism had proven to be not just futile but counter-productive, arousing intense hostility among the Evangelicals. It therefore came to place its spiritual hopes in Pietism, a movement that had grown powerful within the Lutheran camp by the early eighteenth century, and which became an enormously valuable religious tool for achieving Prussian political and social solidarity.[6]

Pietism's root concern was the forging of a Christian spirit that could be recognized as a truly vibrant force in the daily lives of men and women. Its supporters claimed that such a vital spirit was obscured and even totally smothered by the doctrinally-focused confessions and fixed liturgical practices of what amounted to exaggeratedly rote, inert, and ever more politicized belief systems. They, in contrast, stressed the need for a faith born of the personal spiritual experience of each individual that would prove its authenticity by producing obvious, practical, and eminently Christian fruits. The path of Pietism is generally understood

---

5. Cameron, 361–88; Mayeur, VIII, 55–280.

6. See Richard Gawthrop, *Pietism and the Making of Eighteenth Century Prussia* (New York: Cambridge University Press, 1993), for the discussion below; Christian T. Collins Winn, ed., *The Pietist Impulse in Christianity* (Cambridge: James Clarke & Co., 2012); Cameron, 389–416; Mayeur, IX, 411–99, X, 216–28.

to have moved from the work of Englishmen like William Ames (1576–1633), author of *The Marrow of Theology* (1627), to the Dutch Republic through Willem Teelinck (1579–1629), Gisbertius Voetius (1589–1676), and Jadocus Lodensteyn (1620–1677), and into the German Lutheran world with Johann Arndt (1555–1621), Philipp Jakob Spener (1635–1705), August Hermann Francke (1663–1727), and Nicolaus Graf von Zinzendorf (1700–1760). Spener's book, *Pia desideria* (1675), gave the movement its name.

Still, this one term ultimately covered a diversity of spiritual approaches to the Christian life. Pietism could end in very traditional territory. It influenced men like John Wesley (1703–1791), who preached the need for an internal conversion that manifested itself in love for one's neighbor, but that did not shun doctrine, ordinary organized church structures, and "supernatural" devotional practices. A Pietism of the Wesleyan Methodist variety could easily open a man to the practice of good works on a natural level while still retaining a central goal of mystical union with God that tapped into the mainline of Christian contemplative history.[7]

What concerns us here is the quite distinct Pietism of Francke, the chief protégé of Spener.[8] Francke was appointed Professor of Near Eastern Languages at the University of Halle in Prussia in 1692. His Pietism, unlike that of Wesley, and, for that matter, unlike that of Spener as well, was very much tied to a personal experience of despair and disbelief that struck with particular fury at one moment in his life and threatened constantly to return. He became convinced that God would give him that sense of His presence and peace, indicative of his being saved, only if he developed a disciplined practice of charitable work for the good of his neighbor. In his mind, the free gift of God's grace entailed an unending labor on behalf of His law of charity. Moreover, Francke claimed that one would know that he possessed this grace if his labors were crowned with success. Success could not help but witness to God's blessing upon him. A lack of success, inactivity, and failure to maintain the inner personal discipline needed to sustain one's successful enterprise would signify divine disapproval and trigger a return of existential anxiety.

Francke's Pietist work, which he wished to serve as a model for a worldwide Christian renewal, involved the creation at Halle of what are referred to as the *Anstalten* or *Frankesche Stiftungen*: various institutions at whose core lay clearly charitable ventures like his well-known and

---

7. On Wesley, see Mayeur, X, 216–28.
8. Gawthorp, 104–99.

highly-organized orphanage. Since charitable endeavors required money to survive, Francke's foundations also encompassed commercial organizations designed to procure much-needed funds. Educational projects intended to form men with the iron-like inner discipline needed to sustain constant commitment to enterprise and the service of one's neighbor also played a crucial role in his labor at Halle. Francke provided *Lebens Regeln* to guide them: rules that emphasized the task of breaking the individual's self-will and rebuilding it, after the model of his own conversion experience.

Charitable, commercial, and educational *Anstalten* moved forward vigorously under Francke's direction from the 1690s onwards. They were fortunate in finding favor with King Frederick William I (1713–1740) of Prussia, who had himself undergone a similar conversion experience, but independently of that of Francke. By the 1720s, the king was eagerly promoting the *Anstalten*, incorporating Francke's educational ideals into his own plans for the unification of the religiously-divided Prussian population through a common, practical Christian activism replacing the need for an Evangelical-Reformed creedal or liturgical union.

For Frederick William as for Francke, a self-disciplined, constantly active citizenry, alert to the good of one's neighbors in society at large, needed to be successful in order to demonstrate its retention of God's favor. A man in Frederick William's position, and with his political responsibilities, rather predictably saw that success reflected in the benefit and growth of the Kingdom of Prussia. For him, Christian action on behalf of one's neighbor in society had to translate into the co-operation of all individuals and groups in the development of the Prussian state, whose every victory would signify a further confirmation of that divine approval which the king felt himself constantly in need of for his personal spiritual calm.

Prussia, like other German states, was already familiar with what was called "cameralism."[9] This was a set of studies designed to form administrators who could better manage governmental resources effectively. Mobilization of the clergy as the teachers of morals and a morals police seemed to Frederick William to be the most suitable means of drilling the Pietist message into the cameralists, and, through them, into the Prussian population at large. Frederick therefore enlisted the Halle Pietists and their allies to teach the cameralists the God-given duty that

---

9. On cameralism, see H. M. Scott, ed., *Enlightenment Absolutism: Reform and Reformers in Late Eighteenth Century Europe* (Ann Arbor: University of Michigan Press, 1990), 6, 18–19, 149–50, 226–27, 306–07, and *passim*.

underlay their work, and the citizenry their personal responsibility for sharing in the bureaucrat's task in their various stations in life. Francke's pedagogical methodology, with its intense study of the psychology of the pupil and its complex system of surveillance of their behavior, was thus transferred into bureaucratic and civil education at large. And all of this, once again, involved a rejection of "unproductive theological dispute" that "thwarted God's will" by weakening that "internal peace and communal charity that passeth all understanding" which could only be protected by building up the power of the Prussian state.[10]

Before investigating this opening to the triumph of God's will through obedience to that of the Prussian state, let us turn to Britain's development of an analogous system, but one that led to the identification of peace, communal charity, and fulfillment of God's will with the personal victories of the strongest private wills within a particular society. The British approach evolved through the late sixteenth and seventeenth centuries with the aid of national as well as Dutch and German influences. As elsewhere, it was rooted in the pressing need to find a way back to social order in the midst of the religious divisions brought about by the Reformation; and it reflected the growth of a spiritual-minded, but nevertheless nature-focused utopianism that presented itself as a bulwark against threats from both Catholic and Spinoza-inspired atheist forces. Working together with the Whig political movement and its defense of the English propertied classes, the most influential apologists for the final English product were the "physico-theologians" of the school of Robert Boyle (1627–1691), Isaac Newton (1643–1727), and Samuel Clarke (1675–1729), along with the chief Whig theorist, John Locke (1632–1704). Let us examine each of these forces and their spokesmen in turn.

The Elizabethan Settlement had confirmed the power of a state church, ministered to by a hierarchical and professional clergy relying upon an official confession of belief as well as firm guidelines for liturgical services. Pious circles, eager for a more fervid, internal expression of religious belief, were looked upon by this state church and its monarchical partner with deep suspicion, especially when inspired by Calvinist Reformed Christianity to seek a more thoroughgoing "second reformation." Civil War in the 1640s and its aftermath in the 1650s gave to a wide variety of Protestant sects a chance to air all manner of religious convictions, as well as their often quite radical political and social consequences. Quakers, Ranters, Levelers, Diggers, and Seekers brought their

10. Gawthorp, 200–84.

beliefs into the public square to criticize and compete against the equally active but more mainstream Protestants of Anglican and Puritan conviction.[11]

Still, this tense religious environment also gave rise to ever more insistent voices calling for a calming of confessional conflict. While very different in character, Oliver Cromwell (1599–1658), Cavaliers disturbed by the religious contribution to the temporary destruction of the monarchy, political theorists such as Thomas Hobbes (1588–1679), and Samuel Butler (1613–1680), author of a highly influential anti-confessional poem, *Hudibras,* all helped to ensure that a more open Anglican church accompanied the Restoration of 1660. The purely Protestant character of this Anglican "latitudinarian" path was assured with the defeat of the equally tolerant but nevertheless frighteningly Catholic James II (1685–1688) in the Glorious Revolution of 1688. Protestant ascendancy was confirmed through the Hanoverian Succession, as well as the subsequent and lengthy Whig domination of English political life.[12]

Francis Bacon's (1561–1626) adulation of the value of organized, cooperative, experiment-focused labor for the betterment of the human condition had already stirred many scientists' minds and hearts before the Civil War began. Foreign seekers after "universal knowledge" such as Jan Comenius (1592–1670) and Samuel Hartlieb (1600–1662) influenced educated English opinion in a similar way, the latter forming a close connection with Robert Boyle and the private, so-called "Invisible College" (1645), whose ethos led to the creation of the public Royal Society for Improving Natural Knowledge in 1660. It was through the Boyle Lectures, funded by the estate of the great chemist after his death in 1691, as well as the direction given to the Royal Society under the presidency of Isaac Newton and his clerical ally, Samuel Clarke, that the physico-theological position so influential to the Moderate Enlightenment was formulated.[13]

Physico-theology, like Pietism in Prussia, insisted upon the need to

---

11. See Mayeur, IX, 411–499; Cameron, 389–422; Christopher Hill, *The World Turned Upside Down: Radical Ideas During the English Revolution* (New York: Viking, 1972), 70–85.

12. Hill, 278–312; Mayeur, IX, 87–113, 175–76, 191–97, 411–99, 1020–33, 1089–1133; Blanford Parker, *The Triumph of Augustan Poetics: English Literary Culture from Butler to Johnson* (New York: Cambridge University Press, 1998), 1–60; Jonathan Israel, *Enlightenment Contested* (New York: Oxford University Press, 2009), 326–71.

13. Hill, 231–46; Israel, *Enlightenment Contested,* 201–22; Jonathan Israel, *Radical Enlightenment* (New York: Oxford University Press, 2002), 447–76, 515–27; Jonathan Israel, *Democratic Enlightenment* (New York: Oxford University Press, 2011), 51, 174, 199–200.

back away from open Protestant religious controversy. This, it insisted, (along with its German "cousins") only fueled assaults on "true religion" by Catholics and atheists inspired by Baruch Spinoza (1632–1677). As its name indicates, the physico-theologians were firmly convinced that practical investigation of the order of nature proved the design imposed upon it by a Creator God, while mysterious forces such as gravity demonstrated the continued presence of Divine Providence within an otherwise machine-like cosmos. Physico-theologians also called attention to that obedience to the obvious, unquestioned code of Christian morals and charitable behavior that they, like the Pietists, deemed to be the primary focus of a believer's life and action. It was not through doctrinal quarrel, nor abstract Cartesian mathematical speculations leading inevitably to the insane and technologically sterile atheist whimsies of Spinoza, but through practical labor within the machine of nature—for which God stood guarantor—that Christian love for one's neighbor was assured and the Divinity thereby properly worshipped. How this emphasis on "works" could possibly fit together with Luther's original insistence on their total irrelevance to salvation was a doctrinal question; but this was precisely the kind of "fruitless" discussion the physico-theologians were seeking to avoid.

In the Royal Society of London, similar "patriotic associations" such as the Society for the Improvement of Husbandry, Agriculture, and Other Useful Arts of Dublin (1731), a myriad of reading clubs, and, one might add, Freemasonic lodges and gentile café society as well, the class distinctions operative in the world outside could temporarily be suspended for the good of all. These could then become truly godly confraternities and sodalities, "religious orders" with a productive purpose. In such communities, swords were literally beaten into plowshares through practical achievement. In their environment, men could begin an honest, practical ascent of Mount Carmel. For, if the scientist and the practical entrepreneur whose discernible fruits could be weighed and measured and imitated with mathematical exactitude were not in union with God and His plan for the world, who was? Did not Sir Isaac Newton point the way to true service of the God who presided over nature's mysteries and the fellow men He commands us to love infinitely better than silly missionaries battling over the doctrinal suitability of the Chinese names for God and ceremonies honoring their ancestors?

Whig activists were natural allies for those looking to calm doctrinal disputes, though these politicos had their own special motives for joining this common cause. As representatives of British propertied interests, they sought freedom from both state and church interference in the affairs of private individuals; in religion, they maintained unorthodox and proto-Deist tendencies. Consequently, they clashed with both the power- and tax-hungry Stuart Dynasty as well as with Christians whose calls for social justice ranged from traditional attacks upon usury to the outrightly communist attitudes of certain Civil War sects. Their eagerness was for a weak state and church, guaranteeing the greatest liberty for men of substance to pursue their own goals. And it was precisely this liberty and its assurance of social order that was defended by John Locke with his call for Protestant religious toleration and his promotion of a government of divided powers rendered harmless in confrontation with private property interests by a system of checks and balances.[14]

Physico-theologians could join forces with Whigs in the defeat of a Catholic "tyrant" and in their opposition to doctrinal bloodletting. But those still Christian in their heart of hearts might have done well to heed Voltaire's (1694–1778) insight into the real consequence of John Locke's principle of tolerance. This, Voltaire saw, had the ultimate impact of reducing all religious influence to impotence alongside an equally paralytic government, either by reducing religion to the status of "private opinion," or by rendering each religious faction inaudible amidst the cacophony of voices that religious freedom unleashed. Voltaire's insight was not lost on other eighteenth-century disciples of the English experience, not the least significant being James Madison (1751–1836) and his fellow founders of the new American socio-political order.[15]

Physico-theologians and Lockeans, calling for a common-sense, non-dogmatic moral code and a practical life based on common-sense precepts, found vigorous support in a British press that came into its own during the reign of Queen Anne (1702–1714). The press worked mightily to help define the "truly Christian spirit" as one that rejected doctrinal and scriptural quibbling and embraced "practical" morality and "properly controlled" behavior instead. Nowhere was the importance of the press in quieting religious controversy and effecting a reform of manners more obvious than in the work of the two periodicals, *The Tatler* and *The Spectator*, brought out by the joint efforts of Joseph Addison (1672–1719) and Sir Richard Steele (1672–1729) in the years between 1709 and 1714. Both these journals insisted upon the need for men of common sense to

---

14. On Locke, see Israel, *Radical Enlightenment*, 515–527; Juan Fernando Segovia, *La ley natural en la telaraña de la razón, ética, derecho y política de John Locke* (Madrid: Marcial Pons, 2014); Mayeur, IX, 87–113, 175–76, 191–97, 411–99, 1020–33, 1089–1133.

15. See Segovia, *passim*; Israel, *Radical Enlightenment*, 515–27; *Enlightenment Contested*, 751–62; *Democratic Enlightenment*, 68, 123, 125, 650, 676; Peter Gay, *The Enlightenment* (New York: W.W. Norton, Two Volumes, 1996), I (*The Rise of Modern Paganism*), 168–71; II (*The Science of Freedom*), 558–68.

gather together without religious rancor, calm intellectual passions, avoid antagonism, and cooperatively undertake the truly moral business of bettering themselves and their surrounding societies in solidly "pragmatic" ways.[16]

This Prussian-British Christianity—shorn of doctrinal clarity, praising religious tolerance, calling for practical achievement based on an unquestioned moral code, and aiming at an "obvious" common good validated by its "success"—proved to be more susceptible to powerful secularizing tendencies than many of its original proponents perhaps expected. While many of their supporters continued to attend church and read their scripture, Newtonian physico-theology and the thought of John Locke easily and swiftly led others into Deism, an adulation of "common sense," and even, eventually, into outright atheism. While Prussian Pietists continued to proclaim their underlying Christian convictions in perhaps even more pronounced ways than their English counterparts, their cameralist "disciples" pursued policies so uniquely favorable to temporal, utilitarian, statist concerns that any godly preoccupations were very well hidden indeed. And one is really hard-pressed to understand how Pietists could observe such developments and then seriously criticize philosophers such as Christian Wolff (1679–1754). Wolff, who affirmed his Christianity but then tended to look primarily to nature and the functioning of its natural laws to understand God's plan for the world, was hugely influential throughout Europe, but particularly in German countries, as a bridge between confessional and Moderate Enlightenment thought. For some, however—and here otherwise illogical Pietist criticisms were at least justified—he served as a way station to Spinoza.[17]

It is perhaps obvious that as orthodox Christian doctrine lost its hold on the minds and hearts of men and its influence over social institutions, men's idea of what constituted common sense or even natural law or virtue underwent a change. What seemed obvious to a first generation that still knew Christian teaching but simply ceased to engage in theological

---

16. Richard van Dülmen, *The Society of the Enlightenment* (New York: St Martin's, 1992); Ulrich Im Hof, *The Enlightenment* (Cambridge: Blackwell, 1994), 105–67; Donald J. Newman, ed., *The Spectator: Emerging Discourses* (Newark: University of Delaware Press, 2005); Maurice Ashley, *England in the Seventeenth Century* (New York: Penguin, 177), 162, 232–47; Franco Venturi, *Italy in the Enlightenment*, translated by Susan Corsi (New York: New York University Press, 1972), 20, 57, 155, 159, 178.

17. See Israel, *Radical Enlightenment*, 541–62; *Enlightenment Contested*, 164–222, 751–93; Frederick Copleston, S.J., *A History of Philosophy* (Doubleday, Nine Volumes, 1994), VI, 101–34.

dispute over its significance was no longer the same as that of a second generation lacking doctrinal formation and prohibited from seeking it under the penalty of being called "divisive" and "obscurantist." By that time it was clear that no appeal to a supernatural court transcending the practical realm could be made to judge the moral validity of an action, since "God" had already expressed His favorable "will" regarding its goodness through His granting of practical success to the Prussian state, British property owners, and Lockean individualists in their exploitation of a natural order liberated from metaphysical concerns.

Along with metaphysics and doctrine, history had also to be discarded or substantially reinterpreted to rid it of its potentially dangerous effects on the unity- and success-oriented personality. What was thought to be natural and successful *now* turned out to be what Christians had always "really" thought about these matters—or at least where that thought was "really" headed. In such an environment, whoever had the strongest feelings and the will to enforce them became the voice of Heaven in nature and of "true Christian tradition."

Hence, the anti-intellectual, willful proponents of Prussian statist concerns, or the myriad of different people propelled down a naturalist, individualist direction of intellectual, economic, or libertine character thanks to the Whig victory and the materialist and atomistic philosophy of John Locke became the "godly" arbiters of "Christian" teaching and the defenders of the Christian world against atheism and the revolutionary social upheaval threatened by democratic egalitarianism.[18]

British and Prussian influence was crucial to the pre-revolutionary secularization in lands ostensibly loyal to the Roman Church. Still, one must remember that the same naturalist pressures that had already plagued the Church from the High Middle Ages onward—the same pressures that had played a crucial role in the birth and development of the Reformation—had prepared the way for acceptance of this influence in these lands. Intellectually, these included the nominalist opposition of men such as William of Ockham (c.1287–1347) to "abstract concepts" of all kinds, including those positing the existence of a politically and socially active "Mystical Body of Christ." There was also a general revival of interest in Roman law, whose absolutist character, peppered with Christian heretical speculations, was clearly underlined by imperialist political theorists like Marsilius of Padua (1275–c.1342). It was no mere whimsy that brought Thomas Cromwell to republish Marsilius' *Defensor*

---

18. See Israel, *Radical Enlightenment*, 541–62; *Enlightenment Contested*, 164–222, 751–93.

Pacis to justify Henry VIII's rebellion against the papacy.[19] Neither was it surprising that the assertion of sovereign or so-called "regalian rights" over the Church became part of the rhetoric of Catholic states that characterized themselves as agents of the divine will.

The Republic of Venice was one of these. Her endemic quarrels with the Roman Church reached a crisis stage in the early 1600s, when a radical political faction called the *Giovani* gained a dominant influence in the republic. The *Giovani*, who were extremely sympathetic to developments in Protestant countries, also carried on the speculations of both nominalism and Marsilius of Padua, contributing to the development of Reformation "willfulness." The state, they argued, was the sole agent of God in the temporal realm. But, given the constant flux and change of life, this "sacred" state could not act with reference to theological and metaphysical guidelines. Great truths were beyond human definition and application to natural problems. The world was the realm of evil, with the lust for power being the specific sin that lay behind all human endeavors. Hence, the "reformed" Roman Catholic Church's renewed Tridentine commitment to transformation of the earth *ad majorem Dei gloriam* was irrationally utopian. Any institution that sought to intervene in the secular realm in this spirit was *ipso facto* acting absurdly and ineffectively. State action could look for guidance to nothing supernatural, rational, or architectonic. In short, it had to be as power-hungry and willful in its action as the jungle animals over which it was called to ruled.

But the *Giovani* argument was much too radical to win a clear victory in a still too Catholic Europe, and it is instructive that the Venetian Republic needed the help of the French monarchy, which had a more nuanced regalist approach to church-state relations, to end the schism with Rome that broke out under the hotheads' control. The necessity of operating through this more nuanced methodology was confirmed due to the reinvigoration of Catholicism in France by the dawn of the seventeenth century. Its most effective regalist supporters—opponents of the militant Catholic *devot* camp, which was openly dedicated to the transformation of all things in Christ—were those partial to the use of the term *bon français* to characterize their position.

A *bon français*, living in a much more solidly orthodox kingdom than the troubled France of the Religious Wars, no longer claimed to stand above the Catholic-Huguenot battle as the so-called *politiques* and statist

---

19. Georges de Lagarde, *La naissance de l'esprit laique au declin du moyen age* (Louvain & Paris: Nauwelaerts, Five Volumes, 1958), III, 235, 224; also, 374.

thinkers like Jean Bodin (1530–1596) would have done. Instead, he insisted that he definitely sought to do the right Catholic thing—but that God not only helped but simultaneously wished that this "Catholic thing" serve the political interests of France. In making a powerful appeal to patriotism and "French Exceptionalism," the *bon français* implicitly criticized a Catholic who did not accept his approach as being a *mauvais français,* blind to God's special temporal concern for his land.

But the problem was that the *bon français* did not judge "God's will" with reference to a fixed Catholic Tradition and natural law. "Reason of state" was its point of reference, and this, in the mind of the *bon français'* chief standard bearer, Cardinal Richelieu (1585–1642), was expressed in the potentially arbitrary human will of a divine right monarch mystically protected from above. This was simply the program of the *politique* and Jean Bodin wrapped up in a more Catholic guise. Unfortunately for the monarchists, one could—and eventually would—just as easily claim that "God's will for temporal success" was expressed through the human wishes of the French law courts, or a French National Assembly, or the entire French people, or the visions of self-proclaimed prophets asserting that they alone understood what the French masses really wanted.[20] Hence, while not as blatantly stated as the *Giovani* position, the approach of the *bon français* pointed precisely in that same naturalist and willful direction.

Middle- to late eighteenth-century Europe was not a happy time and place for continental Catholic governments. Repeated defeat in war, economic resentment, and frustration over the impact of an unusual string of natural disasters drove most of them down the pathway of fundamental reform from the 1740s onwards. For Portugal and Spain, inability to resist British commercial pressures at home and in the Americas were major incitements to change. Austria shared similar anti-British sentiments. Nevertheless, she was pushed to tinkering with her own system more by her bad military showing, first against the Ottoman Empire in the 1730s, and even more significantly against Prussia in the War of the Austrian Succession and the subsequent Seven Years' War (1756–1763). Severe crop failures that seemed unnecessarily destructive given the state of contemporary science and technology

20. W.J. Bouwsma, *Venice and the Defense of Republican Liberty. Renaissance Values in the Age of the Counter-Reformation* (Berkeley and Los Angeles: University of California Press, 1968), *passim;* A. Lloyd Moote, *Louis XIII. The Just* (Berkeley: University of California Press, 1989), 178–272; Dale Van Kley, *The Religious Origins of the French Revolution* (New Haven: Yale University Press, 1996), 32.

urged certain Italian and German states down the same direction. And France responded to comparable stimuli, both foreign and domestic.[21]

In all the cases cited above, the success stories of rival Prussia and Britain, with their non-doctrinal, Franckian Pietism, cameralism, religiously tolerant physico-theology, cooperative scientific-agricultural-commercial "religious orders," and Lockean individualist-materialism offered themselves as obvious models for thinkers encouraging the reform activity of regalist emperors, kings, dukes, and prince-bishops. Prussia and Britain became the recognized masters of temporal happiness and the art of godly statist and private gain, placing political and economic utilitarianism above the supernatural purpose of society and the individual, and trumpeting this utilitarianism as a charitable boon for society, a proof of God's blessing, and the key to fighting atheism and political radicalism.

Outright supporters of the Moderate Enlightenment were obviously prominent in promoting such changes, but the necessary theological justification for regalist action came through the work of what historians call "Reform Catholicism."[22] Reform Catholicism included in its ranks a wide variety of different but interrelated groups, all of them playing down doctrinal purity enforced by strong ecclesiastical authorities, and replacing the "other worldly" liturgical, and devotional approach encouraged by post-Reformation, Baroque, "Jesuit-inspired" culture with something more "practical" and therefore, they argued, more truly Christian.

Men like Ludovico Antonio Muratori (1672–1750), the Italian priest-historian, whose *Della regolata divozione dei cristianti* (1747) was "the classic statement of Catholic reforming ideals in the eighteenth century,"[23] saw the Baroque ethos as an obstacle to what amounted to a Pietist-like inner moral development. Reformed Catholicism's educational approach wore its supernatural armor much more humbly, and it

21. See Scott, *Enlightened Absolutism*, 1–243; Venturi, *Italy and the Enlightenment*, 103–33, 225–91, and *passim*; Israel, *Democratic Enlightenment*, 270–301, 374–410. Also interesting is Franco Venturi, *The End of the Old Regime in Europe, 1768–76: The First Crisis*, translated by R. Burr Litchfield (Princeton: Princeton University Press, 1989).

22. Mayeur, X, 1–88, 179–298; Hubert Jedin and John Dolan, *History of the Church* (New York: Crossroad, Ten Volumes, 1981); VI, 90, 125, 167, 232–590; Israel, *Democratic Enlightenment*, 110–71, 326–48; Gay, *The Enlightenment*; Françoise Hildesheimer & Marta Pieroni Francini, eds., *Il giansenismo* (San Paolo: SAN, 1994). On Jansenists, see, also, Henry Philips, *Church and Culture in Seventeenth-Century France* (New York: Cambridge University Press, 1997). On Reform Catholicism in general, Scott, 24, 45, 59, 86, 122, 129, 162–63, and *passim;* Venturi, *Italy and the Enlightenment*, 103–33, 225–91 and *passim*.

23. Chadwick in Scott, *Enlightened Absolutism*, 59.

favored useful, productive, charitable activities in the Prussian-British manner. Two of Muratori's eager disciples, Johann Joseph Trautson (1707–1757) and Christoph Anton Migazzi (1714–1803), became archbishops of Vienna. They were joined in their reform spirit by Johann Ignaz Felbiger (1724–1788), Augustinian Abbot of Sagan in Prussian Silesia and the Benedictine Franz Stephan Rautenstrauch (1734–1785).

Both Spain and Portugal contributed to this Catholic Reform program as well. The hugely influential Spanish Benedictine Benito Jeronimo Feijoo (1676–1764), author of the encyclopedic *Teatro critico universal* (1726–1740), clearly followed a solidly physico-theological line, as did Bishops José Clíment (1706–1781) and Felipe Bertrám (1704–1783). Meanwhile, the Portuguese Oratorian, Luís António Verney (1713–1792), with his *O Verdadeiro metodo de estudiar* (1746), called for the introduction of a pragmatic and openly parochial type of education eschewing the more dogmatic and universalist vision; an education "intended to be useful to the Republic and to the Church commensurate to the style and necessity of Portugal."[24]

Lurking in the varied wings of Reform Catholicism was an entire army of French, Belgian, Dutch, German, Spanish, and Italian Jansenists, bringing with them a program that had snowballed since the publication of Cornelius Jansen's (1585–1638) *Augustinus* (1640/1641).[25] Jansenism, by the eighteenth century, promoted a quasi-Protestant theology of grace exaggeratedly emphasizing man's sinfulness. It disdained the temporal-supernatural union promised by both Catholic Reformation mystical theology as well as the ordinary ceremonial and devotional life. It criticized the hierarchy of the Church as despotic, power-hungry, hypocritical, and immoral, while idealizing the "honest consciences" of the lower clergy and laity persecuted by popes and prelates. Although theoretically critical of secularism, the Jansenists promoted a separation of the natural from the supernatural realm while exalting the individual conscience over social authority, thus providing a valuable opening for the Enlightenment to wander down its own naturalist, pragmatic pathway, untroubled by otherworldly scruples.

A Jansenist trio—the natural law theorist Carlo Antonio Martini (1726–1800), along with Maria Theresa's physician, Gerard van Swieten (1700–1772), and confessor, Ignaz Müller (1713–1782)—thus became conspicuous in supporting reform in Austria. The University of Pavia was a conduit for pragmatic, Jansenist-inspired reformism in Italy, though its most famous active proponent was the bishop of Pistoia and

---

24. Scott, 104.
25. On Jansenism's influence, see van Kley, *passim*.

Prato, Scipione de'Ricci (1740–1810), himself a close collaborator of the secularizing Grand Duke Leopold of Tuscany (1765–1790). Jansenists active in the reform circles of Feijóo, Clíment, Bertrám, and the historian-philosopher, Gregorio Mayáns y Siscar (1699–1781) also flourished in Spain. Any "practical" impact of their program could not help but differ very little from that promoted in Prussia, Britain, and by the Moderate Enlightenment in general, despite the fact that the chief supporters of the latter detested Jansenism.

Ironically, but very significantly, the Jesuits themselves also aided the effort to reduce the role of religion to mere cheerleading for the non-doctrinal physico-theological approach. Voltaire, fresh from his conversion to the Newtonian position, but before coming out of the closet as a ferociously anti-Christian Deist, played a major part in this development. It was he who convinced his former teachers on the extremely influential Jesuit *Journal de Trévoux* that the physico-theological direction was the only effective means of fighting Spinoza's atheism. Newton, of course, meant Locke as well, and the Voltaire-friendly Jesuits dutifully helped to enhance Locke's stature in the Catholic world. They, along with Reform Catholics of other stripes, turned the founder of modern individualist and materialist Liberalism into an icon as unassailable as Aristotle in medieval times; a courageous and godly Horatio fighting off the horde of wicked radicals threatening Rome.[26]

Speaking of Rome, all aspects of Reform Catholicism were visible and influential in the Eternal City from the late 1600s onwards, and given open *droit de cité* therein by the reign of Pope Benedict XIV (1740–1758). Benedict, himself a representative of a reformed and more "nature-friendly" approach to canon law, could be counted in its ranks, along with numerous princes of the Church, heads of religious orders, and clerical scholars. Oratorians of the *Chiesa nuova* provided ready recruits for the reformers, an important number of whom met together as the so-called *Circolo dell'Archetto*. The Jesuits gave the Eternal City their most prominent physico-theologian, Ruggiero Boscovitch (1711–1787), who was welcomed to the Roman College with the blessing of the pope. One would not be far off the mark in saying that Benedict's Rome in many respects seemed to be embarrassed by the inadequacy of the supernatural-minded Tridentine Catholic Church as a spiritual force capable of guiding the temporal world; that it was openly eager for help from more serious students of "God-in-nature" so as to serve the divine cause more suitably.

---

26. Israel, *Radical Enlightenment*, 515–27; *Enlightenment Contested*, 751–62, *Democratic Enlightenment*, 110–71, 326–48.

What did the "reformism" of Catholic states actually entail? There is no denying that it did lead to some reforms of an administrative, fiscal, and commercial character that struck at traditional clerical, governmental, and social abuses whose correction was long overdue. Nevertheless, these were tied together firmly with an ethos that required indifference to or outright abandonment of the Tridentine spirit of transforming all things in Christ. This indifference or abandonment was reflected in the growing enthusiasm for the principle of religious toleration, in campaigns against contemplative monasteries and confraternities not engaged in "useful" work, in the expropriation of properties supporting such "pointless" religious and their activities, in the almost total destruction of the Jesuits, the chief symbol of supernatural-natural union, and in the usurpation of control over seminary education so as to create a clergy dedicated chiefly to serving as a civic police force enforcing obedience to a more natural, common sense morality.

Given the more powerful organization of the Catholic Church and continued support for "Tridentine Catholicism," "pragmatic" change in Catholic lands was often effected with more violence than in Protestant countries with weak or divided confessional authorities. Under the reforming emperor Joseph II (1765–1790) elderly religious were turned out on the streets and scholarly Catholic libraries were sold off as valueless scrap paper, while the Portuguese Marquis de Pombal (1699–1782) condemned many Jesuit priests to a living death in Lisbon prisons for a myriad of offences (including inhibiting the growth of the black slave trade in South America in which he had invested). Officials whose hearts bled for their people ended price controls on basic foodstuffs, attacked deeply-rooted devotional practices, prohibited popular outdoor evening diversions that kept men up too late at night for their own good, and reduced the number of holidays. Popular protests against such measures were crushed as indicative of the continued strength of obscurantist forces incapable of understanding what "true Christianity" was all about.[27]

Reforming Catholic governments put intense pressure upon the Roman pontiffs and local episcopacies to baptize their actions. The Holy See, which see-sawed back and forth in its willingness to bend, reached the heights of its "collaboration" with "Catholic" secularization under Clement XIV (1769–1774), who openly cooperated in the destruction of the Jesuits and quietly abandoned the Roman Church's annual Holy Thursday catalogue of illicit state intrusions in the religious sphere. Local prelates, like many of the prince-bishops of the Empire,

---

27. Mayeur, X, 25–55; Scott, 55–219; Venturi, *Italy and the Enlightenment*, 198–224.

backed by reform canonists such as Johann Nikolaus "Febronius" von Hontheim (1701–1790), were much more steadily helpful in this regard, often being among those most actively promoting the doctrinally loose, pragmatic-minded reforms in question.[28]

Catholic rulers making pre-revolutionary changes were concerned more with state interests than with theology, philosophy, or morality. Nevertheless, some of these rulers were still believers; their governments maintained at least some contact with the Church and continued to oppose radical atheism. Consequently, Catholics were reluctant completely to break off support for them. Of particular interest (to us, in the twenty-first century), are the arguments favored by the majority of the most committed defenders of the Roman Catholic Church in the years leading to 1789. These were of two sorts—but both indicated the victory of the anti-intellectual, "practical minded" Protestant-Moderate Enlightenment within Catholic circles.

On the one hand, Catholic apologists openly favored the teachings of Newton, Locke, physico-theology, Pietist reformism, or Christian Wolff —the Protestant bridge from Christianity to the Enlightenment. Seeing in them what they wanted to see, they ignored or refused to admit their progressive reduction of religion to the service of naturalist, materialist, statist, or individualist interests: a process held back only by the continued existence of customary influences—including doctrinal ones—illogically preventing the full logical development of their program.

A second Catholic apologetic approach was the acceptance of a "no enemies on the Right" policy—on the Prussian-British-Moderate Enlightenment model—linked together with a commitment to fideism. Radical atheism and social revolution of the Baruch Spinoza, Denis Diderot (1713–1784), Baron d'Holbach (1723–1789), and Helvetius variety were so much in their minds, that Catholic apologists were ready to ignore any and perhaps even all of the problems of the ideas and actions of the "moderate" naturalists—so long as they proclaimed the good fight against the evil ones. Moreover, their defense against the atheists and social revolutionaries was tied more and more to the encouragement of a blind acceptance of the will of the sacred monarch, in union with the will of the Supreme Pontiff, in the joint battle of throne and altar against radicalism. The possibility that the ideas and programs of the "moderates" might logically lead down a radical path, and that

---

28. Scott, 78–80, 221–43, Mayeur, X, 34; Volumes XXXV–XL of Ludwig von Pastor, *The History of the Popes* (London: K. Paul, Trench, Trübner, Forty Volumes, 1906–1913), are filled with examples of papal actions and counter-actions in response to state demands, with Clement XIII (Volumes XXXVI and XXXVII) being the most resistant.

monarchs and pontiffs failing to recognize this could actually be doing damage to the full Catholic message was not addressed.[29]

Post-revolutionary, Catholic counter-revolutionaries fought a serious battle for the reinvigoration of the full tradition of the Roman Church, intellectually as well as spiritually and sociologically. They based this upon an understanding of the full meaning of the Incarnation for nature, society, and the individual that was destructive to Protestant as well as Moderate and Radical Enlightenment interpretations. The impact of this counter-revolutionary movement upon the development of modern Catholic social doctrine was immense.[30]

Nevertheless, the "no enemies on the Right" argument, along with recourse to a Catholic Fideism to defend it, has continued to prove to be stronger than the counter-revolutionary "incarnational vision." Appeals to fight the "true danger to the Faith"—the atheist, social revolutionary threat—by linking arms with the supporters of moderate Liberalism—the child of John Locke and the Whig Movement, in "Christian" union with physico-theology—have repeatedly proven more persuasive. It is this appeal, in the form of American Pluralism, with its call for a "truly religious" tolerance and "truly charitable" fight for "individual freedom" against "tyranny" that, in our own time, has most effectively devastated the authority of the Church and crushed the real Catholic tradition; a tradition that unites the supernatural, nature, society, social authority, and the human person *ad majorem Dei gloriam*. And it is an anti-Catholic, anti-traditional, anti-intellectual, blind, fideistic obedience to the arbitrary will of the Supreme Pontiff, in closer union with liberal states today than altar and throne were ever linked together in the past, that has been used to block all criticism of the acceptance of this appeal and what it *really* means.

What acceptance of the "no enemies on the Right" argument *really* means is, in effect, the acceptance of Luther over his more radical opponents, on the basis of an arbitrary willfulness with strong pre-Reformation roots, but only effectively "incarnated" in history since 1517. That means acceptance of a worldview that adopted a more "moderate" approach for establishing its reign, one that may indeed today use the sugary language of "freedom" and "charity," but which, once established, can go whither the strongest materialist and libertine states and individuals wish it to go, blocked only by the crumbling remnants of

---

29. Israel, *Democratic Enlightenment*, 140–47, 326–48; van Kley, 218–34.

30. For the Catholic counter-revolutionary argument and its problems, see John Rao, *Removing the Blindfold: Nineteenth-Century Catholics and the Myth of Modern Freedom* (Kansas City: Angelus Press, 2014).

true Catholic belief and custom. In short, it means support for a power-hungry Triumph of the Will that, as Gawthrop notes in focusing on the problems of Prussian Pietism, is the central thrust of the entire modern experiment:

> In light of the demonstrated connections and affinities between Lutheran Pietism and Anglo-American Puritanism, it should be evident that these psycho-cultural tensions, which have haunted German history in perhaps an archetypal way, are endemic in the very nature of modernity itself. Although the Prusso-German path toward modernization was characterized by an unusual degree of primacy given the collective state power, its deeper significance will elude us if we fail to focus on the Promethean lust for material power that serves as the deepest common drive behind all modern Western cultures. Thus, when we look upon such figures as August Hermann Francke and Frederick William I, we should not simply dismiss them as embodying something alien, but rather see them as possible reflections of ourselves.[31]

31. Gawthorp, 284.

6

Luther's Disembodied Grace and the Graceless Body Politic

Christopher A. Ferrara

Introduction: Political Religion

T HE STATE OF our once Christian civilization at the end of half a millennium of total depravity is the end result of a single histori- cal development imposed in one way or another by violent rebellion since 1517. Jerrold Siegel describes this development rather euphemistically as "a fundamental orientation toward politics chosen by early modern Europeans in order to free themselves from the intel- lectual and spiritual influence of the Catholic Church...."[1] The result, as Christopher Dawson famously observed, is "the reversal of the spiri- tual revolution which gave birth to Western culture and a return to the psychological situation of the old pagan world...."[2]

If any one man can be said to be the first parent of this civilizational debacle, it is Martin Luther, whom Ignatius von Döllinger described as "the most powerful demagogue and the most popular character that Germany has ever possessed." "From the mind of this man, the greatest German of his day," wrote Döllinger, "sprang the Protestant faith."[3] From Protestantism sprang the irresistible forces that brought about the destruction of the Christian commonwealth and the inevitable conse- quence of that destruction: the subordination of the spiritual to the temporal power in the modern state system.

1. Pierre Manent, *An Intellectual History of Liberalism* (Princeton, NJ: Princeton University Press, 1995), viii (preface by Jerrold Siegel).
2. Ibid., 18.
3. Hartmann Grisar, *Luther* (London: Kegan, Paul, Trench, Trubner & Co., Ltd., 1913), vol. 3, 1932–34 (Kindle ed.).

As Cardinal Manning remarked, "All human differences are ultimately religious ones."[4] Pierre-Joseph Proudhon, writing in his *Confessions of a Revolutionary*, likewise admitted, "It is surprising to observe how constantly we find that all our political questions involve theological ones."[5] Luther's theological revolution could not have failed to produce political revolution. In a pious paean to the great heresiarch, entitled *The Political Theories of Martin Luther*, the American academic and federal bureaucrat Luther Hess Waring declared of his namesake:

> Thus the ecclesiastical Reformation led to a political one.... The Reformation was not only a religious and intellectual, but a political revolt.... [Luther] was, or became ... the instrument, not merely of a religious reformation but of a many sided-revolution. It would be a great mistake, a grievous error, to regard the movement of which Luther was the source and the center as purely religious.[6]

In his *Essay on Catholicism, Liberalism and Socialism*, Don Juan Donoso Cortés put the matter this way:

> The real danger to human societies commenced on the day the great heresy of the sixteenth century acquired the right of citizenship in Europe. Since then, there is no revolution which does not involve for society a danger of death. This consists in the fact, that as they are all founded on the Protestant heresy, they are all fundamentally heretical.[7]

This essay will focus on Luther's seminal role in the emergence of the modern nation-state: the graceless body politic that emerges precisely from his system of grace as a mere external imputation of righteousness that rejects the transformation in Christ and thus the role of the Catholic Church in the transformation of both individual and society.

As we shall see here, it was Luther, almost a century before Hobbes and Locke, who first accommodated politics to irremediable Original Sin. His successful rebellion against Rome and the Empire opened the way to destruction of the Christian commonwealth and its replacement by a mass of citizens no longer coextensive with the Mystical Body of Christ and the great liturgical polity the Church had administered. We are living in the final stages of that civilizational catastrophe.

---

4. Cited in Wilhelm Röpke, *A Humane Economy* (South Bend: Gateway Editions, 1958), 4, 75.

5. Quoted in Don Juan Donoso Cortes, *Essay on Catholicism, Authority and Order*, (New York: Joseph F. Wagner, 1925), 1.

6. Luther Hess Waring, *The Political Theories of Martin Luther* (New York: G. P. Putnam's Sons, 1910), 266–67 (Bibliolife reprint).

7. Don Juan Donoso Cortés, *Essay on Catholicism, Liberalism and Socialism* (Dublin: William B. Kelly, 1974), 267.

Rise of a Religious Demagogue

When Luther burst upon the ecclesial scene in Germany, conditions were ripe for the triumph of demagoguery that marked his entire career: the resentment-breeding privileges and perquisites of the Catholic clergy and the ecclesial bureaucracy, the Renaissance splendors of the papal court, the wide penetration of the humanist "new learning," the fiscal demands of Rome upon the empire. People north of the Alps were ready to hear, and Luther was ready to tell them, that it was not God who had ordained the plotting, planning, intrigues, dynastic ambitions, and immoralities of the Renaissance popes of Borgia, Rovere, and Medici.

And yet, contrary to popular impression, it cannot be said that late medieval Catholicism as such was a source of colorable pretexts for rebellion. As the Protestant historian Euan Cameron admits with a rather clinical candor:

> The Christianity of the later Middle Ages was a supple, flexible, varied entity, adapted to the needs, concerns, and tastes of the people who created it. . . . It was not an inflexible tyranny presided over by a remote authority. It threatened, but it also comforted; it disciplined but it also entertained. If it were *only* a question of piety and worship, we should be hard put to find signs of real mass dissatisfaction with the Church. It was not its *primary* function, then, which made the Church on the eve of the Reformation so vulnerable. It was rather the tangle of *secondary* roles, duties, responsibilities and their consequences which caused most of the trouble. . . .[8]

Of course it was not medieval Christians who "created" the Christianity of the Middle Ages, but rather the incarnate God who founded the Church that engendered Catholic social order as a developing spiritual, moral, and sociopolitical totality down through the centuries of Christendom. This was a work of the Holy Ghost: the continuing miracle of the conversion of an entire civilization.

It was left to Luther and his swarm of progeny literally to *create* religion—his religion—as a distinct category of social order.[9] Luther's demagogic exploitation of legitimate grievances over abuses of ecclesiastical authority was only the bow from which he launched the arrows of a furious theological attack on the papacy and the Mass. And the

---

8. Euan Cameron, *The European Reformation* (Oxford: Clarendon Press, 1991), 19.
9. On the creation of the sociological category "religion" in the sixteenth century, see William T. Cavanaugh, *The Myth of Religious Violence* (New York: Oxford University Press, 2009).

bull's eye of the target was just what the Catholic Church alone offered: an economy of grace and salvation in which man participates via the sacramental system. Eliminate the need for this, if only rhetorically, and the emancipation of the body politic from the Catholic Church becomes not only possible, but absolutely essential.

Luther assailed with implacable fury the very idea of a system of grace that builds up a Mystical Body composed of souls who first achieve the state of grace in baptism, restore it when lost through confession and penitence, and maintain it—in a bond of unity with fellow Christians also in the state of grace—through participation in the Holy Eucharist. In short, Luther made war on a Mystical Body coextensive with a body politic that was also a liturgical polity, whose soul is the Church.

Luther the proto-Protestant was the first to devise an entire religion accommodated to his personal failings. A plague of designer religions, all variations on his original theological contrivance, has ever since led to the breakup of the Mystical Body, a civilizational default to the power of the state, and the consequent relentless descent of our civilization into a condition of total depravity. Yet this has happened in the midst of a profusion of man-made religions that has misled thinkers like Charles Taylor into concluding that our secular age is in fact deeply religious in its own, perhaps not apparent, way. What Taylor cannot account for from his secular academic perspective is our focus here: the operation of divine grace in the one Mystical Body of Christ, without which *religion* qua religion—meaning multivariate Protestantism—must degenerate ultimately into various well-disguised forms of political activity. Indeed, it was thanks to Luther, writes Cameron, that "religion became mass politics," following which "other ideologies, ultimately more secular in tone, would take its place." Today, in our secular age, what Charles Taylor has called the "buffered self" that is no longer threatened by "spiritual forces"[10] replaces the Catholic subject under the ultimate authority of the Church Universal.

Sola Fide and the End of Grace

Luther's decisive blow against the Mystical Body, his masterstroke of religious demagoguery, was his great dogma of *sola fide*, which dispenses with the operation of the sacraments and thus the role of Catholic Church in the salvation of souls. Accommodating his religion to his

10. Charles Taylor, *A Secular Age* (Cambridge, MA: The Belknap Press of Harvard University Press, 2007), 38, 300, and *passim*.

own sins, Luther declared that the grace of faith in Christ as Savior does not perfect nature but merely covers over its defects, which remain irremediable even after baptism. Justification, therefore, does not effect real sanctification, does not produce the new man to whom Saint Paul refers, but rather merely imputes to the believer a righteousness that can never be his in the wayfaring state.

Because man does not *become* good under the influence of grace, his nature having been corrupted irremediably, there is for Luther no infused supernatural *personal* virtue of charity, but only a divine favor by which God overlooks a fallen nature that can never be elevated in this world. *This does not mean that Luther denies regeneration as such.* He declares, rather, that regeneration can never in this world produce a soul pleasing to God apart from the extrinsic righteousness God has imputed to it once the grace of faith is accepted. Good works, therefore, are merely byproducts of the fiducial faith of the "regenerated" (in Luther's sense) soul; they are not the fruit of an inner sanctification but merely the evidence of God working through the "regenerated" sinner.

Therefore, the good works a man performs under the influence of grace are not at all his works, but entirely God's. Luther's God literally cannot say on the Day of Judgment, "Well done, good and faithful servant," for the servant has not actually *done* anything of his own merit even as enabled by grace. Nor can Luther's Christ declare, "Be perfect even as your heavenly Father is perfect." As Luther put it, "True and real piety which is of worth in God's sight consists in *alien works and not in our own*. If we wish to work for God we must not approach Him with our own works but with foreign ones."[11]

From the dogma of *sola fides* it follows that Luther could not abide the existence of Catholic saints. The lives of the saints, including their miracles, were proof of their inner sanctification and true regeneration under the influence of sacramental grace, whereas Luther's life was a continuing proof of its absence. Thus Luther, writes Hartmann Grisar, "was always fond of imputing weaknesses and sins to the Saints. Their works he regarded as detracting from the Redemption and the Grace of Christ, which can be appropriated only by faith. Certain virtues manifested by the Saints and their heroic sacrifices Luther denounced as illusions, as morally impossible and as mere idolatry." As Luther boldly declared, "The Apostles themselves were sinners, yea, regular scoundrels.... I

---

11. Hartmann Grisar, *Luther*, Vol. 5 of 6 (Kindle Locations 1114–16). Unless otherwise indicated, all quotations from Luther's writings are from this six-volume work, cited by volume number and page (x.xxx) as to both the print and Kindle editions.

believe that the prophets also frequently sinned grievously, for they were men like us."[12] By which he meant, men like Luther.

Nevertheless, Luther expected a great flowering of acts of charity once men, freed from the burden of a guilty conscience and the intolerable demands of the Church for penance and good works, simply allowed God to work through them. Laboring to escape the consequences of his own teaching, Luther tried to have it both ways: freedom from the judgment of the Law in one who has been justified solely by faith—and by the Law he meant even the natural law as set forth in the Commandments—but obedience to the Law whose judgment no longer threatens the one justified. The Law, Luther insisted—conflating the Mosaic regime Saint Paul had in view with the moral law enunciated in the Gospel—"is not given to the righteous, i.e., it is not against them. . . . Sin does not reign over the just, and, to the end, it will not sully them. . . . The Law is named merely for those who sin, for Paul thus defines the Law. . . ."[13] Luther's conflation of the Mosaic Law with the law of the Gospel remains a fundamental tenet of evangelical Protestantism to this day.

Now, if the "justified" are no longer under the sentence of the Law that they nonetheless are to obey as God works through them (their works not being their own) then effectively there is no law, indeed no morality, but only the divine action. Hence it was Luther's own teaching that spawned the Antinomianism he himself vehemently but incoherently opposed with expedient rhetorical adjustments of his position as the occasion demanded. But, as we shall see, Luther was forced to acknowledge that what happened in the wake of his "liberating" Evangel was exactly the opposite of the moral revival he predicted, although he resolutely refused to assign any of the blame for the rapid collapse of morals to the rapid spread of his own teaching.

Given that his new religion required an irremediable corruption of human nature on account of Original Sin—even among the justified under an extrinsic imputation of righteousness—Luther was compelled by his own logic to deny the very existence of natural virtue and natural morality. To quote Grisar: "Natural morality, viz., that to which man attains by means of his unaided powers, appears to him simply an invention of the pagan Aristotle. He rounds on all the theologians of his day for having swallowed so dangerous an error in their Aristotelian schools to the manifest detriment of the divine teaching."[14] As Luther famously declared, "For nothing do my fingers itch so much as to tear

12. III, 3613–17.
13. V, 325–31.
14. Ibid., 1080–82.

off the mask from that clown, Aristotle."[15] Thus, notes Alasdair MacIntyre, it was Luther who "set the tone" for political modernity's rejection of the classical view of human nature, which he repudiated "precisely as Aristotelianism."[16]

The inescapable conclusion of Luther's moral logic is, of course, his infamous denial of free will, culminating in his *De servo arbitrio* (1525). Earlier in his career even Luther had acknowledged what Aristotle and Thomas call the *synderesis*, the innate moral faculty in man directing him toward the choice of good and the avoidance of evil. But he moved rapidly from trivializing the *synderesis* to dispensing with it entirely, as it could not be reconciled with his system. For if, as Luther held, man is incapable of good works without the aid of grace, then his will must otherwise be bound to do evil. And if even under the external imputation of grace man's actions are not his own, but only God's, "regenerated" man conversely is bound to do good. As early as 1519, in a commentary after the Leipzig Disputation, Luther could not have been more explicit in this regard: "Free will is purely passive in every one of its acts. . . . A good act comes wholly and entirely from God, because the whole activity of the will consists in the divine action which extends to the members and powers of both body and soul, *no other activity existing.*"[17]

How, then, to explain the continuing commission of sins by the justified, indeed the rapid collapse of morality in the once Catholic precincts that had been won over to Luther's teaching? This was the conundrum Calvin would address with an argument only a lawyer could devise: that a "regenerated" man who does evil must never have been regenerated in the first place. To this day, Calvin's sophistical solution to the problem remains a staple of Calvinist and evangelical Protestantism, while the risible debate between Calvinists (no free moral will whatsoever) and Arminians (limited moral free will) continues.

Despite the absurdities to which it must lead, Luther's entire theological construct *had* to rest upon a radical rejection of man's freely willed cooperation in his own salvation, because that cooperation necessarily involves the moral accountability of an inwardly sanctified and truly regenerated moral agent, which Luther's new non-sacramental system could not engender. Only the Catholic Church even claimed to provide the means by which man could attain that standard of true accountability before God, which involves radical freedom, not bondage of the will.

---

15. VI, 211.
16. MacIntyre, *After Virtue* (Notre Dame, IN: University of Notre Dame, 1984), 165.
17. II, 231.

Not for Luther was Augustine's admonition that "God has made you without your cooperation, but he will not save you without it."

So, whereas the Pelagian heresy excludes grace from the operation of free will, the Lutheran heresy must in the end exclude free will from the operation of grace. The Augsburg Convention attempts to finesse this embarrassment by a distinction between "civil" righteousness—the moral freedom to choose to behave well in human society through actions that are nonetheless corrupted and unavailing for salvation—and "spiritual" righteousness, meaning the movement toward salvation by fiducial faith alone, in which there is no element of human freedom but only grace. That is, one can choose freely with respect to all works except salvation, which is the work of God alone.

But this attempt to salvage something of the tradition of the virtues and free will for everyday social life while walling it off from the economy of salvation amounts to explaining away the core teaching of Luther himself while retaining the Lutheran brand, as it were, for denominational purposes. For as Grisar notes, following Leo X's bull of excommunication in 1521, Luther insisted that his denial of free will was *articulus ominium optimus et rerum*—that is, foundational to his teaching.[18] That Luther's doctrine on free will reached full maturity only during the period of his "reaction" against the Roman censures does not exonerate the heresiarch from his heresy but only assigns a baser motive to its promulgation.

Finally, reason itself must fall under Luther's onslaught, for it is in the rational soul that the *synderesis* resides, and in the *synderesis* lies the foundation of man's radical freedom in grace and, with this, his personal moral accountability before the judgment seat of the God in whose image and likeness he is made. Thus, reason must go. Human reason, Luther declared in one of his innumerable attacks on the very faculty of the soul engaged in the development of his new theology, is "a crazy witch and Lady Hulda," a "clever vixen on whom the heathen hung when they thought themselves cleverest." In Luther's case, we must admit he had a point.[19]

The considerations just outlined suffice to indicate that Luther's system radically rejects man as the Greco-Catholic tradition conceives him in the light of revelation. Let us count the ways: First, by reducing justification to a mere imputation of righteousness that effects no elevation of fallen nature, Luther exalts grace only to put it out of commission. He *disembodies* grace in the individual, denying its incorporation into the

18. Ibid.
19. V, 126–29.

human substance of body and soul via the regenerated soul with its supernaturally aided *synderesis*. For Luther, there simply is no actual *state* of grace in man, not even through the action of Holy Eucharist, which unites the Mystical Body of Christ. Second, if no human action is pleasing to God save God's action in man, it is clear that, as Grisar puts it, Luther "did away with the olden doctrine of virtue, and without setting up anything positive in its place."[20] Third, as Grisar further observes, by denying any "distinction between natural and supernatural goodness, essential as it is for forming an ethical estimate of man," Luther "practically destroys both."[21]

Now, if there is no inward transformation in Christ, the Incarnate God who lived among us and lives still in His risen and glorified Body, and if there is no indwelling of the Trinity in the soul, then God and Christ become theologically indistinguishable. Luther, however unwittingly, prepared the ground for providential Deism, the only step necessary for exiling God from the social order and a halfway house on the road to practical atheism. In the Protestant theology Luther first created, Christ tends to be reduced to a *concept* easily assimilated to the *Deus absconditus*—the hidden God—of the Deists.

Worse, the reduction of Christ to the *concept* of Christ, as merely the object of an utter fideism, will lend itself to the coming philosophical revolution, which will replace the immanence of divine grace in the soul with the *immanentism* of what we call "god" in the natural order and in ourselves. Thus, even Hegel acknowledges a debt to Luther in propounding his notion of an Absolute Spirit manifesting itself through pure conceptualization: "What Luther began as faith, in the indistinct sentiment and witness of the Spirit, is the same thing that the more mature Spirit is at pains to capture in *the concept* and thus to free itself in the present and therefore to find itself in the present."[22]

Luther's invention of Protestantism, then, is the first step in the simultaneous creation of "religion" and the reduction of religion to disembodied *concepts* in which one professes faith. The immanentization of Christianity results inevitably from the rebellion against the incarnational religion an Incarnate God established for the visible unity of a Mystical Body, leaving individual man alone with his God. Cornelio Fabro assesses the immense damage in this regard:

20. VI, 1065–71.
21. Ibid., 1071–72.
22. Hegel, *Grundlein der Philosophie des Rechts*, 17, in Cornelio Fabro, *God in Exile*, 1151, n. 4.

The division of Christianity occasioned by the Reformation contributed decisively, by elimination of objective authority in the area of faith, to the abandonment of Christianity as a historical religion of salvation in favor of that "eternal Christianity" or "reasonable and mystery-free Christianity" which proved to be the prologue and incubator of the positive and constructive atheism of the nineteenth- and above all twentieth-century philosophical schools.[23]

Lex Luther: Luther's Political Theories

We turn now to the political theories—if we can call them that—that Luther expediently appended to his new theology: the political theory that first gave rise to our graceless body politic. Just as Luther's new religion disembodied grace in the individual by reducing it to a non-transformative external imputation, so would it disembody the operation of grace in the collective of the body politic, beginning with the German principalities, first and foremost at Wittenberg. This emergence of a graceless body politic, no longer coextensive with the united Mystical Body, is another way of describing the emergence of the modern state system.

Luther did not deny the traditional doctrine of the divine ordination of man to life in the state, the divinely imposed duty to obey civil authority in all things except sin, and the evil of sedition. But his politics were modified according to the rhetorical needs of the moment to accommodate a double and self-contradictory movement, away from the Catholic Church and toward a Lutheran confessional state. Luther's rebellion against the Church obviously required the church-state separation of which he is the great pioneer. But it just as certainly required a confessional alliance of civil authority with Luther's new religion. For one thing, the old Catholic order had to be demolished in order to make room for Luther's creation, an impossible task without the coercive power of civil authority. For another, Luther and his Swiss reform counterparts had to fend off challenges to their own authority from the horde of heretical fanatics the Reformers themselves had unleashed via the principle of private judgment—first and foremost the Anabaptists, who were already preaching open rebellion against the emerging Protestant political establishment.

Accordingly, anticipating Locke by more than a century, when it came to the empire and the German princes and electors loyal to Rome,

---

23. Fabro, *God in Exile* (New York: Newman Press, 1968) 1153.

Luther denied any competence of the civil authority in religious matters whatsoever. Political authority was to be limited to the protection of persons and outward possessions; the individual conscience has primacy over the claims of the state. Luther maintained, as Locke would in his *Letter Concerning Toleration*, that as there is no church to teach infallibly concerning the way to salvation, there is no church that could lay claim to the obedience of civil authorities.

But having thus dispensed with the Catholic Church as the politically embedded conscience of the state, Luther turned round to insist that his new religion fulfill that very function. Thus, when it came to the establishment of Lutheranism in Wittenberg and elsewhere, Luther did not hesitate to invoke state power not only for the destruction of the old religion, but also for the imposition of the new orthodoxy. "Some argue that the secular authority have no concern whatever with ghostly matters," he wrote. "This is going much too far. . . . The rulers must not only protect the life and belongings of their underlings, but their highest duty is to protect the honor of God and to prevent blasphemy and idolatry"—meaning public manifestations of the Catholic religion.[24]

The resulting program included local laws revoking the jurisdiction and privileges of Catholic priests and prelates, ordinances compelling attendance at Lutheran services on Sunday under penalty of fines, corporal punishment, forfeiture of property and banishment, and civil penalties for heresies against Lutheranism, not excluding the death penalty. In addition, civil statutes compelled teachers of religion to adhere to the Augsburg Confession as interpreted by the theological faculty at Wittenberg.[25] In a perfect merger of the new church with the old state apparatus, the princes and Imperial Free Cities who had aligned themselves with the new religion petitioned the Imperial Diet, or general assembly of the empire, at Speyer in protest of the imperial ban on Luther and the prohibition of his works, demanding that the Evangel be allowed to spread without hindrance by the emperor. The Protestation of Speyer is the very source of the term "Protestant," the name Luther's innumerable progeny have happily applied to themselves ever since. In another manifestation of this new marriage between church and state, in 1530 the Augsburg Confession, setting forth the articles of the Lutheran religion, was adopted at a mixed gathering of rulers, lawyers and Lutheran theologians and then signed by various electors, princes, and German nobles.

24. VI, 258.
25. Cf. Grisar, Vol. VI, 244–77; Vol. II, 294–309.

It should not be surprising that Protestantism was launched as a political movement, for Luther's invention represented a supreme act of will directed against the entire existing order. The emergence of Protestantism thus led inevitably to the exercise of political power for the imposition of its demands. Luther's religion, to recall Cameron's observation, was a form of mass politics pitted against the age-old sociopolitical status quo of the Catholic confessional state, seeking to insert itself into the church-state configuration, replacing the Church, through the back door of the organs of local government, the front doors in Rome and Vienna being barred shut. As such, it required a political revolution in the imperial states and free cities, not just a religious one, in order to establish itself.

Again anticipating Locke, therefore, Luther developed a theory of revolution also conveniently adapted to the double movement away from the Church and toward a Lutheran confessional state. In line with the tradition, Luther held that the Christian must submit to temporal authority and that the Gospel forbids rebellion and revolution, especially when civil authority was defending the new Evangel. But, of course, these principles were quickly discarded when the emperor or the princes acted in defense of the Catholic Church and to inhibit the spread of Luther's errors. In that case, the emperor and the prince alike were to be resisted by the Christian as citizen even if the Christian as *Christian* was bound to the Gospel injunction against sedition. On the other hand, the emperor and the princes were invited to join in a general rebellion against the pope's temporal power: "If the fury of the Romanists continue," wrote Luther in 1520, "there seems to me to be no remedy left but that the emperor, kings, and princes gird on their armor, attack these pests of the earth, and decide the matter, not by words but by the sword."[26]

The resulting new configuration of the confessional state could only mean a subordination of religion by the civil sovereign in the form of the state churches of the imperial and secular states, including the free cities. It meant, as well, the establishment of the Church of England of which Henry made himself head in 1534 via the Act of Supremacy at the same time Luther and his reformed-church counterparts in Switzerland were using state power to impose and consolidate the new order. As Brad Gregory writes:

> The reformers' rejection of the Roman church left them entirely dependent upon secular authorities for protection, beginning with

---

26. Waring, 140.

Friedrich of Saxony's sheltering of Luther after the latter's excommunication by Leo X and imperial condemnation by Charles V in early 1521. *Simply put, no Protestant regime was even possible save through dependence on secular rulers, without which those who rejected the Roman church would presumably have been crushed by Counter-Reformation ecclesiastical or secular authorities. . . .*[27]

In Germany and Switzerland, as in England, civil authorities were only too happy to take advantage of the opportunities for plunder and the expansion of their own power created by the separation from Rome in the name of the new Gospel. Luther had provided an excellent vehicle for that purpose. What resulted, writes Waring, was the first emergence of "sovereignty, as understood in our age," meaning "absolute political power within the state—supreme power to regulate all affairs within the state—and *yet itself subject to no authority.*"[28]

Whatever the extent of the process of nation building prior to 1517, after that date the process entered a radically new phase. This was not a matter merely of the aggrandizement of power for the highest authority within the sphere of purely temporal affairs, yet preserving the separate and independent authorities of *imperium* and *sacerdotium* in their usual oscillation of conflict over the Christian centuries, but with the former ultimately subject to the latter where the two powers overlapped in their jurisdiction. Rather, as Waring describes approvingly, what emerged was "*the supreme will and power of the state as a unitary totality.*"[29] That is, a totality that no longer included a socially embedded religion uniting but standing over a body politic under the authority of the Roman pontiff.

Destruction of the Liturgical Polity

The modern nation-state as an exclusive moral totality could not have emerged without the destruction of the underlying liturgical polity that was Christendom, organically linked to Rome and the Church Universal. The destruction of the liturgical polity that had made the Mystical Body coextensive with the body politic was the essential task, Luther constantly declared. "On no other point does his hate flame forth so luridly," writes Grisar. "[N]owhere else is he so defiant, so contemptuous and so noisy—save perhaps when attacking popery—as when assailing the Sacrifice of the Mass, that main bulwark of the papacy. One

---

27. Brad S. Gregory, *The Unintended Reformation* (Cambridge, MA: The Belknap Press of Harvard University Press, 2012), 152.

28. Waring, 87.

29. Ibid., 88.

thing is certain; of all the religious practices sacred to Catholics none was branded by him with such hideous and common abuse as this, the sublimest mystery of faith and of Divine Love."

"When once the Mass has been put away," wrote Luther in 1522, "then I shall think I have overthrown the pope completely." Not only the pope, but the Mystical Body itself, leaving behind only what would become a graceless body politic. Whether it was the more gradual approach favored by Luther or the rapid liturgical revolution conducted by the southern German and Swiss "reformers," the abolition of the Mass and other traditional Catholic rites was, as even the Protestant scholar Euan Cameron observes, "indubitably a radical and unheard-of departure. The traditional sacrificial Mass had been the focus of the liturgical rhythm: performed daily by the priesthood, watched by the laity, deemed to have a quantitative and qualitative value for the good of the soul."[30]

The loss of precisely that quantitative and qualitative value for the good of the soul, the principal channel for the mediation to man of God's redemptive and inwardly transformative grace, could not fail to have disastrous social and political as well as spiritual consequences. Luther, with the aid of the state, literally destroyed the visible Mystical Body wherever the population adopted his new religion and its new liturgy, as did other "reformers" to the extent they were successful in imposing their variations on Luther's original theme.

Luther's Season of Regret

Inconsistent to the end, Luther would bitterly lament the outcome of his own religious revolution. Above all, he was aghast at the moral consequences of the incalculable loss of grace he himself had wrought with his new dogma of *sola fide* and his relentless attack on the spiritual unity he had labored to destroy. In a sermon given in 1528 he declared:

> That we are now so lazy and cold in the performance of good works, *is due to our no longer regarding them as a means of justification.* For when we still hoped to be justified by our works our zeal for doing good was a marvel. One sought to excel the other in uprightness and piety.
>
> *Were the old teaching to be revived today and our works made contributory to righteousness, we should be readier and more willing to do what is good* [emphasis added].

---

30. Cameron, *The European Reformation*, 248.

Of this there is, however, no prospect and thus, when it is a question of serving our neighbor and praising God by means of good works, we are sluggish and not disposed to do anything.[31]

In his commentary on the Epistle to the Galatians in 1535, Luther complained:

> People talk about Christian liberty and then go and cater to the desires of covetousness, pleasure, pride, envy, and other vices. Nobody wants to fulfill his duties. Nobody wants to help out a brother in distress.
>
> This sort of thing makes me so impatient at times that I wish the swine who trampled precious pearls under foot were back once again under the tyranny of the pope. . . .
>
> Even we creatures of the world do not perform our duties as zealously in the light of the Gospel *as we did before in the darkness of ignorance, because the surer we are of the liberty purchased for us by Christ, the more we neglect the Word, prayer, well-doing, and suffering.*[32]

Having himself been instrumental in drying up the wells of Catholic charity in German society, Luther himself bitterly protested, "Now, when asked to give, everybody protests he is poor and a beggar, and says there is no obligation of giving or of performing good works. *We have become worse than formerly and are losing our old righteousness.* Moreover, avarice is increasing everywhere."[33] Luther explicitly conceded that with the disappearance of Catholic charity, the charity of men in general had grown cold:

> I own, and others doubtless do the same, that there is not now such earnestness in the Gospel as formerly under the monks and priests when so many foundations were made, when there was so much building and no one was so poor as not to be able to give. But now there is not a town willing to support a preacher, there is nothing but plundering and thieving among the people and no one can prevent it. Whence comes this shameful plague?[34]

And, as Grisar notes, "it was precisely of Wittenberg and his own surroundings that Luther complained so loudly." Luther even lamented that his own morality had suffered:

---

31. IV, 212.

32. *Commentary on Saint Paul's Epistle to the Galatians*, Chapter V; electronic text version, Christian Classics Ethereal Library, www.ccel.org/ccel/luther/galatians. viii.html.

33. IV, 212–13.

34. VI, 54.

I confess of myself, and doubtless others must admit the same, that I lack the diligence and earnestness of which really I ought to have much more than formerly; *that I am much more careless than I was under the papacy*; and that now, *under the Evangel, there is nowhere the same zeal to be found as before* [emphasis added].

Never, however, did Luther acknowledge that the rapid collapse of morality following the destruction of Catholic social order in Wittenberg and elsewhere had anything to do with the success of his rebellion against Rome, the consequent plunder of the Church in Germany, the destruction of the Catholic network of charity, the abolition of the Mass, and the rise of supreme sovereignty. It was always, as Grisar notes, "due to the devil and to people's carelessness, but not to his teaching."

Where once Luther's complaint had been the interference in temporal affairs by the spiritual power represented by the pope and his minions, now he complained of the interference of the princes in the spiritual affairs of the reformed churches. But there was no stopping what he himself had set in motion. In "all the attempts made to infuse life into the branch torn away by Luther from the universal Catholic Church the secular power never failed to interfere," writes Grisar. "The state had stood sponsor to the new faith on its first appearance and, whether in Luther's interest or in its own, the state continued to intervene in matters pertaining to the church. This interweaving of politics with religion failed to insure to the new church the friendly assistance of the state, *but soon brought it into a position of entire subservience—in spite of the protests of the originator of the innovation.*"[35]

The Religious Wars

Luther's call for separation of church and state had resulted in a divorce from the Catholic Church followed by its remarriage to the Lutheran church. But the second marriage produced unending conflict with the first spouse, a conflict inextricably linked to the struggle for political power.

Only months after his death in February of 1546, the imperial states whose official religion was now founded upon the Augsburg Confession formed the Schmalkaldic League, launched their unsuccessful war against the empire, and were crushed by the imperial army of Charles V. But the Lutheran heresy was by now uncontainable politically as well as spiritually. The rather ludicrous Augsburg Interim of 1548—which

35. III, 557–61.

attempted a politically negotiated compromise of the Catholic religion by permitting the marriage of Lutheran clergy and communion under both kinds while mandating Lutheran reintegration into the Catholic Church—and the even more ludicrous Leipzig Interim did nothing to prevent further Protestant rebellion.

Ultimately, with the Peace of Augsburg in 1555, Charles V gave back everything he had won with the victory over the Schmalkaldic League as Protestantism attained both political and religious legitimacy in the empire via the principle *cuius regio, eius religio*, which allowed the princes of the empire to elect the religion of the state, either Catholicism or Lutheranism. The stage was set for the politico-religious wars that followed as the virus of Protestantism spread from the empire to France and England, provoking the French civil wars raging from the 1560s to the 1590s, the English Civil Wars from 1642–1649 and the Thirty Years' War from 1618–1648. As Cavanaugh notes, the rise of the nation-state (beginning with Luther's call for the unification of Germany) was the cause, not the solution to the Thirty Years' War.

Sovereignty Enshrined: Historical Landmarks

The agreements comprising the Peace of Westphalia (1648) enshrined in the empire the sovereignty of the nation-state as the new and unchallengeable locus of constitutional and territorial authority, whose official religion—as already decided at Augsburg—would be determined and controlled by civil authority. The German states, the Netherlands, and Switzerland gained substantial or complete autonomy from the Holy Roman Empire, even if certain imperial prerogatives remained, while the Church was essentially stripped of her indirect temporal authority over the sovereign states.

After 1648, writes John Galgiardo, "the Empire was never again to function to any significant extent as a supra-territorial government." Pope Innocent X, in his bull *Zelo domus Dei*, denounced offending provisions of the Westphalia accords as "null, void, invalid, iniquitous, unjust, damnable, reprobate, inane, empty of meaning and effect for all time."[36] The papal protest was futile. The transfer of the sacred from the Church to the state had already taken place in a baptism of blood, and at Westphalia political modernity received its sacrament of confirmation.

In England, in a dramatic manifestation of the new Protestant and

---

36. In Daniel Philpott, *Revolutions in Sovereignty* (Princeton: Princeton University Press, 2001), 87.

graceless body politic in action, in the year following the Peace of Westphalia, Charles I, a monarch of unacceptably papist tendencies, was beheaded after a mock trial by his own subjects. Thereafter, the political control of official religion reaches perhaps its most bizarre extreme under Cromwell with the *Humble Petition and Advice* of 1657. During the Interregnum between the execution of Charles and the restoration of the monarchy, a group of members of Parliament submitted their *Humble Petition* to Lieutenant-General Cromwell, requesting "His Highness the Lord Protector" declare that "the true Protestant Christian religion, as it is contained in the Holy Scriptures of the Old and New Testament, and no other, be held forth and asserted for the public profession of these nations. . . ." This "true Protestant Christian religion" would be determined by "a Confession of Faith, to be agreed by your Highness and the Parliament . . . and recommended to the people of these nations, that none may be suffered or permitted, by opprobrious words or writing . . . to revile or reproach the Confession of Faith to be agreed upon as aforesaid. . . ."[37]

In *Leviathan*, first published in 1651, Hobbes had already recommended precisely what the *Humble Petition* contemplated: that the political sovereign shall serve as the Protestant equivalent of a pope. Hobbes's liberal prescription for liberal disorder arises from his belief that, given the fragmentation of religion inherent to Protestantism and the consequent emergence of sects contending for political power, "the only way of saving royal authority, and thus civil peace," as Pierre Manent observes, "was to detach completely the king's power from religion by making the king fully sovereign over it."[38]

Locke, "the confused man's Hobbes," will then follow to prescribe his own liberal cure for liberalism, fully developing the themes Luther himself had first ventured: the attack on the Aristotelian-Thomistic conception of man and the tradition of the virtues; the principle of private judgment; the primacy of individual conscience; and the total incompetence of civil authority in matters religious—except when it comes to suppressing the threat posed by Catholics and Protestant "fanatics" who reject the reasonable, mystery-free Christianity outlined in Locke's *Reasonableness of Christianity*, a work even Luther would have found heretical. Locke's Law of Toleration, the ultimate liberal solution to the religious chaos religious liberalism had unleashed, would become the governing principle of political modernity. All religions were to be

---

37. *Humble Petition and Advice* (1657), Article 11.
38. Manent, *An Intellectual History of Liberalism*, 21.

tolerated, not only by the state but by every other religion—with the exception, of course, of Catholicism, which must be exempted at least until it is tamed, as it certainly has been.

In 1688, the Glorious Revolution permanently precluded a Catholic monarchy in England, and Locke triumphantly returned from his exile in Holland on the royal yacht. By 1700, writes John Bossy, "the world was full of religions."[39] But by then the foundations of political liberalism had been solidly established, and all that was necessary to erect the superstructure was the revolutionary destruction of the confessional state even in its vestigial form.

At the same time, the New Philosophy, essentially philosophical Protestantism run amuck, led inevitably to an attack on the very existence of any kind of Christian commonwealth. The erosion of philosophical certitudes, beginning with the very nature of man as an ensouled creature, necessarily undermined whatever theological certitudes were still held in common by Christians, including the need for the soul's redemption by grace, and thus had undermined any agreed basis for a Christian state. As Jonathan Israel observes, "[O]nce the main thrust of dissent ceased to be theological and became philosophical, there set in an inexorable slackening and loss of coordination in church-state collaboration in the cultural, educational, and intellectual spheres."[40] From 1650 onward the reigning New Philosophy "rapidly overthrew theology's age-old hegemony in the world of study . . . and led a few openly to challenge everything inherited from the past."[41]

Only in America, however, did the graceless body politic finally rid itself of even a captive and vestigial religious organ under state control. Even this was reviled as a remnant of popery by the colonial radicals, a motley group of descendants from dissenters from the Church of England—the "Protestants of Protestantism" as Edmund Burke called them. By July 1789, when the Bill of Rights was ratified, the process was complete. All religions, above all Catholicism, were to surrender any claim to authority over the central government of the world's first working model of an officially secular nation-state, holdover Protestant religious customs aside. The Framers had erected the graceless body politic *par excellence* wherein which every Christian believer, as Pierre Manent so memorably observes, is expected to act politically as

---

39. Cavanaugh, *The Myth of Religious Violence*, 74.

40. Jonathan I. Israel, *Radical Enlightenment: Philosophy and the Making of Modernity* (Oxford: Oxford University Press, 2001), 8.

41. Ibid., 4.

"an atheist under the true God, under the God in whom he believes."[42] It is in America that the state first becomes fully supreme in the modern sense described by Westel Willoughby:

> [N]ot only as giving ultimate validity to all law, *but as itself determining the scope of its own powers*, and itself deciding what interests shall be subjected to its regulation,... [t]he state is distinguished from all other persons and public bodies.... [I]t sets to itself its own right and the limits to its authority.... *Obligation, through its own will, is the legal characteristic of the state.*[43]

On September 20, 1870, Pope Pius IX raised the white flag of surrender at Castle Sant'Angelo. The Masonic armies had won. Rome was incorporated into the Kingdom of Italy and the Roman pontiff's eleven centuries of sovereignty over the Papal States came to end. In that same year, the Third Republic was constituted in France. Fifteen years after that, Pope Leo wrote the epitaph of Christendom in *Immortale Dei*:

> There was once a time when ... the religion instituted by Jesus Christ, established firmly in befitting dignity, flourished everywhere, by the favor of princes and the legitimate protection of magistrates; and Church and state were happily united in concord and friendly interchange of good offices. The state, constituted in this wise, bore fruits important beyond all expectation....

> Christian Europe has subdued barbarous nations, and changed them from a savage to a civilized condition, from superstition to true worship. It victoriously rolled back the tide of Mohammedan conquest; retained the headship of civilization; stood forth in the front rank as the leader and teacher of all, in every branch of national culture; bestowed on the world the gift of true and many-sided liberty; and most wisely founded very numerous institutions for the solace of human suffering....

> A similar state of things would certainly have continued had the agreement of the two powers been lasting.... But that harmful and deplorable passion for innovation which was aroused in the sixteenth century threw first of all into confusion the Christian religion, and next, by natural sequence, invaded the precincts of philosophy, whence it spread amongst all classes of society.

> From this source, as from a fountain-head, burst forth all those later tenets of unbridled license which, in the midst of the terrible upheavals

---

42. Manent, op. cit., 83.

43. Westel Woodbury Willoughby, *An Examination of the Nature of the State* (New York: The Macmillan Company, 1911), 193.

of the last century, were wildly conceived and boldly proclaimed as the principles and foundation of that new conception of law which was not merely previously unknown, but was at variance on many points with not only the Christian, but even the natural law.[44]

Six years later, in *Au milieu des solicitudes* (1891), Leo counseled the Catholics of France to resign themselves to the advent of the post-Christian nation-state. By the turn of the twentieth century a now graceless body politic was well on the way to becoming, as John Rao says, a "death camp ruled by willful passion that now extends throughout the globe."[45]

Conclusion:
End Point of the Lutheran Trajectory

When Martin Luther was able to burn Leo X's bull of excommunication and defy the imperial ban with impunity, he became Patient Zero in an epidemic that would spread throughout the Western world. The first symptoms of the contagion were a severance of the relation between the body politic and the Mystical Body in the imperial states and free cities that adopted Luther's new religion. In those places the grace of the sacraments, above all the Holy Eucharist, was bled out of the body politic as a moral totality, including its organs of government, in the manner of a hemorrhagic fever. As we have seen, even Luther lamented the consequent sudden collapse of morality. As Luther's and his fellow Reformers' religion was essentially a feverish ideology, state control over its doctrine and praxis was inevitable, followed by the just-as-inevitable total subordination of what passed for Christianity by the nation-state, which is depicted in the liberal narrative as our savior from religious strife when it was actually the primary beneficiary of religious strife— strife that had originated in the tortured soul of Patient Zero.

We owe it all Luther. "The traces of that one mind," writes Waring in his appreciative study of Luther's political theories:

> are to be seen today in the mind of the modern world. Had there been no Luther, the English, the American, and the German peoples would be acting differently, *would be altogether different men and women from what they are at this moment.* . . . Luther was thus the liberator of modern thought.[46]

---

44. Leo XIII, *Immortale Dei* (1885), nn. 22–24.

45. John Rao, *Removing the Blindfold* (Forest Lake: Remnant Press, 2012), 284.

46. Waring, *The Political Theories of Martin Luther*, 264, 268.

The great liberator freed men from the Church only to lay upon them the shackles of the state. But, as Waring notes with inexplicable satisfaction:

> [T]he ecclesiastical reformation led to a political one. *The sphere of the state was extended to include everyone within its borders and to include temporal affairs of every kind.* On the whole, the supremacy of the common law of the land upon everyone within its borders, *including the clergy,* triumphed universally with the Reformation.[47]

The overthrow of the Church by the Protestant Reformers could only leave the individual helpless before the power of the state. Protestant Man, alone with his God, can do no more in opposition to the state than to cast the one vote allotted to him. For him there is no appeal to higher authority, no defender of freedom beyond fifty percent plus one of the governing electorate, no idea of what true freedom really is.

In his critique of Kierkegaard, the supposed revivalist defender of faith against the arid rationalism of political modernity, John Rist notes that he too, adrift in the heaving sea of private judgment, succumbed to the "Protestant tradition of man as isolated ethical individual," so that he broke even with the established Lutheran Church of Denmark. "Radical choice," writes Rist, "in and of itself ... like many another modern ethical trend, is as much as bastard of the Protestant Reformation, of the thesis of man alone with his God, as are the sub-Kantian theories of autonomy with which [the Reformation] is now associated."[48]

A Christian alone with his God, deprived of the grace of the sacraments—above all the Bread of Life—is man alone with his *concept* of God. And even if the living God has not altogether abandoned him, if only in virtue of his baptism, he no longer belongs to the visible Church and the incarnational religion that were the social matrix of a body politic united in grace and thus immunized against the worst excesses of willful passion in the realm of the political.

"Where the people are Catholic and submissive to the law of God, as declared and applied by the Vicar of Christ and supreme pastor of the Church, democracy may be a good form of government," wrote Orestes Brownson in 1873. "But," he continued:

> combined with Protestantism or infidelity in the people, its inevitable tendency is to lower the standard of morality, to enfeeble intellect, to abase character, and to retard civilization, as even our short American experience amply proves. Our republic may have had a material expan-

---

47. Ibid., 266 (internal quotation and citation omitted).
48. John Rist, *Real Ethics* (Cambridge: Cambridge University Press, 2002), 58–59.

sion and growth; but every observing and reflecting American, whose memory goes back, as mine does, over fifty years, sees that in all else it is tending downward, and is on the declivity to utter barbarism.[49]

"The third and last stage of Protestantism is Individualism," wrote Brownson in 1845. And it is this rugged religious individualism that renders the professing Christian impotent before Hobbes's mortal God as the isolated member of a graceless body politic.

Brownson wrote of an "old difficulty" in this regard: that while religion is essential for the maintenance of true liberty against the tyranny of the majority, Protestantism itself is a majoritarian religion. "Protestantism," he argued, "is not and cannot be the religion to sustain democracy; because . . . like democracy itself, it is subject to the control of the people, and must command and teach what they say, and of course must follow, instead of controlling, their passions, interest, and caprices." Hence the Protestant religion has declined in tandem with the body politic that embraced it. The end result is now nothing less than a return to paganism. "When Catholic societies prevaricate and fall," wrote Donoso Cortes in 1851, "it happens that paganism immediately gains a foothold in them, and we behold ideas, customs, and institutions, and the entire society relapsing into paganism."[50]

The only way back from the abyss at the end of the declivity, of course, is reintegration of the body politic with the Mystical Body and the universal liturgical polity that Luther and his progeny destroyed. Indeed, as John Milbank has warned, "Only a global liturgical polity can save us now from literal violence."[51] But for the past fifty years, Rome itself has been determined to bar any such return to civilizational sanity. In 1870, Pius IX merely raised a white flag of surrender to Mazzini and Garibaldi. In 1962, the Church inexplicably raised a white flag of surrender to the zeitgeist itself.

Above all, the liturgical reforms designed to appeal precisely to Protestants have, incredibly enough, done more than Luther himself demanded in his war on the Mass as the great bulwark of Catholic Christendom. In his landmark work on the subject, Klaus Gamber observes that *"much more radical than any liturgical changes introduced by Luther,*

---

49. Orestes Brownson, "Introduction to Last Series," Brownson's *Quarterly Review* (January 1873), in *The Works of Orestes A. Brownson* (Detroit: H.F. Brownson, 1887), Vol. XX, 285.

50. Juan Donoso Cortes, *Essay on Catholicism, Authority and Order* (New York: Joseph F. Wagner, Inc., 1925), 74.

51. John Milbank, "The Gift of Ruling," *New Blackfriars*, Vol. 85, No. 996 (2004), 238.

as far as the rite was concerned, was the reorganization of our own liturgy—above all the fundamental changes that were made in the liturgy of the Mass."[52] What Euan Cameron called an unprecedented rupture when it happened in German states and free cities in the 1520s and 1530s has been imposed even more radically on the Catholic Church herself by the pope and the bishops—the bare validity of the New Mass aside.

At the same time, ecumenism and dialogue have replaced opposition to the errors of the Protestantism and the necessity of a return to the one true Church for Christian unity with a pan-denominational and even a pan-religious indifferentism that denies in practice the identity of the Mystical Body with the Catholic Church. Even as their various sects descend into various states of moral and doctrinal decrepitude, Protestants are now unquestionably accepted as "brothers and sisters in Christ." Catholic churchmen hail the "growing unity" between Catholics and Protestants, without seeming to notice that the progress toward "unity" consists entirely in the Protestantization of Catholics, beginning with hierarchy.

With liturgical unity shattered by a vernacular rite that no longer conveys mimetically what it provides sacramentally, there has, of course, been a consequent loss of grace even within the Mystical Body itself. To quote Gamber again: "[T]he real destruction of the traditional Mass, of the traditional Roman rite with a history of more than one thousand years, is the wholesale destruction of the Faith on which it was based, a Faith that had been the source of our piety and our courage to bear witness to Christ and His Church, the inspiration of countless Catholics over many centuries."[53] The great majority of Catholics are now *de facto* Protestants—indeed, very liberal Protestants whose practice and views on contraception, abortion, divorce, and "gay marriage" are now more liberal than even the views of the most conservative Protestant evangelicals, who condemn the papacy today not because it is the whore of Babylon but because it has gone liberal. Even Luther, who likened contraception to sodomy, would view with amazed incomprehension the liberal wreck that is most of the human element of the Catholic Church today.

John Paul II called the result silent apostasy, although he did virtually nothing about it. But now we have a pope who sounds for all the world like Luther himself: a pope who continually mocks the orthodox, coddles the heterodox, panders to sexual sins, above all divorce and remar-

52. Klaus Gamber, *The Reform of the Roman Liturgy* (New York: Una Voce Press and the Foundation for Catholic Reform, 1993), 43.
53. Ibid., 102.

riage, ridicules the traditional Mass as "a kind of fashion,"[54] describes the dogma of transubstantiation as a mere "interpretation," informs Protestants that all who are baptized belong the same "church of Christ" as Catholics do, no matter what heresies they profess or sins they condone, and publicly informs a Lutheran woman, during Sunday ceremonies in a Lutheran church in which he participated, that it is a matter to be decided between her and the Lord whether she should receive Holy Communion in the Catholic Church.[55]

We have a pope who presided over a ludicrously misnamed Synod on the Family that labored, under his minute control, to obscure and undermine the revealed truth he seems incapable of uttering, but that was just affirmed by a Synod of the Orthodox Church in America:[56]

> God has established marriage as a lifelong, exclusive relationship between one man and one woman, and all intimate sexual activity outside the marriage relationship, whether heterosexual, homosexual, or otherwise, is immoral, and therefore sin.

We have a pope who condemns insistence upon that very certitude as "rigorism" and Pharisaism, reducing it to a mere "objective ideal" that must be accommodated to "the concrete complexity of one's limits." And now that same pope has traveled to Sweden to honor *precisely* Luther—the greatest heresiarch of all time. The abomination took place on October 31, 2016. Francis's participation in this celebration of the 500th anniversary of Luther's rebellion included a joint liturgy with *faux* bishops of the Swedish Lutheran Church, including its female "primate," who purports to be an archbishop. The liturgy featured this common prayer, among others:

> The ecumenical journey enables Lutherans and Catholics to appreciate together *Martin Luther's insight into and spiritual experience of the gospel of the righteousness of God,* which is also God's mercy. . . . *Thanks be to you, O God, for the many guiding theological and spiritual insights that we have all received through the Reformation* [emphasis added].[57]

---

54. "Pope Francis on February 14: "Old Mass? Just a Kind of Fashion!", February 15, 2014 @ rorate-caeli.blogspot.com/2014/02/important-pope-francis-on-feb-14-young.html.

55. Visit of Pope Francis to the Evangelical Church of Rome, November 15, 2015 @ https://youtu.be/ooCWoXpFQo?t=1292.

56. Statement of the Holy Synod of the OCA on Sincerely Held Religious Beliefs Regarding Marriage, June 16, 2016 @ oca.org.

57. "Common Prayer, from Conflict to Communion: Lutheran-Catholic Common Commemoration of the Reformation 2017," https://www.lutheranworld.org/sites/default/files/dtpw-lrc-liturgy-2016_en.pdf.

In sum, the human element of the Catholic Church has undergone a thoroughgoing Protestant Reformation! Irony of ironies, Lutheranism, having failed catastrophically as a religion, has achieved its greatest victory over the Church as an ideology. If Luther is in a place where laughter is possible, he is laughing now—intermittently with his tormented screams.

If the salt loses its savor, it will be trampled underfoot. But today the Church endures the spectacle of a pope who seems to welcome the trampling. With the suave assurance of an Argentinian ideologue, Francis declared to the world in one of his many magazine interviews, "*States must be secular. Confessional states end badly. That goes against the grain of history.*"[58] The man from Argentina seems not to have noticed that the grain of history is a trail of blood beginning at the feet of the man whose rebellion against God he himself commemorated. The Catholic confessional state did not simply "end badly," but rather was *ended* badly by the wave after wave of civic zombies who contracted their disease from Patient Zero or his descendants.

But for all of this we must not despair. In fact, the Bergoglian pontificate is a sign of hope. In the midst of Luther's calamitous ascendancy, Erasmus, now a chastened humanist, wrote to King Ferdinand words that apply with equal force to the state of affairs under this bizarre pontificate: "God grant that this bitter and drastic remedy, which, in consequence of Luther's apostasy, has stirred up all the world like a body that is sick in every part, may have a wholesome effect for the recovery of Christian morals." Grisar's comment on Erasmus's rude awakening is also helpful to us in our current circumstances:

> Catholics can see easily enough why the rise of Protestantism tended to bring back many humanists, among them Erasmus himself, to a more whole-hearted support of the Church. Erasmus ... frequently spoke of Luther's work as a "remedy." It was a remedy above all for himself and for the more serious elements among his own party, whom the sight of the outward effects and internal consequences of the new teaching served to withdraw from the abyss towards which they were hurrying.[59]

The spectacle of the Lutheran abyss provoked the Counter-Reformation. And now that a neo-pagan abyss looms before us, toward which no less than the pope seems determined to drag us, there is a kind of

---

58. Interview with *La Croix*, May 17, 2016; English translation @ www.la-croix.com/ Religion/Pape/ INTERVIEW-Pope-Francis-2016-05-17- 1200760633.

59. III, 249, 257.

great awakening of many members of the Mystical Body who before were sleeping the slumber of the great renewal. Now they recognize for what it is the end point of a trajectory traditionalists have been tracing since its origin in the irenic ambiguity of the Second Vatican Council.

At that end point is our beginning, even if it will probably mean dramatic events for all of humanity before the Mystical Body and the body politic—in whatever remains of our civilization—are united again in grace. In this regard it is fitting to close with the prophetic words of Sister Lucia of Fatima, filled with dread but also with glorious promise in the light of eternity, before which all earthly calamities pale:

> I felt my spirit inundated by a mystery of light that is God and in Him I saw and heard: the point of a lance like a flame that is detached, touches the axis of the earth, and it trembles: mountains, cities, towns and villages with their inhabitants are buried. The sea, the rivers, the clouds, exceed their boundaries, inundating and dragging with them, in a vortex, houses and people in a number that cannot be counted. It is the purification of the world from the sin in which it is immersed. Hatred, ambition, provoke the destructive war. After I felt my racing heart, in my spirit a soft voice said: "In time, one faith, one baptism, one Church, Holy, Catholic, Apostolic."[60]

60. *Pathway under the Gaze of Mary* (World Apostolate of Fatima: 2013), 244 (267 in Portuguese edition).

7

Religious Evolution and Revolution in the Triumph of *Homo Economicus*

Rev. Richard A. Munkelt

We are suffering from a metaphysical disease, and the cure must therefore be metaphysical.
                                        E. F. Schumacher, *Small is Beautiful*

ONE OF C. S. LEWIS's more popular works, *The Great Divorce*, is a commentary on William Blake's fanciful and gnostic literary creation, *The Marriage of Heaven and Hell*, in which Lewis dutifully reminds us by way of allegory that what Blake sought to join together in a perverse union must be strictly sundered. But Lewis's title would be of greater intellectual service and provide a deeper cultural understanding if it were applied to the Protestant Reformation of the sixteenth century. In that context we should understand by the phrase "great divorce" the alienation between heaven and earth wrought by the new form of Christianity that Protestantism represented. Ironically, the Reformation began in Lewis's own country with a great divorce, not only between king and queen, but also between England and the Bride of Christ, the Catholic Church.

A state of alienation between heaven and earth is contrary to the original intention of the Christian religion, which was and is the reconciliation of those two ultimate poles of reality, nature and super nature. According to the old theological reckoning, the Incarnation and the propitiatory sacrifice of the God-Man, Jesus Christ, restored a spiritual intimacy between God and the believer through the salvific gift of divine grace, which is a participation in the life of God here and now. Thus, having long been estranged by human sin, heaven and earth were reunited through the ordinary channels of grace, the sacraments of the Church of Christ. This reunion was poetically expressed through Christianity's ancient bridal symbolism concerning the Bridegroom and His ecclesial spouse, as well as rationally articulated through the Pauline theology of the Catholic Church as the Body of Christ animated by the Holy Spirit.

In place of this vision of theological reconciliation, the magisterial founders of Protestantism—Luther, Calvin, and Zwingli—effected a novel and radical separation of Creator and creature by dint of their well-known and complementary doctrines of the total sovereignty of God and the total depravity of man.[1] Prostrate in sin, man had no role to play in the work of salvation, and assimilation of the human to the divine was condemned as a popish fantasy. The divide between man and God could not have become more profound. With human effort in the matter of salvation out of the question, human life and work could give its undivided attention to mundane pursuits. Enter the worldly striving of *homo economicus,* economic man.

It will be the burden of this essay to tell something of the story of his rise to power, thanks in large measure to the European religious upheaval of the 1500s. Accordingly, several questions are posed herein and answered in the course of what may be described as an exercise in speculative history. First of all, who is economic man? From where did he come? What role did religion play in his ascendancy? And how did he make the modern state his servant? I shall contend that the embryo of economic man was formed in the womb of Classical Christianity, i.e., Catholicism, which constituted an evolution in the mentality of pagan antiquity; that he was then born in the Middles Ages but swaddled and constrained by custom and regulation; and that finally he grew into full stature and socio-political dominance in the wake of the cultural revolution unleashed by Neo-Christianity, i.e., Protestantism.

The immediate and most manifest consequence of a militant Protestantism on the march was to divide Christendom, an ongoing division that could not but engender and encourage forces directed toward the de-Christianization of Europe.[2] Pierre Bayle is one of the more spectac-

---

1. The *locus classicus* in Martin Luther's *oeuvre* in regard to these two doctrines is *De Servo Arbitrio.* For a translation of, and introduction to, this work, see *On the Bondage of the Will,* tr. J.I. Packer and O.R. Johnston (Westwood, NJ: Fleming H. Revell Co., 1957). John Calvin's principal theological treatise, *Institutes of Christian Religion,* amply testifies to these teachings; for a translation see online, *Christian Classics Ethereal Library,* http://www.ccel.org/ccel/calvin/institutes. See also, *John Calvin, Selections from His Writings,* ed. John Dillenberger (Garden City, NY: Anchor Books, 1971).

2. See Mark Greengrass, *Christendom Destroyed, Europe 1517–1648* (New York: Viking, 2014).

ular early examples of the new intellectual shock trooper in the campaign to undermine the political and cultural hegemony of Christianity. Armed with his Calvinist doctrine of total depravity and a Lockean view of religious tolerance, Bayle provocatively theorized on the possibility and advantage of an atheistic state.[3] The tragic failure, furthermore, to reunite Europe under the banner of a single faith in the Thirty Years' War, the war itself a sanguinary result of the religious rebellion of the previous century, virtually guaranteed that Europeans would begin to explore new forms of cultural and social identity to replace a Christianity exhausted by internecine strife. On the large scale, the burgeoning of the nation-state, under the motto cuius regio eius religio, would gradually extinguish the idea of a universal Christian order; and on the small scale, individuals would begin to pursue mundane vocations and doux commerce with ever-greater avidity and scope.[4] Hence, the Neo-Epicureanism and naturalistic mechanico-quantitative trends in the Scientific Revolution of the seventeenth century (culminating later in the methodological atheism of the physicist, Pierre-Simon Laplace) and the intellectual rejection of Christianity in the radical Enlightenment of the eighteenth century seem almost to follow with historical and logical necessity from the pan-European religious convulsion that shook Christendom to its foundations in the period of the High Renaissance.[5]

---

3. See chapters on Bayle in Ronald Beiner, *Civil Religion: A Dialogue in the History of Political Philosophy* (Cambridge: Cambridge University Press, 2011). Bayle's political toleration is based on indifferentism, which is intolerant of all religious claims to truth. Toleration is a smoke screen for civil religion, whether of the so-called natural or secular type. From the idea of a confessional state it does not logically follow that it must persecute; but the secular state must persecute religion by either outlawing it or, against its nature, forcing it into the sphere of the private. For the strange tale of the rise of "Christian secularism" (a contradiction in terms unbeknownst to the author) see Larry Siedentop, *Inventing the Individual, The Origins of Western Liberalism* (Cambridge: Belknap Press, 2014). In an otherwise engaging story of the birth of the "liberal" concept of the individual from ancient Christian egalitarianism and notion of conscience, Siedentop fails to see how liberal secularism (astonishingly "the embodiment of Christian moral intuitions," 362) assumed in turn (after the Church) the right to impose and enforce its own system of belief. Similarly, Perez Zagorin seems unaware of the deleterious effects on religion of the secular pluralist strategy of a free market in religion, reducing all religion to meaningless subjectivism; see, Perez Zagorin, *How the Idea of Religious Toleration Came to the West* (Princeton: Princeton University Press, 2003). Protestantism, to its own religious and socio-political demise, eventually embraced the secular strategy in order to protect limitless dissent and non-interference.

4. The idea of the civilizing effects of commerce stems from Montesquieu.

5. The primary influence of the Renaissance on the reformers was the humanist elevation of rhetoric as the supreme art. Luther and Calvin were rhetoricians first and foremost in the dialectical battle for the soul of Christianity.

Though the European Restoration after Napoleon gave Christian civilization a stay of execution, modern pressures toward nationalism culminated in the double conflagration of two world wars that left the religio-culture of Europe in ashes. Then, across this civilizational wasteland spread the secular and materialistic rivalry of those economic siblings, capitalism and socialism.

Nothing so exemplifies modern secularity and materialism than the alienated man par excellence, *homo economicus*. As a social model, he represents modern man's estrangement from his supernatural vocation and the contemplation of eternity, an aspiration that the West considered our highest calling, from the time of the Parthenon to the age of Chartres Cathedral. Economic man can be defined as a self-interested creature who seeks to maximize returns on private capital as he chafes under cultural constraints. He knows law but not honor, he has no country, and economic utility is his god. In the body politic he is the stomach, a necessary organ to be sure, but one which in modern times has succeeded to rule the head.

The economic sense of utility is the pleasure one gets from the satisfaction of material desires. It is measured by the quantity of things demanded or consumed. It functions, therefore, in modern commercial societies as a marginal signal of price for producers and so as a measure of fiat or conventional, as opposed to natural, value, that is to say, exchange value.[6] In other words, demand determines supply, and the intersection of the two reveals, in theory, the equilibrium price that allows markets of wanted, not necessarily needed, commodities to clear. Throw in constant innovation and you arrive at the economic promised land of infinite appetite and endless growth, i.e., limitless production, consumption, and accumulation. But as with any psychic disorder that exhibits neither a mean nor moderation, advanced economies based on the social ideal of the *popolo grasso* suffer consequences such as credit fever, environmental degradation, collapse of fertility rates, loss of solidarity, and axiological confusion, to name a few.[7] These consequences act like so many symptoms of a spiritual disease that is a kind of psychosocial bulimia. The underlying causes of this disease—which Keynes did

---

6. For discussions of the meaning and significance of use and exchange values for Aristotle and St Thomas Aquinas, see Scott Maeikle, *Aristotle's Economic Thought* (Oxford: Clarendon Press, 1995) and Christopher Franks, *He Became Poor: The Poverty of Christ and Aquinas's Economic Teaching* (Grand Rapids: William B. Eerdmans Publishing Co., 2009).

7. Not unlike "externalities" or "market failures" in economic parlance, *mutatis mutandis*. For critiques of neoclassical economics, see the following: Joseph Stiglitz, *Freefall: America, Free Markets, and the Sinking of the World Economy* (New York: W. W.

not hesitate to describe as a "disgusting morbidity"[8]—are the spiritual emptiness and the loss of cultural identity that are fostered by the ubiquitous money motive and the total economic regime.

Economic man is in one sense apolitical and amoral. From another perspective, however, he is always angling to get the ethico-political order to accommodate, or better serve, his possessive practices. Because he has effectively captured the state in modern times and turned its legal machinery in favor of the life of acquisition, economic man is the author of the modern regime and so the paradigm of modernity. Like wind and water working on a rocky landscape, the titanic forces of the modern mass market erode and reshape traditional culture. For its part, the market is no longer a means at the disposal of the commonwealth but the very end of human social life. As such, notwithstanding the fact that there have always been self-interested people, it is the new and great misalliance between economics and politics that distinguishes the modern age from all previous ages. The offspring of this misalliance are collective alienation (the reduction of the bonds of society to anonymous exchange), enormous economic disparities, and all manner of fiat rights and dubious forms of self-expression, blithely arrogating to themselves such venerable terms as art, liberty, and gender in a semantic anarchy that defies the natural common sense of humanity. And yet, all this spells further opportunity for the man of the market, who will both form and flatter conventional taste, while brooking no obstacles of nature or culture in the path of dubious progress and unlimited profit. Economic man is, therefore, the inventor of the fake culture of rootless consumerism, or paraculture, and the paratheology of omnipotent utility, seductively clothed in the demagoguery of a negative and undefined freedom.[9] Not long ago one of the last noticeable vestiges of Christian

---

Norton & Co., 2010). Stiglitz baldly states (p. 281), "I have explained how the world is rife with externalities"; Ian Fletcher, *Free Trade Doesn't Work, What Should Replace it and Why* (Washington, DC: U.S. Business & Industry Council, 2010). Fletcher explodes David Ricardo's theory of comparative advantage; Jonathan Schlefer, *The Assumptions Economists Make* (Cambridge: Harvard University Press, 2012). In neoclassical theory, Schlefer arrestingly explains (73): "The very concept of society is banished." This is a legacy of the individualism inherent in Protestant theology and Protestant-inspired early modern theories of the social contract emerging out of the solitary life of man in the so-called "state of nature."

8. Quoted in Meikle, 103.

9. Man is a cultural being. Real culture, by my lights, would be a traditional society bound together by a political theology. Because they have no respect for tradition and no explicit theology, market societies have no culture. On the other hand, because market societies try to hold people together through economics alone and have an implicit anthropology and anti-theology, they may be said to have culture of a sort, viz., paraculture.

civil society in America became extinct when the country opened itself up for business on Sunday. Sunday morning is now given over to a new devotion, that of the "soccer mom." How quaint seems the painting by Edward Hopper.

Before the advent of modernity, Classical Christianity represented an evolution or development from antiquity. In many respects, it can be seen as, and to some degree saw itself as, the perfection of natural religion and an improved, not to say true, philosophy. St Justin Martyr typifies this outlook. And for all the putative anti-intellectualism of Tertullian, he made skillful use of his classical education and Aristotelian reasoning, condemning the false philosophy of syncretistic Gnosticism, not the true philosophy of Christ.[10] Moreover, Catholic rituals were, and are, unashamedly analogous to certain forms of pre-Christian piety. Even the idea of the divinity of man, a virgin birth, or a god who died and came back to life, had pagan antecedents. The flamboyant Empedocles declared himself a god. And Caesars became divine while they sat on their thrones. But certainly with Christianity something was also new, startlingly new. For no one in antiquity could anticipate or envision that an historical, and what is more, an apparently ordinary man, albeit of extraordinary charismatic gifts, a poor Jew crucified with criminals, would found and launch a worldwide religion based on his worship, one that would supplant Western paganism. But we must leave that great mystery aside and concentrate on something less sublime but more germane to our topic. And that is the fact that Classical Christianity promoted a new vision of work, and thus of economic activity, that departed from the ancient pre-Christian ethos. Closely connected with this change was the wholesale Christian desacralization of the world via the doctrine of *creatio ex nihilo*—nature was no longer divine, as it had been for the pagans.

Yet, for all its changes, Classical Christianity also maintained a number of strong philosophical and cosmological continuities with pagan antiquity, especially with respect to the schools of Plato, Aristotle, and the Stoics. In particular, and perhaps most outstanding, the Church reaffirmed a teleological and providential universe, one in which the

10. See David Lindberg, "Science and the Early Church," in *God and Nature: Historical Essays on the Encounter between Christianity and Science*, eds., David Lindberg and Ronald Numbers (Berkeley: University of California Press, 1986), 26. Likewise, St Paul does not condemn philosophy as such in Col. 2:8. St Peter, furthermore, seems to require it in 1 Pet. 3:15, if we are expected to give an explanation or reasons for our Christian hope.

effects of the artistic hand and purposive government of the deity over the cosmos could be seen with the rational eye of the mind. Creation thereby extolled a Supreme Being and exhibited a moral order and thus a natural (moral) law, to which Jew and gentile alike had access.[11] To this day, the Catechism of the Catholic Church cites Cicero for his definition of natural law.[12] Consequently, the Church, like the ancients, has always esteemed virtue and the contemplative life as the true end of man, high above commerce and all other non-liberal arts. Though man had lost divine favor and suffered an impairment of his faculties on account of an original act of disobedience against his Creator, Classical Christianity saw in the grace of Christ the interior amelioration of fallen human nature rather than the mere overlooking of sin as in Protestantism. Whereas the Church brought about change in the midst of continuity with the ancients (hence, an evolution), Neo-Christianity broke decisively with both antiquity and Classical Christianity, causing a cultural rupture with the intellectual and spiritual inheritance of Western Civilization. It viewed man as hopelessly corrupt, rejected the theory of teleology for presuming to know the ends of things established by divine will, and embraced a highly voluntaristic God, inspired by late medieval nominalism. Indeed, Luther considered himself something of an Ockhamist and follower of the *via moderna*.[13]

During the period of the Scientific Revolution, Neo-Christianity inclined to the newly emerging mechanistic worldview and moved away from the reigning Aristotelian or hylomorphic Scholasticism going back

11. See St Paul, Romans 1:20 and 2:14–15.

12. Catechism of the Catholic Church (CCC), #1956.

13. Nominalism put great stress on the omnipotent will of God and the individual character of reality. Luther might be described as an unmitigated nominalist. For an illuminating discussion of Luther's ambivalent relation to Ockham and his school as a source of modernity see Michael Gillespie, *The Theological Origins of Modernity* (Chicago: The University of Chicago Press, 2008). Gillespie, however, fails at first to see that divine grace for Luther is not an interior and ontological assimilation of man to God. To the extent that Lutheran grace gives a powerful experience of God, it is only the experience of excited affectivity. Yet Gillespie's narrative does progress to a realization that Luther's God is so remote, abstract, and incomprehensible that "For us, he is thus not a personal God at all but resembles the Greek concept of fate governing and determining all things." For an exoneration of nominalism for producing the Reformation, see Francis Clark, *Eucharist Sacrifice and the Reformation* (Devon: Augustine Publishing Co., 1967). Clark writes, "The Reformers undoubtedly found more in Ockhamism that was apt for their purpose than in Thomism, but their title to originality is none the less intact; the change from the theology of Gabriel Biel to that of Martin Luther was not an evolution but a revolution."

to the Catholic Middle Ages.[14] God remotely presided over inert matter, whose motion was externally caused and governed by laws of force decreed by the deity. With form and finality banished, only two of Aristotle's four causes remained to rule the universe, the material and efficient. Leaving behind the question of direction and ends, all was considered to be, whether in the heavens or on the earth, so much matter in motion subject to the laws of inertia and gravity. Thus a somewhat incongruous Protestant natural theology (incongruous for reasons to be explained ahead) preferred to see nature as a machine rather than as an organic teleological whole ontologically dependent on God, thus making of God a Supreme Mechanic, whose purposes are known only to Himself, rather than a Supreme Designer, whose purposes are manifest in the natural direction of things. The world-machine of Newton was typical of the age: "Unlike the world conceived by Aristotle, in which inherent mind-like principles imbued matter with purposive development, the Newtonian world possessed no inherent activity and no inherent direction."[15]

In the human sphere the mechanistic revolution and the Protestant revolution combined to treat fallen man, not as the rational animal of both pagan antiquity and Classical Christianity, but rather as a material body fundamentally and predictably driven by appetite. In the human microcosm, man and appetite were subject to the law of inertia as were moving chunks of physical substance in the macrocosm. This plumped large for economic man, who, as a producer and consumer, is principally concerned with appetite and in making reason subordinate and instrumental in its service. As David Hume in Presbyterian Scotland would famously aver in his *Treatise*, "[R]eason is and ought only to be the servant of the passions."[16] Since man, for the Neo-Christian mental-

---

14. See "Reformation Theology and the Mechanistic Conception of Nature," Gary Deason, in Lindberg and Numbers. After identifying the inertness of matter as the fundamental tenet of mechanism, Deason states that "the mechanical philosophers turned to the Protestant doctrine of the radical sovereignty of God in arguing for the passivity of matter" (170). For more on this topic see Margaret Osler, "Mechanical Philosophy," *Science and Religion: A Historical Introduction*, ed. Gary Ferngren (Baltimore: The Johns Hopkins University Press, 2002). And also, Margaret Osler, *Divine Will and the Mechanical Philosophy: Gassendi and Descartes on Contingency and Necessity in the Created World*, (Cambridge: Cambridge University Press, 1994). For the Puritan attraction to "useful knowledge" and experimental philosophy see Joel Mokyr, *A Culture of Growth, The Origins of the Modern Economy* (Princeton: Princeton University Press, 2017), 227–46.

15. Lindberg and Numbers, 185.

16. David Hume, *A Treatise of Human Nature*, ed., L.A. Selby-Bigge (Oxford: Clarendon Press, 1978), 415. In "Of Commerce" Hume proposes that "it is requisite to govern men by other passions, and animate them with a spirit of avarice and industry, art and

ity, is not to preoccupy himself with God mystically, sacramentally, or even rationally (but only emotionally, religion being a matter of feeling for Goethe and Schleiermacher), the human arena is properly restricted to worldly affairs in which the individual might find signs and assurance of his divine election through earthly success.[17] Work for salvation is rejected in favor of disciplined work for earthly ends. Leisure is spurned as mere idleness and the devil's workshop; Catholic ceremony, feast days, and monasticism all dismissed as unproductive. The Reformation, therefore, played a significant historical, psychological, and sociological role in unchaining the Promethean spirit of economic man and securing his social preeminence.[18]

I hasten to add that although some of the major purveyors of the new science of mechanical natural philosophy were Catholic—Galileo, Gassendi, Descartes, for instance—the Catholic mechanists tended to be resolute in their defense of the immaterial soul, the sacraments, and man's ability to know God through both reason and revelation, thus enabling a higher calling, a metaphysical or transcendental vocation, consistent with the idea of the contemplative life as recommended by the ancient philosophers. However, the English Protestant Francis Bacon and the French Catholic Descartes both saw science as having the relief of man's temporal condition as one of its ends, if not the primary goal. Some mechanists tried to overcome a perceived antagonism between teleology and mechanism, e.g., Leibniz. Gassendi, having

luxury." David Hume, *Essays Moral, Political, and Literary*, ed., Eugene Miller (Liberty Fund, Indianapolis: 1987), 263.

17. This thesis was first propounded by Max Weber in his famous opus, *The Protestant Ethic and the Spirit of Capitalism*. For an equally insightful work on the same topic, see Amintore Fanfani, *Catholicism, Protestantism and Capitalism* (New York: Sheed and Ward, 1935), which includes a critique of Weber, particularly in regard to his opinion that the capitalist spirit did not precede Calvinism. Fanfani's thesis can be summed up in his own words: "Protestantism encouraged capitalism inasmuch as it denied the relation between earthly action and eternal recompense" (205). My essay expands on this point of view.

18. See Jan de Vries, *The Industrious Revolution: Consumer Behavior and the Household Economy, 1650 to the Present* (Cambridge: Cambridge University Press, 2008). De Vries explains: "The intellectual origins of this new understanding [of the human personality and consumer demand] must be sought in an unlikely quarter, the theologies of the Calvinists, and, especially, of their Augustinian cousins the Jansenists. Both shared the view that man is driven by passions (such as avarice, pride, envy, and lust) reflecting a deep sinfulness, the legacy of the Fall. Jansenists of the 'Port-Royal' school (such as Blaise Pascal and Pierre Nicole, but also the Huguenot Pierre Bayle) went on to assert that these passions notwithstanding, God's providence made it possible for fruitful social relations to emerge from the patently anti-social passions of self-interest and self-love, or *amour propre*" (58–59).

Christianized Epicurus to his satisfaction, chided Descartes for pursuing physics without final causes for fear of leaving the order of the universe to chance. Robert Boyle, the Protestant chemist, was also worried by Descartes' disregard of teleology. Yet both Gassendi and Boyle ascribed the operation of final causes to God rather than to nature, Boyle going so far as to deny secondary causes altogether.[19] And behind, and contemporary with, the Catholic mechanical philosophers, were other Protestants such as the influential Isaac Beeckman, the Calvinist atomist, who schooled Gassendi and Descartes in Epicureanism, and Thomas Hobbes, the English Protestant, who openly subscribed to materialism. In sum, among the mechanists, the nomological, as opposed to the teleological, description of nature played to the ever-increasing prospects of materialism.

While Catholic mechanists tended to be critical of materialism, the Protestants, apart from Hobbes, were more hesitant.[20] Leibniz feared that Newton's *divine sensorium* had turned God into a world soul. However, the hugely influential John Locke, the gentrified Hobbes, speculated that man might be nothing more than thinking matter. Significantly, one can even detect in the Protestant founders themselves a nascent materialism conducive to an economic worldview through their shunning of the supposed non-biblical Greek inheritance of anthropological dualism, in accordance with their depiction of man as a creature of the flesh, a thoroughly carnal being. Calvin states, "Everything, therefore, which we have from nature is flesh."[21]

This is not to say that there were no Protestants with a penchant for old-style metaphysics and a disdain of materialism. There were. But they were not major thinkers, and their influence proved limited and transient. In this regard, the Cambridge Platonists come to mind. But Protestant thinkers generally eschewed metaphysics as a Catholic, Scholastic, and even pagan endeavor, with the notable exception of Leibniz, who showed something of an appreciation for Scholasticism, secondary causality, and Catholicism.

To the extent that Protestants engaged in natural theology, it was generally on the basis of natural philosophy or physics rather than meta-

---

19. Deason, 180: "The Bible, [Boyle] said, makes no reference to nature as a cause (not even as a secondary or cooperating cause) but sees all of creation as the direct work of God."

20. This, notwithstanding the idealisms of Leibniz, Bishop Berkeley, and Jonathan Edwards, which were culturally less significant for their breathtaking denial of matter, a violent intellectual reaction to the growing threat of materialism.

21. *Institutes of Christian Religion*, chapter iii, translation in *Christian Classics Ethereal Library* online at http://www.ccel.org/ccel/calvin/institutes.

physics, which has to do with the ultimate nature of being and existence. In other words, the question and cause of motion, not the *ratio entis*, guided their theology. After all, they had no time for the *analogia entis*, the analogy of being, God and man being entirely incommensurate. It was the mechanics of matter in motion that principally occupied the scientific investigations of Protestants. Moreover, the Neo-Christian demand for a strict separation of Creator and creature meant that material nature was passive dead weight and God not just the primary cause but the only cause of its operation. This kind of thinking managed to influence the Catholic occasionalists, such as Malebranche, whose thought had a direct impact on Hume and his skepticism concerning natural causality. With increasing emphasis on inertia, God could be disregarded, so much so that Laplace would finally declare that he had no need of the God hypothesis in his physics. In contrast with the cosmological determinism of Laplace, the universe could also be seen in early modern times in the way that Epicurus and Lucretius saw it in ancient times, as an everlasting combination of atoms and the void, of necessity and chance.

In any event, the more Neo-Christian thinkers favored some sort of religious hybridization, oddly mixing into the original Protestant teaching elements from the Catholic intellectual tradition in natural theology, the more they deviated from the letter and spirit of the magisterial founders of Protestantism.[22] Many Protestants, however, felt compelled to do this because Luther's attack on natural reason and Calvin's attack on free will with its implication of human automata left them without an adequate intellectual defense of their faith and a framework of education. For the overwhelming psychological emphasis in the spirituality of the Protestant founders was on the affective rather than the cognitive.

---

22. Packer and Johnston write (46): "It was in her capacity as the prompter of and agent of 'natural' theology that Mistress Reason was in Luther's eyes the Devil's whore; for natural theology is, he held, blasphemous in principle, and bankrupt in practice." Calvin's vague openness at first to natural theology is deceptive. In the end, voiding St Paul's endorsement (Rom. 1:20), Calvin rendered natural theology impossible: "[W]e have not the eyes to see this [evidence of God in creation] unless they be illumined by the inner revelation of God through faith," *Institutes*, chapter v, in Dillenberger, 348. Concerning Romans, Calvin confuses the speculative and moral orders. Paul is saying that it is possible by the use of natural reason alone based on evidence to arrive, through the book of creation, at a belief in the one spiritual deity or maker of heaven and earth; a monotheism. Furthermore, gentiles *did know of* the one God, at least some; Calvin admits to Plato. But generally, according to Paul, moral failure caused by irrational passions, the consequence of the Fall, led to theological error, impiety, and worship of the creature rather than the Creator.

Hence, Melanchthon, Luther's ally, had to revive Scholasticism among his co-religionists in spite of Luther's fulminations against it and Arminius, the Reformed Dutchman, sought to amend the problematic determinism of Calvinist religion by restoring some notion of psychic freedom.[23] However, this only served to increase the doctrinal anarchy set in motion by Luther, Calvin, and Zwingli—who, of course, opposed each other on various theological topics—and to further loosen Christianity's hold on culture.[24] The spiritual continued to give way to the material until the vision of man as a soulless machine fueled by economic interest and functioning in a Newtonian social world of competition triumphed in the eighteenth century.[25] Theories of ethical affectivity and psychological associationism from Hume to J.S. Mill purported to provide a mechanics of the mind, paving the way from the cognitive staples of idea and object to behaviorism's stimulus and response.[26] And James Madison called down the mechanical philosophy from the heavens and brought it into the political world of his countrymen when he wrote a constitution that set forth the procedural mechanics of a federal government—without reference to a higher power or Creator—in order to establish an equilibrium among multiple social forces, sects, interests, and factions in an extended commercial republic.[27]

But to comprehend more fully the ascent of economic man, let us go back and delve deeper into that evolution of Christianity out of pre-

---

23. "Calvin was perfectly aware that the determinism of divine predestination was 'dreadful indeed' to humanity." Diarmaid MacCulloch, *The Reformation, A History* (New York: Penguin Group, 2003), 237.

24. MacCulloch observes (654–55) that, in accord with indifferentism, the Arminians tied the promotion of religious toleration with anarchy in biblical interpretation as a way of "clarifying the real truths of Christianity." (The preposterous nature of the Arminian project seems quite lost on the author.) Furthermore, "the flourishing economy and growing power of the Netherlands . . . was one good reason for taking seriously the idea of toleration."

25. Consider La Mettrie's *Man a Machine*. E. F. Schumacher quotes Darwin from his autobiography: "My mind seems to have become a kind of machine for grinding general laws out of large collections of fact." *Small is Beautiful: Economics as if People Mattered* (New York: Harper Perennial, 1973), 103. Karl Popper noted that La Mettrie has been updated: man is a computer.

26. Theories of moral sentiments, emotivism, and hedonism replaced the rational and teleological foundations of the natural law in a complete revision or elimination of the subject.

27. The age-old political problem was that of how to eliminate factions. Remarkably, Madison's solution was to multiply them (*Federalist 51*), an idea anticipated by Voltaire (*Philosophical Letters*) and Montesquieu (*Persian Letters*).

Christian times, to which I alluded above; for Neo-Christianity cannot be understood except in terms of Classical or Catholic Christianity, nor the latter without regard to pagan antiquity. As the art of providing for the material well-being of the individual and the community through exchange, economics, like the poor, has always been with us. However, in antiquity, unlike in modernity, in both the East and the West, economics and economical practices were understood to be subordinate to the common good, as cared for by the state. While commercial exchange waxed and waned in ancient times, no doubt contributing to the rise and fall of civilizations, there were powerful meta-economic restrictions in the form of social norms and religious adherence that kept commerce and industry from becoming the ruling concern and aim of ancient peoples. Accordingly, over the millennia of antiquity, economic development, output, and technological progress seem flat compared to that of the astonishing technical innovation and exponential economic growth that have characterized the brief period in the West from the Industrial Revolution at the beginning of the nineteenth century to the present day. Let us consider some of the reasons why antiquity remained relatively underdeveloped economically speaking. I should quickly add, however, that despite their economic stagnation, the ancients bequeathed to our race innumerable cultural glories that remain unsurpassed, especially in comparison with the aesthetic and literary banalities of our contemporaries, for all their material abundance.

There are three fundamental biases in ancient culture that help account for the flat economic growth of antiquity: political, aristocratic, and productive. The political bias refers to the fact that political, not economic, life was esteemed above all human occupations. Civic virtue, moral rectitude, and military valor were the themes celebrated by the ancient poets. Aristotle said that politics is the architectonic art and, famously, that man is a political animal. No doubt man's origins in small communities ingrained in the species a concern for solidarity and social order. And of course, the Greek polis was the archetypal fraternal political order. Moreover, participation in politics required a preference for, and means of, leisure as opposed to economic activity. This ties in with the aristocratic bias of antiquity. The dominant aristocratic culture of the ancients utterly disdained work and commercial enterprise. The system of status and the ethos of honor obliged the well born and high-minded to engage in political leadership, military endeavors, religion, patronage, and intellectual pursuits of a theoretical nature. To soil one's hands with commerce was shameful. As regards the intellectual life, one historian notes that "Euclid and Archimedes regarded the application of theory to practical or, worse, profitable ends with withering contempt."[28] Recall that the ugliest of the pagan gods and lame to boot, namely Hephaestus, the divine blacksmith, was the only worker deity. And as if to heap derision upon his technical vocation, the Greeks spun tales of Hephaestus' wife, Aphrodite, the beautiful goddess of love and pleasure, occasionally making a cuckold of him. Furthermore, the mythic fate of Prometheus and Daedalus testified to the pernicious nature of technical novelty.

Artisanal production and commercial dealings were to be left to the lower classes, foreign merchants, metics, and untold numbers of slaves.[29] The aristocracy, i.e., the leading citizens consisting of large landholders, constituted a leisured rentier not a producer class, and so was generally unconcerned with capital formation and investment, industrial mobilization, and technical innovation. Custom was king and novelty highly suspect. Classical times were considered a descent from a Golden Age and not about material progress toward a better future. The rest of the citizenry, for their part, were mostly farmers of small and medium property as well as artisans, the former being concerned with prudent household management from whence the very word economics is derived (*oikos*, house, and *nomos*, law). Production for markets was incidental rather than the central factor of material life. Self-sufficiency (*autarkeia*), rather than trade, was the ideal. Tranquility (*ataraxia*) and civic cooperation were preferred to competition. The use value of things was held above exchange value.[30] And private property as well as travel and transportation were extremely insecure; better to hold on to what you have than risk what you have in order to get more.

---

28. Peter Green, *The Hellenistic Age, A Short History* (New York: Modern Library, 2007), 54.

29. Slave societies did not innovate and create labor-saving machinery because slave labor was cheap, but rather because "production and physical work were associated with low-prestige culture and inferior social standing." Mokyr, 120. In this regard, the ancient Sybarites were proverbial.

30. Simply put, use values have to do with the worth of natural necessities, i.e., things that are needed for the cultivation of our humanity or the good life, objectively understood. Exchange values have to do with the worth of things insofar as they are wanted, i.e., insofar as they are valued on the basis of personal desire or preference. Use value is objective, though associated prices will be affected by scarcity, while exchange value is subjective and equivalent to the price elasticity of demand. Non-market societies are those where need and use values in exchange (and in wealth acquisition) predominate, market societies where exchange values based on want are primary. In this respect, ancient societies were of the non-market type. Non-market societies are natural for limiting exchange and acquisition primarily according to the needs of virtue and what is sufficient for the good life, secondarily according to scarcity. Market societies are unnatural, artificial, or formalistic for being driven purely by demand and for rejecting

The state often financed its projects through taxation, liturgies (aristo-cratic benefaction), and tribute. Capital markets, labor markets, and an independent banking system were in short supply or non-existent. Credit was not publicly and corporately organized. It was mostly per-sonal rather than institutional and contractual, unlike today. That pre-cursor of feudal obligation, the Roman system of patronage (*clientela*), well illustrates the point. In general, economies of scale were found only in public works, such as building construction, mines, arms produc-tion, e.g., naval arsenals, and grain supply, although there was pottery manufacturing. Finally, there are the widespread ancient sumptuary laws and the striking examples of pre-modern suppression of economic activity, such as at Sparta, which virtually outlawed economic life, and during certain Chinese and Japanese dynasties, which closed the door to commerce. The pre-Christian world was a place where economic man, if he existed, lived in the shadows. Then came Christianity.

The period of the consolidation of the Christian religion and empire, heir to the Roman Empire, is both an extension of antiquity and a tran-sition to modernity; hence, the commonplace historical designation of the Middle Ages. In the womb of the Christian age is the embryo of modern economic man or, to switch metaphors, economic man begins to emerge from the shadows into the early light of day during the Cath-olic era. Why should that be? Answer: cultural evolution, the Catholic religious evolution of late antiquity. Here are some main characteristics of the cultural development and social transformation inaugurated by the triumph of the Church of Christ over the pagans.

First, Catholic Christianity undermined the ancient aristocratic bias by elevating the status of work, or at least removing from it any oppro-brium, even if the greatest labor was to work in the fields of the Lord spreading the Gospel. After all, the apostles of Christ came from a hum-ble background, which means they had to work to support themselves and their families. And Paul, though having enjoyed something of a Hebrew and Hellenistic education, worked as a tentmaker and pro-

---

any objective limit on demand apart from unacceptable prices or insurmountable scar-city. See Meikle and Franks for elaboration. Thus, we may distinguish between three kinds of economy: subsistence, need, and want economy. Need is not to be confused with subsistence; the former is perfectly in accord with flourishing, or prosperity both material and spiritual, but within the limits set by nature. Strangely, Siedentop considers (363) the economic "satisfaction of current wants or preferences without worrying much about the formation of those wants or preferences" a departure from liberalism, whereas it seems to me that that belongs to liberalism's very nature. Liberalism has no "lasting moral value" precisely because it rejects all claims to a permanent and objective moral foundation.

claimed to the Christian community, in *The Second Letter to the Thessalonians*, that those who didn't work had no right to eat. Although the Judeo-Christian story of the fall of man from paradise in the Genesis account consigned man to a life of toil as a consequence of his sin, work was considered a good because it was part of man's vocation to subdue the earth, formerly a deity, in the service of man and the true God who created all. As time went by, large numbers of Christian men and women lived under the Benedictine rule and motto of prayer and work, *orare et laborare*. Such a saying, as indicative of a noble or higher calling, was unthinkable in pagan antiquity. And by the late Medieval period, there were many monasteries that were not only holy places of worship but also commercially successful enterprises, such as those in England that were engaged in the lucrative wool trade. To be sure, the monasteries employed lay workers. But that only reinforces the suggestion of a vertically integrated corporation with the abbot as chief executive officer, which was a good thing, maintaining the physical plant and contributing to works of charity, unless it occasioned laxity on the part of the monks. Not surprisingly various medieval reform movements proliferated on behalf of a return to spiritual rigor and evangelical poverty, such as the Carthusians, but especially the new orders of friars (e.g., Franciscans and Dominicans), what with their emphasis on mendicancy.

Second, as mentioned above, the Judeo-Christian doctrine of the creation desacralized material nature. Cosmic nature was no longer divine and eternal. It was not even *being* in the strict and proper sense of the term. As created or participated being, nature was nothing in comparison with Uncreated Being itself, which enjoyed being essentially, the *ipsum esse subsistens*—the absolute, self-subsisting, and supernatural Being, namely, God. Thus was born the concept of the supernatural, an idea wholly foreign to the pagan mind. By contrast, Plato's highest principle, the Idea of the Good, and Aristotle's Prime Mover were not endowed with will, and though separated from matter, they were part of one fixed and eternal cosmic system. Plato in the *Timaeus* called the physical universe a living god. In keeping with the idea of supernatural divinity, then, the whole physical order became so much ordinary raw material available for human appropriation and use. No longer were there sacred and inviolable woods or cattle and the like. All was available for production and consumption, all ready for commodification and sale. This evidently gave a boost to the concept of property. That said, Classical Christianity also retained the image of nature as *speculum Dei*, a mirror in which God's thoughts were reflected through a system of natural symbols or emblems. In that sense nature was neither sacred nor profane, but iconic.

The question of private rights of property came to the fore during the late medieval period in the ecclesial crisis surrounding the arrival of the Franciscan Spirituals. The Spirituals preached radical poverty and condemned property, believing that Christ had done so. The popes, however, tended to uphold the right to property and rejected the radical claims of the Spirituals. Nonetheless, Classical Christianity viewed nature as first and foremost God's property and man the steward of the deity's created estate. Moreover, God gave creation to man in common, but permitted man to divide it up for the sake of the common good, if that were more favorable to peace and prosperity. In the age of the Reformation, however, God became remote for no longer being sacramentally available. Thus the Lord became an absentee landlord, allowing the steward to assume the role of a proprietor and to become a man of private dominion. No longer was property tied to obligation, virtue, charity, or distributive justice according to the needs of the commonwealth, as it had been in the Middle Ages, at least in theory. Rather, the security of private property, self-proprietorship, rights to the fruits of one's labor, and performance of contracts became increasingly matters of central concern after the Reformation for Protestant political philosophy and jurisprudence.[31] The commons, common tillage and pasturage, succumbed to enclosure. And as private property became more secure, selling to markets and risk taking for economic ends and accumulation were emboldened. Accordingly, the economic or commercial classes in virtue of their weighty capital were able to accumulate not just property but also power, thus ascending to the position of political brokers. But we have gotten ahead of ourselves.

The third important Christian development had to do with the new prominence given to the faculty of the will. Emerging Christianity thrust the will to center stage in both the theological and psychological realms. The supernatural God was free to do as He pleased, to create or not to create, to contemplate the actual world and all possible worlds, to issue laws, suspend or change them as He wished. This theological voluntarism was diametrically opposed to ancient necessitarianism, which had replaced the poetic caprice of the gods with a philosophical religion of fatalism, although the poets anticipated this move through the idea of the preordained and implacable destiny of all things, namely, *Moira*. The fixed order of the universe of pagan, especially Stoic, antiquity, allowed no room for a free creator and personal God of intellect and will. The Stoic god was rather a material world soul, a thinking fire, by

---

31. See Stephen Buckle, *Natural Law and the Theory of Property, Grotius to Hume* (Oxford: Clarendon Press, 1991).

nature limited and responsible for the rational and benevolent order of the cosmos, a providence of sorts. This god was neither capable of existing apart from its cosmic body nor dispensing with the plan of the universe. On the other hand, the less popular Epicureans—considerably less because not civic-minded—endorsed Democritean randomness. But the random motion of atoms occurred in a stable, eternal, and infinite void. Even their happily indifferent gods were made of atoms, deities who had no thought to, or providential care of, the multiple worlds continuously and fortuitously confected by swerving and colliding particles that were both material and indivisible. Furthermore, Plato's Demiurge could not reach the voluntary heights of the Christian God, for the Demiurge was a fabricator not a creator. He had to fabricate the world within the bounds of the forms and the preexisting material receptacle, like a potter and his clay. Moreover, Aristotle's God was not only *not* a creator, He was forever only thinking of Himself and nothing more. Finally, in Plotinus's system, the Intellect and World Soul flow forth from the first principle, the One, with an emanationist necessity; the One, blinkered by perfection, does not choose to generate all things, nor does it think the possibility of other worlds.

The Christian God is eminently a being of free will and He endows man with a similar power. Will power, therefore, began to assume a major independent role in man's psychological makeup, whereas the pagans had appeared to confuse will and practical reason. After all, God is love according to St John the Evangelist, and love or charity is located by the Scholastics in the will. From St Augustine to Henry of Ghent, not to mention the Franciscan nominalists of the late Middle Ages, voluntarism was in the ascendancy. Aquinas's intellectualism was discarded by many theologians. Henry went so far as to speak of reason as the servant of the will, holding up a lamp so as to allow the master to see, while it is the will that chooses the direction of the mind and body it inhabits. Unlike the will of God, however, man's will was impaired by an original disobedience toward the Creator in the face of a divine command not to eat of the tree of the knowledge of good and evil. Contrary to the intellectualist doctrine of Socrates, St Paul taught that to know the good was not necessarily to do the good. The problem of man was not so much a problem of ignorance as of malice in the will. Will needed to be repaired by divine grace. Will is a faculty of desire, affection, or appetite. Man is, therefore, fundamentally a creature of desire. If the will is not directed to God, through God's gracious assistance, it will be turned toward matter, and concupiscence will reduce speculative reason to instrumental reason, that is, to rational self-interest in the satisfaction of mundane wants.

Nevertheless, for Classical Christianity, according to the normative Thomistic perspective, the will is a rational appetite and takes its cue concerning the true and the good from reason and the objective nature of things, whereas Neo-Christians, such as Melanchthon and Camerarius, make the will non-rational, affective, and autonomous.[32] Instead of will following reason, the rational faculty follows the will, an independent appetitive power that is indifferent to the aims of reason and nature. Late medieval nominalism built the bridge to Protestant modernity through its teaching regarding not only the omnipotent and sovereign will of God but also the radical indifference of the human will.[33] This anti-teleological and anti-eudaimonistic doctrine replaced the participatory character of the human relationship with God with a forensic and contractual relationship, so as to keep human agency (and nature) and divine agency (and grace) safely and clearly distinct. Protestantism rejected an independent human agency as Pelagian, but accepted voluntaristic indifferentism, that being congenially anti-Aristotelian, and in keeping with its notion of total divine sovereignty and the outward nature of the human-divine relationship, retained the theology of contract. In Geneva, the capital of Calvinism, everyone had to sign a contract of belief and practice. As society was deemed consensual and

---

32. Risto Saarinen, *Weakness of Will in Renaissance and Reformation Thought* (Oxford: Oxford University Press, 2011), 216: "Both Melanchthon and Camerarius detach the power of the will from the cognitive-rational faculty and associate it strongly with passions or affections. In denying the freedom of the will, Melanchthon also strips the will of its rationality."

33. William of Ockham taught that God could command us to commit murder, adultery, or even hate him because none of these acts are intrinsically immoral. Human acts have no moral qualities, only God's will and human intention make for good or evil. Ockham posits both a divine and human liberty of indifference, meaning that neither God nor man is ordered to the good. Human will, inasmuch as it is not ordered to the good or happiness, can commit evil for evil's sake. In sum the will, whether divine or human, is an autonomous and morally neutral power. Ockham seems, in voluntarist fashion, hell bent on securing a maximum of freedom for both God and man. Combine this with Ockham's belief that natural agents act from necessity not finality and the cosmic foundation of a teleological, eudaimonistic, and rational ethics of virtue is destroyed. There is nothing really beyond efficient causality. So if God commands us to obey right reason, on what criteria is right reason based? Two further relevant points: Ockham envisioned a secular state without reference to religion and the medieval Hume, Nicholas of Autrecourt, is unthinkable without various aspects of Ockham's skeptical-friendly philosophy. Finally, even though not an atomist himself, Ockham's natural philosophy inspired mechanistic accounts of change and Hobbes's atomism. On this last point see "Ockham's Philosophy of Nature" by Andre Goddu in *The Cambridge Companion to Ockham*, ed., Paul Vincent Spade (Cambridge: Cambridge University Press, 1999), 149.

artificial, rather than natural (man being anti-social thanks to the Fall), the pact with God made it possible to identify the faithful according to Protestant teaching in order to create a political society of the reformed. And though the true church of the elect is invisible, the socio-religious contract could function as a sign of election.

Given the central role of fallen will, what keeps man, according to Classical Christianity, on the right path upward, and heaven and earth in mutual communion? Grace in the first place, certainly. But also a human nature that is intrinsically ordered to the love and knowledge of God, an order that is not effaced by sin. Even fallen human nature can know without revelation the existence of God and is capable of responding to the invitation of grace so that man, despite the wound to his nature, may freely cooperate in his own natural fulfillment and eternal salvation.[34] This orthodox Christian and Catholic anthropology speaks to a teleological ethics of virtue in keeping with ancient moral philosophy, except for the additional necessity of the theological virtues of faith, hope, and charity. In other words, notwithstanding the Fall, human beings still share a common nature whose end is happiness, imperfect in this life and perfect in the next, i.e., beatitude or the vision of God. Man without grace is capable of some good, but perfect and salvific good requires faith and divine grace. If cooperation with grace obtains, the desire for material things is tamed or limited and the soul directed to and governed by a transmundane contemplation, a contemplation whose highest aspirations were similar to those of Plato, Aristotle, and Plotinus—although now, in a Christian context, one which recognizes the need for divine assistance, unlike the self-reliant and Pelagian pagan philosophers. Man's supernatural perfection begins on earth through the divine gifts of faith, hope, and charity, which in turn lead one to the physical channels of grace, the sacraments of the Church, which function to provide spiritual alimentation for the soul on its journey *in Deum*. For Classical Christianity, grace is, to reiterate, a participation in the divine life. Hence, through grace heaven and earth, super nature and nature, are thus reconciled and intimately united. But the fruit of grace, which is personal holiness, required constant care and effort on the part of the Catholic Christian, using prayer and the sacramental means provided by the Church. Temporal matters, however important they may be, came second to the work of personal sanctification.

Moreover, in keeping with antiquity once again, the Church insisted that man was a corporate being, a political animal, for whom there was

---

34. This is neither Pelagian nor semi-Pelagian because grace both initiates the process of salvation and consummates it.

a *summum bonum.* This objective and supreme good is grounded in a teleological universe, which spoke to the possibility of a qualified happiness here—happiness understood objectively as the virtuous life—and a perfect or completed happiness in the next life, if one died in state of grace.[35] The supreme good and end of man qua man is the basis of the common good. As such, the Church's social teaching aimed at preserving an organic and cooperative human society rather than fostering a mechanical one of competing interests, each out for its own advantage. This, along with the Church's traditional praise of voluntary poverty in imitation of Christ, and the apostolic and ultimate communal destination of goods, imposed fundamental restraints on the over commercialization of society, even though the late medieval Christian world was becoming increasingly urbanized and increasingly suffused with capitalist practices.[36] These practices were barely held in check by feudalism and guild corporatism, and, though heavily regulated, were nonetheless stimulated by, among other things, the Church's recognition of the natural right of private property, vocational choice, and the gradual liberalization of rules governing credit, interest, and the deployment of capital.[37] Certainly the move beyond the slave economy of antiquity to a more egalitarian system of free peasantry, along with a healthy tension between capital, labor, and customary protectionism within the late

35. In contrast, Keith Thomas, speaking of new attitudes on the part of early modern Englishmen, writes that "[M]ost people . . . chose in practice to devote their main energies to the business of making this life as fulfilling as possible. Most commonly, their goal was subjective happiness, something quite different from the objective happiness of the Greek *eudaimonia*. . . . Thomas Hobbes observed that what pleased one man displeased another and that total satisfaction was unobtainable, life being a matter of desire succeeding desire, ceasing only in death. . . . Locke also denied that there was any one prescription for human flourishing, any single end which everyone should pursue." Keith Thomas, *The Ends of Life, Roads to Fulfillment in Early Modern England* (Oxford: Oxford University Press, 2009), 266.

36. See James Murray, *Bruges, Cradle of Capitalism,* 1280–1390 (Cambridge: Cambridge University Press, 2005).

37. The usury prohibition was relaxed, mitigated through the assumption of risk, or hidden as in bills of exchange. The organization of credit starting in Italy by family banks was paralleled by the Church's establishment of the "monti di pieta," non-profit banks that could make loans at five percent per annum. Even something like fractional reserve banking began to appear through overdrafts. See Edwin Hunt and James Murray, *A History of Business in Medieval Europe,* 1200–1550 (Cambridge: Cambridge University Press, 1999) and Robert Lopez, *The Commercial Revolution of the Middle Ages,* 950–1350 (Cambridge: Cambridge University Press, 1976). For exceptions to the ban on usury, e.g., foregone profits (*lucrum cessans*), as settled practice in late medieval Europe, see Gregory Clark, *A Farewell to Alms, A Brief Economic History of the World* (Princeton, Princeton University Press, 2007).

medieval religio-cultural unity did much to improve man's earthly lot, while not reducing him to an isolated and alienated player in an all-pervasive market game. A major sociological change comes in, however, with the shift from need to want, from use value to exchange value, in ever-greater production for markets, and in a focus on accumulation and consumption.[38]

Suppose, now, one were to argue, based a new interpretation of Christian scripture, that man can do nothing to secure his salvation, that human nature is totally corrupt and no longer directed to anything but the fulfillment of individual appetite. What then? As suggested, here begins the story of the sixteenth-century religious revolution of Protestantism and the liberation and triumph of *homo economicus*. Pressed by the magisterial Protestant reformers, it is the core and novel doctrines of the total depravity of human nature in conjunction with the total sovereignty of God that made possible the maturation of economic man. Nature was left utterly profane, even malevolent, like the forest in *The Scarlet Letter* (from the viewpoint of the Puritans) or Melville's whale. Nature was to be subjugated, her secrets torn from her, her veins opened up for resource exploitation. The analogy of being, linking human being and divine being, was destroyed. Luther and Calvin, through a hyperbolic belief in the sovereign will of God, could not tolerate any meritorious agency on the part of man lest it derogate from the divine sovereignty. For Calvin, man can do nothing on his own and is saved because God from all eternity arbitrarily predestined some for heaven while damning others, without foreknowledge of any merit in cooperating with grace—contrary to St Augustine, an occasional hero of the reformers through highly selective reading. What God has decreed will inexorably be. Grace is really nothing more than election. It is not the

---

38. Certain Scholastics, St Thomas Aquinas among them, have been identified by libertarian economists as anticipating modern ideas of subjective value and demand-supply market pricing through the notion of "common estimation." Nothing could be further from the truth. For the Scholastics in general, values and prices based on common estimation presupposed objective use values that were grounded in a culture that had a true understanding of human nature and its perfection, i.e., Christian culture. The cultural context was necessary to inform right valuations and justice in exchange. Only within that context could the common estimation be consistent with the just estimation, with just prices and wages, which the Scholastics never failed to recognize as of preeminent consideration in the socio-economic realm. If all this seems archaic, particularly the idea of a just price, a price not the mere outcome of market forces, then consider the American presidential election of 2016. Candidates debated the minimum wage, free college tuition, loan forgiveness, and both presidential finalists condemned over pricing by drug and other kinds of companies. The form these socio-economic issues assumed was sometimes entirely medieval in spirit.

internal transformation and repair of the soul as it was and is in Classical Christianity. For Luther and Neo-Christianity, grace is merely a pall covering the festering and irremediable wound of sin. It didn't heal or remove it: *simul justus et peccator*. Without the requisite equivocation, this is an astonishing piece of anti-intellectualism for its denial of the principle of non-contradiction. But the rhetorical strategy of the reformers had little time for such principles.

The Protestant notion of righteousness or justification is, therefore, external, imputed as it were to the perennially corrupt believer. Contrariwise, Catholic theology upholds a transformation or spiritual renewal of the inner man through the grace of Christ, so that the image of God in man is restored and the justified person (on account of faith and the sacraments, beginning with baptism) no longer a slave to sin.[39] Moreover, though God's gratuitous pardon, or divine inattention to sin, was attendant for the Neo-Christian on an act of faith in Christ, not even this act could be attributed to the believer, so utterly unworthy and impotent was he to participate in, or contribute to, his own salvation.

With work for salvation out of the picture, the effect of Protestant anthropology, despite itself, could not help but turn man to the world and worldly endeavor, and so contribute to the gradual secularization of the European home base of Christianity. The logic of total depravity, furthermore, leads to the subordination of religion to the secular order. There is no need of an independent ecclesial organization as the visible means of reaching eternal life. Election is individual, hidden, gratuitous, and predetermined. All that is required for society is the enforcement of contracts and the suppression of attempts to harm others in their person or property, a point strongly emphasized by Locke. Instead of preserving an independent institutional status, Protestant religion drove itself into the political misadventures of quietism or institutional confusion (of clergy and magistracy) or separatism. Roland Bainton writes, "Lutheranism developed in the direction of Caesaropapism, Calvinism developed theocracies, while the smaller sects avoided both by separation."[40] Anglicanism was created by an Erastian act of parliament in 1534, which eventually led to the proliferation of sects, civil war, and regicide.

---

39. See Rom. 6:6; Gal. 3:27; Eph. 3:16, 17, and 4:23, 24; Col. 3:10.

40. Roland Bainton, *The Reformation of the Sixteenth Century* (Boston: The Beacon Press, 1952), 54. Brad Gregory writes of the revolutionary church-state thinking in the Calvinist stronghold of the Netherlands: "Dutch magistrates oversaw and regulated religion no less than did Charles II in England or Louis XIV in France. But they did so differently. They broke with more than a millennium of Christianity . . . by making the

The pilgrim's personal and eternal fate had nothing to do with the workings of the public order except to submit to it, according to a certain Protestant reading of Romans 13. By contrast, in the theory of the hierarchical polity of medieval Christendom, the Church was both independent of the state and the morally superior institution, as the soul to the body. From John of Salisbury's *Policraticus* to Pope Boniface's *Unam Sanctum*, princes were the servants of priests.[41] Late medieval men such as Dante and John of Paris dissented from this position, giving equal rank to emperor and king. The road to Erastianism, from Marsilius of Padua to Jean Bodin and Thomas Hobbes, was completed by the Neo-Christian dismantling of Christendom. Secular modern politics that followed from the subordination and then privatization of religion became indistinguishable from the modern economic regime, now the global model of social life, for the *Machtpolitik* it affords nation-states.

Let us consider further the intellectual and social consequences of magisterial Protestant doctrine. Insofar as it denies free will, rejects natural and human finality (because the ends decreed by God are utterly wrapped up within the *deus absconditus*), suppresses or minimalizes the natural law in favor of revealed divine command, makes conscience subjective, and negates the value and capacity of speculative reason to know divine things, it puts man according to his completely fallen human nature squarely on the practical and inertial trajectory of ever-expanding consumption and aggrandizement of the individual. Protestant thinkers like Grotius, whose reasoning was placed in the service Dutch commercial interests, emphasized individual subjective rights and gave individualistic human nature a mere inclination to social life. From Grotius to Kant, man, according to the trend in Protestant anthropology, became sociable not political, but sociable only with a view to security and trade, to truck and barter in peace. Kant marveled at man's "unsocial sociability." Finally, Kant replaced natural law and virtue ethics altogether with an ethics of duty

---

faith a private matter of individual preference." Brad Gregory, *The Unintended Reformation, How a Religious Revolution Secularized Society* (Cambridge: Harvard University Press, 2012), 164. Gallicanism, it is to be noted, was a complex and ambiguous church-state arrangement. "The French church, which called itself 'Gallican,' meant different things to different parties.... To church leaders, Gallicanism meant an autonomous organism that bowed to neither pope nor king, and leaned at times to a conciliar view of church governance." William Beik, *A Social and Cultural History of Early Modern France* (Cambridge: Cambridge University Press, 2009), 176.

41. These positions found a basis in scripture, e.g., Matt. 28:18 and John 19:11.

grounded in the formalistic rationale of the categorical imperative, a move that could only result in the supremacy of human or positive law. But as Dostoevsky and Nietzsche thought to ask, why should anyone be moral, why should morality be imperative, if there were no Supreme Being and effective higher law? Just out of fear of human law and punishment or respect for ungrounded human rights? This cannot but bring a smile to the face of the *Übermensch*. The problem of finding a rational and objective ground for ethics after the death of God, without sliding into the morass of relativism, is the insoluble dilemma of modernity. Inextricably bound up with this problem is the specifically economic question: who or what creates value? Standing against the fiat of super nature and nature is the fiat value of demand creation and triumph of the will.

Thomas Hobbes, furthermore, enshrined Calvin's bleak picture of human nature in his theory of the original state of nature, in which man leads a solitary and self-seeking existence fraught with violence and insecurity, only to escape from this brutish and nasty sphere through the auspices of the social contract.[42] From a venerable aristocratic perspective based on honor, a gentleman's word secured an agreement. Now along with the covenantal theology of Calvinism everything was to be secured by written consent or contract. All this proclaimed the artificiality of social life as a collection, not a body, of individuals whose individualistic purposes were ultimately personal advantage and accumulation within the tenuous confines of a social truce.

The newly assertive bourgeois man of Protestant respectability became the praiseworthy model of shrewdly dealing with one's selfishly motivated and spiritually alienated fellows in a mechanical world ruled by chance and risk, the realm of economic man. But even the great man with a pedigree, beginning in the eighteenth century, began to hanker after more and more land. Thus, in Protestant countries land enclosure helped to create, along with new scales in manufacturing that displaced the artisan, what became the landless proletariat of the Industrial Revolution.[43] Then when the successful middle classes finally sought unlimited material prospects and stopped leaving enterprise behind for land

---

42. "For both Hobbes and the Calvinists, the antidote to wickedness and disorder was arbitrary power." Michael Walzer, *The Revolution of the Saints, A Study in the Origins of Radical Politics* (New York: Athenaeum, 1974), 159.

43. "The privatization of common land ... served not the cause of peasant protection but instead favored the formation of large-scale agrarian capitalism." Jürgen Kocka, *Capitalism, A Short History*, tr., Jeremiah Riemer (Princeton: Princeton University Press, 2016), 76.

and title, the general transformation of social life into economic life was complete.[44] The accent on the free contract, moreover, allowed economic activity to become increasingly impersonal, apolitical, amoral, and indifferent to custom and culture.

The Neo-Christian idea of man's fundamentally depraved and self-serving nature (*incurvatus in se*)[45] culminated in the liberal socio-economic theories of such men as Thomas Mun, William Petty, John Houghton, Nicholas Barbon, and Bernard Mandeville, for whom the seven deadly sins became economic virtues.[46] But most significantly, the tenets of Protestant anthropology can be seen underlying the monumental work of Adam Smith, *The Wealth of Nations*. Smith envisioned a commercial society based on his "system of natural liberty" in which economic self-interest freely pursued would enrich the individual and unwittingly serve the common good, now reduced to material prosperity.[47] But the Romulus of market economics would have its Remus in the form of socialism, and the two would be at each other's throats for political hegemony with the advance of the modern era. If Marx is the father of socialism, Rousseau is its grandfather, what with his denial of the right of private property, the essence of socialism, which denies the dignity of man as an individual. This flew in the face of Lockean England.[48] In order to gain the upper hand on capitalism in view of its

---

44. This social phenomenon began in earnest during the industrialization of Europe in the nineteenth century. In a former age, successful businessmen sought to buy nobility. "[T]he de la Poles of Hull cheerfully deserted their great enterprise for the earldom of Suffolk" (Hunt and Murray, 53). For the business class of the Middle Ages, "capital accumulation and entrepreneurial growth were a long way from being the dominant goals they later became. Instead, profit and business success remained a means to the end of the good life," that is, a life of leisure in a country manor (Kocka, 47). This would appear to lend credence to Weber's opinion that the "spirit of capitalism" was not pervasive before the Reformation, if we understand by that spirit the belief in the business of indefinite wealth creation as a vocation and end in itself, perhaps the supreme end.

45. A phrase Luther emphasized in his *Lectures on Romans*.

46. For an illuminating discussion of the proto-Smithian economic views of Mun, Petty, Houghton, and Barbon, among others, see Joyce Appleby, *Economic Thought and Ideology in Seventeenth-Century England* (Los Angeles: Figueroa Press, 2004). In *The Fable of the Bees*, Mandeville made raw selfishness and prodigal expenditure the basis of national prosperity. De Vries notes (63): "After generations of Protestant efforts to sacralize everyday life, Mandeville's poem asserted that profane commercial life is, in effect, all there is."

47. Adam Smith, *An Inquiry into the Nature and Causes of the Wealth of Nations*, ed., Edwin Cannan (Chicago: The University of Chicago Press, Two Volumes, 1976), II, 208.

48. One of Rousseau's themes, contra Locke, was that freedom could not be preserved and enjoyed without equality. Freedom by itself leads to inequality, and that to oppression. Rousseau tried to solve the problem of freedom, the Enlightenment's great

efficiencies based on market pricing, socialism has had to morph into state capitalism, as we see in the great Chinese experiment of the twenty-first century.

With the cultural displacement of the aristocratic value of *otium* by the bourgeois value of *negotium*, the forces of capital were able to brandish a political leverage that made the state submissive to their will. And without the brake of religion, and in the face of the perceived need of national states to win the battle of comparative economic and technological advantage, capital became the overriding concern transforming politics into political economy and thence, via the hedonic "marginal revolution," into plutocracy.[49] This state of affairs has its origins in the Protestant supposition of the individualistic, anti-social, and appetitive nature of man—every society having its basis in a metaphysical theory of human nature.[50] Thus, when government, rather than providing the means for the cultivation of virtue and moderate wealth (the classical political *telos*), was reduced to enforcing contracts and channeling the acquisitive passions of man into productivity, then the state assumed its modern role as mere referee in the economic arena. Hence, the triumph of pragmatic reason, a metaphysics without metaphysics, of the apparent good (*bonum apparens*) over the true, moral, and noble good (*bonum honestum*), and of the unlimited commercialization and secularization of human life.[51]

---

aim, by asserting the necessity of the general will, i.e., the formation of a citizen body whose will was only for the public interest and whose positive legislation secured civil freedom because law would be self-imposed rather than imposed by any other or higher authority. But this, for Rousseau, required the abolition of private property.

49. One can readily understand industrial policy under the Meiji Restoration after Admiral Perry sailed into Tokyo bay with decks full of canon. The Japanese though, unlike the West, attempted both to modernize and preserve traditional culture. Marginal analysis utilizes the limit concept in calculus (as compared with averages) to maximize results. The need economy employs marginal analysis selectively, the want economy indiscriminately. The latter case might be termed "marginalism."

50. See U.S. Supreme Court Justice, Anthony Kennedy, Wikiquote page, online. "At the heart of liberty is the right to define one's own concept of existence, of meaning, of the universe, and of the mystery of human life." And yet, "the law has a moral foundation." It would appear that the official legal philosophy of the United States is that of metaphysical nominalism. Anyone but a nominalist would say that at the heart of liberty is the right to search for and embrace the truth, unless of course there is no truth, which would seem to be the relativistic and contradictory implication of Kennedy's remarks. Given the first quote, what possible moral foundation could the law have, other than the ethically sterile and self-defeating ideologies of relativism or positivism?

51. While there is much to be said for the philanthropy made possible by the generation of enormous wealth in the present secular order, there is also much in the direction of public funding and private giving that is not for the glory of God or of man according

The liberation then domination of economic man was largely made possible by the fragmentation of European religion through the culturally tumultuous Protestant revolution, which, despite all its intentions to the contrary, turned man toward the world. As R.H. Tawney observed in his *Religion and the Rise Capitalism*, "For to the Puritan, a contemner of the vain shows of sacramentalism, mundane toil becomes itself a kind of sacrament."[52] In the absence of a culturally unifying religion there was nothing to restrain the commodification of human life and work. Protestant religion was not equal to the task of subordinating and moderating economic endeavors—indeed, we have seen that it did just the opposite—because it had brought about the great divorce of heaven and earth only to see men increasingly engrossed with the art and prospects of worldly gain. However sincere many Protestants may have been about reform, the great aftershock of the Protestant-inspired great divorce was first a fatal undermining of Christendom, then the gradual reduction of the West from Christian empire to nations, from nations to markets, and from markets to a modern realm of maniacal consumption, aimless pluralism, and the relentless topicality and popular banalities that come with secularization. But total secularization is, of course, not only banal, but, from a moral and spiritual point of view, nefarious in its distraction from divine things through constant demand creation and in the arbitrary redefinitions of human life itself according to relativistic categories.

In the furtherance of his control of the state, economic man came to justify his takeover first by an appeal to a Newtonian or mechanical view of nature, then to a Darwinian universe of competition and "gales of creative destruction," after to a Freudian psychology of libido, and finally on the basis of a Hegelian theory of the historical inevitability of global negative freedom and business, a la Locke and Smith, as Francis Fukuyama confidently asserted.[53] But against the idea that the modern

---

to his divine and moral calling. But this is to be expected in secular liberal democracies in which the question of the proper ends of human life is deliberately put into a state of confusion and subjective discernment.

52. R.H. Tawney, *Religion and the Rise of Capitalism, A Historical Study* (New York: Harcourt, Brace & Co., 1926), 199. See also Tawney's *The Acquisitive Society* for his comments on obsessive economism.

53. Schumpeter coined the phrase "creative destruction," which he thought was of the essence of capitalism; see Joseph Schumpeter, *Capitalism, Socialism and Democracy* (New York: Harper & Row, 1950). For the thesis that Hegel's Lockean prophecy about capitalism and liberal democracy has come true, see Francis Fukuyama *The End of History and the Last Man* (New York: The Free Press, 1992).

economic regime based on insatiable want, rather than natural needs, springs from human nature or is a necessary end to history, rather than a contingent fact, comes a sober remark from Hegel himself: "[T]he need for greater comfort does not exactly arise within you directly; it is suggested to you by those who hope to make a profit from its creation."[54]

This, by the way, helps to explain America's continuous and bloody foreign policy failures in the Middle East. Man, by nature, is so much more than an economic being. Many people do not want to live according to the dogmas of secularism. To set about trying to make the world safe for shopping is a dangerous strategy and an assault on man himself according to his cultural personality. The stated reductive goal of secularizing the Arab world by imposing liberal socio-economics—and what follows, viz., diversity (which is simply a uniformity prescribed by liberalism), gender equality, and the like[55]—is an open declaration of war on the Arab people and their ancient political theology, in the name of a new and alien theology whose idol is the gadget and whose high priests are the oligarchs of Silicon Valley. Artificial intelligence is aptly named.

The rejection of economic secularism is not as such the rejection of economics, markets, and technology. It is the critical part of a positive aim to recover an equitable economy based on sustainable rather than maximal growth. Such an economy would promote decorum in the conduct and architecture of social life, a geometric equality, family-friendly wages, and a responsible solidarity rather than jejune individuality; an economy that would respect the limits of nature and the true

---

54. G.W.F. Hegel, *Philosophy of Right*, tr., T.M. Knox (Oxford: Oxford University Press, 1942), 269, para. 191. Max Weber later echoed this judgment: "A man does not 'by nature' wish to earn more and more money, but simply to live as he is accustomed to live and to earn as much as is necessary for that purpose" (Weber, 60). Similarly, we find this in Anthony Giddens, *Capitalism and Modern Social Theory, An Analysis of the Writings of Marx, Durkheim and Max Weber* (Cambridge: Cambridge University Press, 1971), 69: "Schmoller has shown, Durkheim states, that economic phenomena cannot be adequately studied in the manner of classical economic theory, as if these were separate from the moral norms and beliefs which govern the life of individuals in society." Recently, Brad Gregory has written: "But neo-classical economists no less than the champions of consumerist self-fashioning are quite wrong in thinking that the practices of never-ending, material acquisitiveness are an unavoidable given of human nature.... Such a claim naturalizes acquired, contingent human behaviors in order to justify them and preempt analysis" (Gregory, 242).

55. Both intriguing and amusing, Schumpeter considered feminism "an essentially capitalist phenomenon" (127).

good of man, in which the market is considered a means, not the end of human life.[56] Like any machine or algorithm, the market mechanism is unintelligent apart from the transcendent judgment or decision of its human masters concerning the good to be pursued. Compared to the metaphysical questions of being, human nature, the objective good, and the good life, economic laws, such as they may be, as well as matters of scarcity and modes of allocation, are all trivial.[57] Economics is a practical science concerned with securing the material welfare of the political community. As it was for Aristotle and Aquinas, it is a distinct discipline though subordinate to ethics (politics and morals).[58] Political economy then, rightly understood and generally speaking, involves the public "allocation of ends" guiding the private "allocation of means." But in the modern period an obscurantism came into play in the form of a false devotion to an aleatoric or Neo-Epicurean ideology, that of the blind automaton of the self-regulating market.[59]

The total economic regime bequeathed by Protestantism, however

56. See Samuel Bowles, *The Moral Economy, Why Good Incentives Are No Substitute for Good Citizens* (New Haven, CT: Yale University Press, 2016) and Tim Jackson, *Prosperity Without Growth, Economics for a Finite Planet* (London: Earthscan, 2009). Essentially, Jackson's work is an intriguing critique of the Keynesian paradox of thrift. He writes (p. 203): "In short, the cultural drift that reinforces individualism at the expense of society, and supports innovation at the expense of tradition, is a distortion of what it means to be human." After quoting Hume regarding the assumption of human knavery and the goal of private interest as the basis of government (16), Bowles cites "a founder of the neo-classical paradigm" as saying: "The first principle of economics is that every agent is actuated only by self-interest" (21). Beating Hume in his own game of experimental method, Bowles subsequently remarks, "Natural observation and experimental data indicate that in most populations, few individuals are consistently self-interested, and moral and other-regarding motives are common." But all this is just to say that the modern economic regime is built on the false Protestant paradigm of total depravity.

57. For example, the growing, pricing, and, say, legal sale of marijuana will involve all manner of economic considerations. But these are trivial in relation to the non-trivial issue of whether to legalize marijuana in the first place, for that issue will involve substantive meta-economic questions of medicine and ethics.

58. CCC #2426: "Economic activity, conducted according to its own proper methods, is to be exercised within the limits of the moral order, in keeping with social justice so as to correspond to God's plan for man."

59. "Economic liberalism was the organizing principle of society engaged in creating a market system. Born as a mere penchant for non-bureaucratic methods, it evolved into a veritable faith in man's secular salvation through a self-regulating market." Karl Polanyi, *The Great Transformation, The Political and Economic Origins of Our Time* (Boston: Beacon Press, 1944), 141. David Wotton points out that the "feedback mechanism"

unwittingly, affects everything from the soul to science. Books of popular science written by modern scientists great and small incessantly preach exactly what you would expect from the secular Neo-Epicurean worldview they have imbibed from the breast of the regime. The self-organizing universe came from nothing. It is ruled by chance. Everything is matter. As with endless consumer preferences, there are even interminable worlds, in which every possibility is realized. No need for God. Computers think. But man really doesn't, as free will is a myth (*pace* the "atomic swerve"). All this is so much metaphysical nonsense and materialist pathology. Moreover, in the biblical scholarship of the "Jesus Movement" one frequently comes across these words: the *diversity* of the early Church, *Gnostic* Christianity, gradual *consensus* among differing Christian sects, and *patriarchal suppression* of female leadership. Slogans all, and the shadows of our age, in the reimagination of the past to fit the liberal narrative. Who can escape the cave of the total economic regime?

Permit me to summarize by way of definition and deviation. From a pre-modern perspective, economics could be said to be the social art of supplying man, by way of production and exchange, with material and intellectual needs insufficient in external nature (scarcity) but according to the limit or end of internal nature, i.e., according to the flourishing or perfection of human nature. Economic man changes "needs" to "wants" and dispenses with the limit or end. This deviation, suggesting that economic man did not fully come into his own until the modern age, has had baleful cultural consequences. It was, I have argued, stimulated by the theology and anthropology of Protestantism.

I shall conclude on a note of both consternation and optimism, optimism for those who understand that man's old persuasion, the longing for the sublime, the Infinite, for Being rather than the finite idols of non-being, will continue to reassert itself against unnatural efforts to suppress it. Having replaced all supernatural hope and the natural bonds of society with the inorganic paste and promise of indefinite economic growth, what would happen if the modern economic regime suddenly became unglued, not to say unhinged, as it almost did in 2008? What would Western society fall back on or into? One shudders to

---

or "self-regulating machine" is the basis of Hume's theory of the balance of trade and Smith's concept of the market; its absence among the Greeks and Romans helps explain why they "failed to develop a general theory of economic behaviour." David Wootton, *The Invention of Science, A New History of the Scientific Revolution* (New York: Harper-Collins, 2015), 441.

imagine.[60] The Great Depression had Christian civil society to fall back on; had the Great Recession become the Second Great Depression, the modern order would likely have cashed in the nihilism it has assiduously cultivated for total civil disorder. But if there is any historical certainty, it is this: the culture of *homo religiosus* will outlive the paraculture of *homo economicus*. *Religio vinculum societatis semper.*

60. The vexed question of growth, employment, and myriad externalities cannot obviously be addressed here in all its immense complexity. But it seems, in general, that the ratio of consumption to conservation and savings should to be weighted in favor of the latter, which could create new jobs while inducing a healthier socio-economic environment; other possibly beneficial economic proposals place hopes in schemes of zero marginal cost along with a sharing economy a la the digital revolution. In his monumental 2016 work on the future of American growth, Robert Gordon cites various technical reasons for its likely continued decline (e.g., inequality, education, demographics, government debt, globalization, climate change); but then he makes this striking normative statement: "[S]igns of social decay are everywhere in the America of the early twenty-first century." Among other reasons for this decay, Gordon points to anarchy in the institution of marriage and the not unrelated growing rates of incarceration. Robert Gordon, *The Rise and Fall of American Growth, The U.S. Standard of Living since the Civil War* (Princeton: Princeton University Press, 2016), 608. For a further related and important study, see Jonathan Last, *What to Expect When No One's Expecting, America's Coming Demographic Disaster* (New York: Encounter Books, 2013).

8

The New Protestant Bargain

The Influence of Protestant Theology on Contract and Property Law [1]

Brian M. McCall

Introduction

I T IS IMPOSSIBLE to dissociate morality (or ethics) from theological doctrine. As Richard Weaver explained in the last century, ideas have consequences.[2] More precisely, Amintore Fanfani observed that moral doctrine is inseparable from theological doctrine.

> [M]oral doctrine is bound up with, or, better, founded on, the theological doctrine, and if for scientific convenience, it may be considered apart, in reality it is only another aspect of the same fact; it is a system of corollaries deduced from a system of postulates. Theology provides the principles, morals their application, and the two are indissolubly linked.[3]

Therefore, a change of theological doctrine will inevitably be accompanied by a change in the norms governing behavior. Since human law is related to and developed in light of the customs and mores of the com-

---

1. This chapter is based on a lecture entitled "El Impacto de la Doctrina Protestante sobre la Propiedad y el Contrato" given as part of the conference entitled "Las Consecuencias Politico-Juridicas del Protestantismo a los Quinientos Anos de Lutero" sponsored by the International Union of Catholic Jurists and held at Anahuac Universidad Norte, Mexico, on April 28 and 29, 2016. A Spanish version of this chapter will also appear in the published proceedings of the conference.

2. See Richard Weaver, *Ideas Have Consequences* (Chicago: University of Chicago Press, 1984).

3. Amintore Fanfani, *Catholicism, Protestantism, and Capitalism* (New York: Sheed & Ward, 1955), 3.

munity for which it is made,[4] these changes will eventually find their way into law. As Harold Berman and John Witte have noted regarding the Reformation, "such a fundamental transformation of . . . the religious beliefs" could not have "taken place without substantial changes in legal thought."[5]

The novel doctrines of Protestantism after these past five hundred years have had their effects on morality and law. Obviously, Protestant novelties have not been the only influence upon law and are not solely responsible for the contents of modern law. Other political, social, and economic forces have had their influence. Some of these other factors beyond theological dogma—such as large-scale wealth redistribution in England upon dissolution of the monasteries—were also bound up with the emergence of Protestantism. Yet, although scholars may differ on the precise extent to which Protestant theology influenced the legal system, it can hardly be denied that there has been some impact. At a minimum, certain aspects of Protestant theology correlate with and therefore provide theoretical support for certain changes in Western legal systems in the past 500 years.

In this chapter we will consider how certain aspects of Protestant theology relate to two legal institutions: contracts and property. We will proceed by summarizing briefly certain Protestant theological doctrines and how they changed the fundamental jurisprudential assumptions of Western law. After this, we will consider how some particular aspects of post-Reformation contract and property law are supported by, or at least are consistent with, novel aspects of Protestant theology. In making this argument, I do not intend to suggest that the original founders of Protestantism necessarily overtly intended to overturn long established jurisprudential principles or particular aspects of contract and property law. In fact, in many ways, early Protestants such as Luther and Calvin explicitly argued in favor of traditional moral and legal norms relating to economic activity developed on the foundation of Catholic principles.[6] Yet, even if one who introduces novel ideas does not intend the logical consequences of those ideas, or even foresee them, the ideas may still be the seeds of that unintended development. One calling into question only an aspect of an existing legal and moral order may unin-

---

4. See Brian M. McCall, "Decorating the Structure: The Art of Making Human Law," *The Journal of Catholic Legal Studies* 53 (2014): 23–91.

5. Harold J. Berman and John Witte, Jr., "The Transformation of Western Legal Philosophy in Lutheran Germany," *Southern California Law Review* 62 (1989): 1573–1659, 1576.

6. See e.g., Fanfani, 190–92.

tentionally pull down the entire order. As R.H. Tawney observed, "If it is true that the Reformation released forces which were to act as a solvent of the traditional attitude of religious thought to social and economic issues, it did so without design, and against the intention of most reformers."[7] We will not, therefore, concern ourselves with the original subjective intentions of early Protestants but rather their objective ideas.

Protestant Theology

In a sense, it is inaccurate to speak of Protestantism or Protestant theology, because from its earliest days in the sixteenth century it has not been a monolithic institution. It quickly divided into different denominations and sects adhering to different doctrines. "As of 1980 David B. Barrett identified 20,800 Christian denominations worldwide...."[8] Yet, several core areas of belief can be identified with Protestantism generally and at least with the Protestant denominations of the sixteenth through the eighteenth centuries, a period when contract and property law underwent significant change. Although various Protestant denominations will develop different interpretations of, and develop different conclusions from, these core principles, the starting points all mark a break with traditional Catholic doctrine.

One of the central tenets of Protestantism that dates from Martin Luther's earliest revolt relates to the prerequisites of justification and salvation. Luther argued that faith alone, *sola fides*, justified a soul.[9] Whereas Catholic theology holds that although salvation is impossible without faith, it alone is insufficient and must be accompanied by good works which, when joined to the merits of Christ, merit salvation in the life to come. According to Protestant teaching, however, works are of no consequence to the justification of a soul or its state after death. This original germ of an idea produced in certain variations of Protestantism other related concepts. Faith, which was the exclusive means of salvation, was also a completely free gift of God that could not be merited by any human action. This thought led to the development of various forms of Predestination theology. If only faith saves and if only God bestows faith, then God must have predestined from the beginning who would get this justifying gift. The emphasis on Predestination further

7. R.H. Tawney, *Religion and the Rise of Capitalism* (London: John Murray, 1929), 84.

8. "Denominationalism," *Dictionary of Christianity in America* (Downers Grove: Intervarsity Press, 1990), 351. This figure includes not only Protestants but also Roman Catholic and Orthodox but even eliminating these groups the number is still enormous.

9. Berman and Witte, 1581.

undermined the value of human acts as it emphasized that good or evil acts bore no causal relation to the fate of the predestined soul after death. Even the act of faith lacks human agency as it is completely pre-destined by God.

The devaluing of human acts and an active role for man in working out his salvation is related to another core belief, the total depravity of human nature. Although created to be good by God, human nature, according to Protestant theology, was totally and irreversibly corrupted by original sin. Christ's redemptive action makes salvation possible, but not by reforming human nature; it merely covers over its depravity through faith. This total depravity devastated the two faculties, intellect and will, that are instrumental to human acts, that is, to free moral acts. As Harold Berman and John Witte explain, "The Lutheran reformers . . . taught that a person's will and reason are both essentially corrupted by his innate egoism. That was the meaning of the Lutheran doctrine of 'total' depravity. It embraced the depravity both of human reason and of human will. . . ."[10]

Notwithstanding their denial of any supernatural or eternal conse-quences of human action, Lutheran and later Protestant denominations did not therefore advocate that people act in a totally depraved way in civil society. They realized that this doctrine would lead to civil anarchy (and in the case of early Lutheranism almost did). In response, Luther developed a concept of the two kingdoms to explain why people should try to act morally in their daily lives while at the same time denying moral action had any effect on salvation. As Berman and Witte explain, "The belief that both human will and human reason are essentially defective and that good works are not a means of union with God led Luther, Melanchthon, and the other reformers to their central theologi-cal teaching that God has ordained two distinct realms, or kingdoms, in which mankind is destined to live—the earthly and the heavenly."[11]

This concept enabled them to deny any efficacy in the supernatural realm to human works while advocating adherence to biblical moral prohibitions, such as obedience to authority and the prohibition on usury. The two kingdoms were essentially separate and unrelated (although, in theory, God stood over both). From the human perspec-tive, the works one did in the earthly kingdom had no impact upon his place in the heavenly although they did impact life in the earthly king-dom. This dualism preserves the need for following legal and moral norms in the earthly kingdom but divests that activity of supernatural

---

10. Ibid.
11. Ibid., 1585–86.

consequences. It makes these laws merely necessary for a peaceful and secure life on earth.

In this devaluation of human actions and their eternal consequences, we can detect the seeds of efficiency jurisprudence. Moral and legal rules are merely necessary to make the earthly kingdom run smoothly. That divests those rules of their gravity and nobility. Honoring those norms does not result in eternal consequences but merely political, economic, and social efficiency in the earthly kingdom.[12] Combined with the total depravity theory, which could easily be co-opted to excuse violations of normative standards (we cannot help being depraved), these Protestant notions, intended or otherwise, undermined traditional Catholic legal and political philosophy.

Early Protestants did, in fact, argue for adherence—and, in the case of the Puritans, strict disciplined adherence[13]—to the moral precepts of the divine law; nevertheless, these doctrines undermined in many ways the traditional Catholic doctrine supporting moral and hence legal obligations. Traditional Catholic teaching approaches moral acts from a different perspective. First, it maintains a more optimistic view of human nature.[14] While recognizing that the faculties of reason and will have been wounded due to original sin, Catholicism still maintains that man can come to know moral truths through the use of reason and can obey them by an act of will; and, therefore, that he can work toward the perfection of his nature, at least on the natural level. With the assistance of grace, a conquering of concupiscence—the *fomes peccati*—is still arduous, but possible. Although works alone are insufficient for supernatural perfection, justification, and salvation, the natural powers are not totally depraved. Thus, conformity to the divine and natural law is possible, especially with the assistance of grace. Grace not merely covers over depravity but medicinally treats it.

Secondly, the Catholic recognition of the potential for supernatural merit for good works (by those who have the Faith and are in a state of sanctifying grace) provides a stronger, supernatural foundation to the call to obey the law. Rather than merely making life in the Lutheran earthly kingdom more tolerable, good works are relevant in determining eternal happiness. Economics and the laws governing it—contract and property—relate directly to the earthly kingdom; but for the Catholic,

---

12. See Harold Berman, *Law and Revolution II: The Impact of the Protestant Reformation on the Western Legal Tradition* (Boston: Harvard University Press, 2003), 75–76.

13. C. Scott Pryor and Glenn M. Hoshauer, "Puritan Revolution and the Law of Contracts," *Texas Wesleyan Law Review* 11 (2005): 291–360, 330–36.

14. See Berman and Witte, 1581.

life in this world cannot be separated from the heavenly kingdom, which must permeate the earthly. Works matter in both realms; therefore, the kingdoms are not separate but interdependent. Economic works, as well as any other type of works, will affect not only natural but also supernatural ends. Failure to conform action to norms results in more than an inefficient earthly kingdom. Although clinging to the biblical rules of action because they are the law of God, the Protestant doctrine removes concrete supernatural or eternal consequences from failure to observe these laws, leaving only earthly economic consequences.

The exclusive reliance on individual faith (or individual predestination) led to a new understanding of the church. Protestantism reduces the value of and need for a visible communal church, since salvation is a matter of isolated, and for some, predestined individuals. Beginning with Luther, Protestantism reduces the visible communal church to an invisible tenuous grouping of individual believers. According to Harold Berman, Luther eliminated the idea of the church as a visible body that made laws for believers. Rather the church is an "invisible community of all believers, in which . . . each is a 'private person' in his relation to God. Each responds directly to the Bible as the word of God."[15] As Berman indicates, this notion of the invisible church is connected to another Protestant tenant, *sola scriptura,* the belief that God's revelation is contained solely in the scriptures, the meaning of which is discovered directly by each individual. The elimination of the visible church combined with the doctrine of *sola scriptura* led to a redefinition of the faculty of conscience. Traditionally, for Catholics, reason is the higher faculty through which we come to know truths. Conscience is the faculty by which we apply those truths to concrete situations. For Luther, conscience becomes superior and through it each person not only applies truths but also comes to knowledge of truths. As Berman states, "Conscience . . . is derived directly from faith; it not only applies principles of divine and natural law to concrete situations but also is a source and an embodiment of our understanding of those principles."[16] Thus, in contrast to the visible hierarchical Church—with laws, courts, and jurisdiction, and priestly administered sacraments—Protestantism substituted the isolated individual, invisibly connected to other individuals who were saved, if predestined, by faith alone and whose actions and works had no consequence beyond the transitory earthly kingdom. These isolated individuals came to know God's revelation as isolated individuals solely through the scriptures and the operation of their indi-

15. Berman, *Law and Revolution,* 40.
16. Ibid., 75.

vidual subjective consciences. As Berman and Witte explain, this stark difference placed a completely different emphasis on law:

> [T]he Roman Catholic Church made salvation conditional upon compliance with the traditions and laws of the visible corporate church. They believed it was only through these traditions and laws that God's will was revealed. The Lutheran doctrine of salvation, on the contrary, rested on the belief that knowledge of God's will—what the Lutherans called spiritual knowledge, as contrasted with temporal knowledge—was to be derived from the Bible alone. The Bible contained the whole Christian revelation and all that was requisite for human salvation.[17]

Catholicism approached salvation as a complex series of interdependent human relationships and works. As a result, there was very little in the realm of human action that did not concern the Church in some way. The jurisdiction of the church courts, another visible communal aspect of the Church, stretched not only from internal church discipline to marriage, intestacy, and inheritance, but also covered property and contract. The institution of church courts was based on the idea that—through scripture, reason, and Tradition—the Church can know moral truths and, therefore, can judge and regulate activity in society. The Protestant doctrines of individual interpretation, justification by faith alone, and *sola scriptura* strip this communal structure away, leaving the believer alone with his Bible, his depraved nature, and his depraved conscience. Those who make laws for the earthly kingdom are, like all believers, on their own. As Berman and Witte note, "Christians exercising political jurisdiction were to be guided not by the organized church but by their own consciences."[18]

All of these doctrines—the depravity of human nature, the two kingdoms, *sola fides*, *sola scriptura*, and the elimination of a visible hierarchical church—coalesce to reinforce a positivist view of law, notwithstanding some verbal references to natural law concepts by Protestant theologians and jurists. Law is understood as simple precepts coming directly out of the Bible or the unaided conscience of the civil rulers. This biblical positivism was most strongly expressed in English Puritanism. As Pryor and Hoshauer explain, "Puritanism's material principle was the scriptures. Neither tradition nor reason could stand over biblical revelation for the Puritan; 'the appeal to scriptural authority [was] the very life of Puritanism.'"[19]

---

17. Berman and Witte, 1582.
18. Ibid., 1590.
19. Pryor and Hoshauer, 313 (internal citations omitted).

In contrast, Catholic jurisprudence understood laws as comprising a spectrum of general principles contained in natural and divine law, together with contingent determinations made by human authorities using their natural reason (aided by grace, divine revelation, and Church Tradition) and human experience derived from customs.[20] The Catholic approach was more nuanced, recognizing the unchanging nature of the general principles but the contingent nature of the particular determinations.

Protestant approaches generally fell into one of two positivist categories. One understood law as precepts posited by the Bible that required no human determination; civil rulers were mere instruments to enforce divine precepts. The other emphasized that law was unnecessary to salvation and, therefore, it is only useful for political or other ends.[21] To the latter way of thinking, civil rulers are independent actors free to posit whatever precepts seem most effective for the earthly kingdom. The concept of predestination was easily adapted to weaken the subjection of local or national laws to higher universal law. Locally posited laws began to break free of the *jus commune* developed and nurtured by the Catholic Church for centuries. Whereas, before, local laws were understood to be subject to universal law, now the law of a place was increasingly viewed as being divinely ordained to be what it is. In England, in particular, this translated into a sense of divinely-ordained historical development. English law "was superior, at least for England, to 'foreign' law,"[22] because it was divinely predestined to develop as it had.

A certain strand of Protestantism that was dominant in Scotland developed the Lutheran notion of conscience as an innate sense by which men know the truth. Known as Scottish Common Sense Realism, this exaltation of an individual's ability to sense what is right and wrong took root in America. Herbert Hovenkamp explains:

> When Scottish Common Sense Realism obtained a foothold in America during the 1760s and 1770s, it imported two ideas about value formation. The first was a unique kind of empiricism that claimed to despise speculation and abstraction. The second was a rationale for individual self-determination that Scottish Realists called the "moral sense." The moral sense enabled a person to know instinctively the difference between right and wrong. "Moral science" was the discipline that used the moral sense to discover the principles of ethical conduct,

---

20. See McCall, "Decorating the Structure."
21. Berman, *Law and Revolution,* 75–76.
22. Ibid., 264.

just as the physical sciences relied on the other five senses to discover the natural principles of the universe.[23]

This idea of the moral sense, combined with the elimination of a visible church to adjudicate moral questions, added to a tendency toward removing legal restraints on behavior. The idea of the moral sense supported "a broad rationale for individual self-determination in every aspect of human activity."[24] These attitudes led to a breakdown of an authority to preserve the divine law and enforce it, particularly with respect to economic matters. This first took the form of the elimination of church courts, or a severe limitation of their jurisdiction, and then a reduction of the role of the civil government in judging economic activity.

In the next section, we will observe how all of these influences upon legal theory affected economic regulation. The weakening of moral agency, the dismantling of a visible juridical church, the emphasis on autonomous individual conscience and the moral sense all supported specific changes in the laws governing contracts and property.

Protestantism and Property and Contracts

Before looking at specific aspects of property and contract law, we need to note how Protestant theology leads to a different understanding of economic activity generally. Property and contract law regulate the ownership, use, and transfer of economic assets and, therefore, the general approach to economic activity will be reflected in these particular fields of law.

The elimination of works from the plan of salvation leads to a segmentation of human life. The doctrine of the two kingdoms reinforces this compartmentalization. Since works, including economic works, have no effect on the spiritual kingdom or the afterlife, they are evaluated solely in light of their usefulness to the earthly kingdom. Such compartmentalization is impossible for Catholicism, which sees every human act as directly relevant to the Kingdom of Heaven and the fate of the actor in the life to come. As Fanfani notes, "A man convinced that wealth is a means for the attainment of his individual, natural ends, which are not and cannot be divorced from his individual, supernatural

---

23. Herbert Hovenkamp, "The Political Economy of Substantive Due Process," *Stanford Law Review* 40 (1988): 379–447, 413.

24. Ibid., 414.

ends . . . will choose such means of acquiring wealth as will not lead him away from his ultimate end or ends related to it."[25]

Two aspects of Protestant doctrine combined to encourage a retreat from the belief that economic behavior should be regulated from a moral perspective. First, the principle of *sola fides* implied that economic acts had no effect on eternal salvation. Therefore, the only legitimate goal of government regulation was the utilitarian one of producing maximum results for the earthly kingdom. Second, the exaltation of the individual, subjective conscience, combined with the destruction of the visible and hierarchical Church—which for centuries exercised her legal jurisdiction to restrain and correct immoral economic activity—tended toward the triumph of individualism and radical autonomy in the economic realm. Individuals could be relied on to interpret scripture for themselves and to know the truth by an innate moral sense (especially according to the tenets of Common Sense Realism) and were, therefore, best suited to apply scriptural texts to their own economic activity.

The principle of individual interpretation of scripture led, in fact, to different individual interpretations. Having eliminated a central visible authority to adjudicate among these various interpretations, Protestantism quickly began to subdivide into different denominations, a phenomenon that continues to this day, producing thousands of radically different sects. In the economic realm, the emphasis on the individual using his common sense conscience, guided only by his own interpretation of biblical rules, led to a policy favoring deregulation of economic activity. Fanfani explains:

> In substance what was required was that the state should no longer impose a special rhythm on economic life with a view to the attainment of certain ends, but should leave the individual free to realize his own ideals for himself, and should confine itself to ensuring that he should not be impeded in so doing.[26]

As a result, laws "are passed to safeguard an individualistic conception of property and the complete autonomy of the individual in economic matters and to defend economic freedom even against the power of the state itself."[27] The individual's freedom of choice becomes the test of justice, just as individual interpretation of scripture becomes the touchstone of doctrine, leading to the radical conclusion that "[a]ll

---

25. Fanfani, 24–25.
26. Ibid., 88.
27. Ibid., 103.

profit is just when there is full freedom."[28] If economic activity has a moral implication, the application of any moral norms should be left to individuals, and the civil government's role in economic activity is limited either to maximizing the scope for individual freedom (classical liberalism) or intervening to maximize wealth creation for the nation (mercantilism).

On the other hand, Catholicism's elevation of objective reason over subjective conscience, emphasis on the consequences of good and evil works, and a visible juridical hierarchy to maintain doctrinal uniformity had produced a very different attitude toward laws regulating economic activity. As Fanfani notes:

> Catholic ethics, in virtue of the ends they set before man and society and of the Catholic conception of human nature and creation, is necessarily in favour of State intervention, and cannot, for instance, approve when the State concedes full and unlimited "freedom of labour," wholly regardless of consequences to the worker and society— even if this neglect could be justified by the conviction, denied by Catholic philosophy, that the conciliation of interests comes about automatically.[29]

The Church led the civil jurisdiction by example, and ecclesiastical jurists were intimately involved in the development of contract and property law. Ecclesiastical courts heard many property and contract cases throughout the Middle Ages. Other parties not falling within the jurisdiction of ecclesiastical courts could and often did voluntarily submit contract and property cases to ecclesiastical courts.[30] The Church and church jurists were intimately involved in the development of economic laws that placed restraints on individual economic freedom up to the eve of the Reformation.

The effect of this change of spirit from Catholic to Protestant, according to Fanfani, is that economic efficiency, encouraged by greater autonomy of action, becomes the sole, or at least predominant, criterion for judging the economic activity regulated by contract and property law.[31] The activity regulated by contract and property law is evaluated purely in terms of natural ends and, therefore, finds its sole focus in what seems best or most productive in the earthly kingdom dominated by autonomous individuals. The morality of the economic means chosen is left to the individual conscience. Professor Hovenkamp argues that

28. Abbé Baudeau, quoted in Fanfani, 101.
29. Fanfani, 140.
30. See Berman, 35.
31. See Fanfani, Chapter 2.

the result of Protestant theology is "the prevailing belief that laissez faire was *the* Christian economics—even if it produced inequalities of distribution."[32]

Contract Law

England became one of the most uniformly Protestant countries in Europe, whereas in Germany the Treaty of Westphalia left the status of religion to the individual German princes, resulting in a patchwork of Protestant and Catholic states across the land. Therefore, the effects in English, and hence American law, are more pronounced, leading Pryord and Hoshauer to conclude, "In short, it was the social practices of Puritanism, ultimately grounded in Puritan theology, which effected the development of contract law in England."[33] Protestant theology contributed to a shift in the underlying basis of contract liability, shifting from *causa* to consideration and promise to bargain. English law also developed in the direction of strict liability for breach of contract, eliminating or weakening excuses for non-performance.

Roman law, from which Catholic contract law developed, required that to be enforced by law an agreement between parties must have a *causa*. The Roman jurist Ulpian explains, "If there is no additional ground (*causa*), in that case it is certain that no obligation can be created, [I mean] on the mere agreement; so that a bare agreement does not produce an obligation...."[34] The mere fact of parties reaching agreement was insufficient to give rise to an obligation. A *causa* could be found in one of the so-called real contracts (*contractus realis*), i.e., forms of transactions Roman law recognized as giving rise to an obligation (sale, hire, deposit, etc.), or in observing a recognized form of stipulation (*stipulatio*). Buckland succinctly explains the difference between Roman law and contemporary contract law thus:

> All that Ulpian means is that you cannot in general sue on a mere pact as such: you must show that your agreement is one of those which the law makes actionable. His way of putting the matter expresses the great difference which exists between the Roman attitude towards agreement and that of our law. With us an agreement is actionable unless there is some reason why it should not be so. With the Romans an

---

32. Hovenkamp, 420.

33. Pryor and Hoshauer, 298.

34. Digest 2.14.7.4, English translation quoted in Ernest G. Lorenzen, "Causa and Consideration in the Law of Contracts," *The Yale Law Journal*, 28, No. 7 (May, 1919): 621–46, 624.

agreement was not actionable unless there was some reason why it should be so.[35]

The emphasis is on the determination by civil law of which types of pacts (agreements) were enforceable obligations as opposed to the subjective agreement of the parties making such determination (as in modern contract law). Catholic jurists building on Roman law concepts "concluded that a morally binding promise should also be legally binding if it is part of an agreement (a *pactum,* or consensual obligation) that is itself morally justified. The object or purpose (*causa*) of the contract had to be reasonable and equitable."[36] Based on this principle that the law determines what constitutes a *causa* for enforcing agreements, Catholic theologians and jurists developed two significant restraints on the freedom of contracts that went beyond Roman law: the prohibition on enforcing usurious contracts and the requirement that contracts must be made at a just price.[37]

The Catholic reliance on an objective standard of justice to determine which agreements created an obligation as determined by civil law conflicted with the new Protestant theology and jurisprudence, which emphasized individual and subjective determinations. Although Protestants initially accepted these Catholic restraints on usury and agreements made for an unjust price,[38] the greater emphasis on subjective determinations and individual autonomy led to the weakening of these restraints. Eventually this produced the opposite approach, described by Buckland, which presumed subjective agreements created obligations regardless of the contents of those agreements. Freedom of contract, explains Professor Hovenkamp, "ingrained Protestant values. Each person bore responsibility for the most fundamental decisions about religious belief, ethical practice, and economic status. The purpose of the state and the church was not to dictate external values, but merely to cultivate and reinforce those values that were confirmed in each person by his own perceptions."[39]

35. William W. Buckland, *Elementary Principles of the Roman Private Law* (Cambridge: Cambridge University Press, 1912), 232.

36. Harold J. Berman, "The Religious Sources of General Contract Law: An Historical Perspective," *Journal of Law & Religion* 4 (1986): 103–24, 110.

37. See Brian M. McCall, "Entender los males económicos modernos a la luz de la doctrina social Católica," *Verbo* 52 Nos. 525–526 (May/June/July 2014): 487–509; Brian M. McCall, *The Church and the Usurers: Unprofitable Lending for the Modern Economy* (Ave Maria: Sapientia Press of Ave Maria University, 2013); and Berman, *Law and Revolution,* 161.

38. Berman, *Law and Revolution,* 161–63.

39. Hovenkamp, 419.

The undermining of the Roman concept of *causa* was replaced, in England at least, by the concept of consideration as bargained for exchange. Whereas contractual promises supported by a *causa* were enforced previously, English law began developing the practice of only enforcing bargains. As Professor Berman notes, "the underlying theory of liability shifted from breach of promise to breach of a bargain."[40] The shift from promises to bargains was reinforced by the English Protestant emphasis on biblical covenants.[41] Pryord and Hoshauer have shown how English Puritanism elevated covenant (as bargain) keeping. "Among the obligations demanded by freedom of conscience, as understood by the Puritans, was keeping one's side of a bargain. Keeping one's promises was an aspect of freedom of conscience because freedom of conscience meant freedom to obey God's law."[42] They even argue that "[o]f all of their contributions to the development of theological doctrine, the Puritan analysis of covenant stands supreme."[43]

Although breach of promise and breach of covenant may seem to be the same concept, for Protestants and particularly Puritans, covenants were interdependent promises given in a bargain, while promises were unilateral. The Puritans read the history of salvation contained in the Bible in a theologically novel manner, as a series of bargains between God and man. Pursuant to the new covenant of grace, as understood by Puritan theology, God promised salvation in exchange for the profession of faith. Salvation was the product of a bargain. Whereas for earlier theologians, the covenant of grace was a merciful gift of God, John Witte explains that these Puritan theologians redefined "the covenant of grace as a bargained contract, voluntarily formed by God and his elect, and absolutely binding on both parties."[44]

Jurists then used that theory of covenanted bargain to ground contract law in bargain which, although freely made, once entered into was absolute. The objectively determined *causae* that must support a promise for liability to arise was replaced by the subjective bargain itself as the basis of liability, and hence there arose the shift from a presumption of not enforcing bargains unless a *causa* exists to the presumption of enforcing bargains. Harold Berman characterizes the shift from *causa* to consideration as a shift from "a *moral* theory to what may be called a bar-

40. Berman, *Law and Revolution*, 339.
41. Ibid., 264.
42. Pryor and Hoshauer, 315–16.
43. Ibid., 320.
44. John Witte, Jr., "Blest Be the Ties That Bind: Covenant and Community in Puritan Thought," *Emory Law Journal* 36 (1987): 579–601, 587.

gain theory of contracts."[45] The older moral theory of contractual liability, "which linked legal liability closely with the sin or wrongfulness of a breach of promise, on the one hand, and the equitable purpose of the promise or exchange of promises, on the other, was attacked in the seventeenth century in England by Puritans, including both lawyers and theologians" and replaced by this bargain theory rooted in the Puritan reading of the Bible as providing divine sanction for liability for bargains.[46]

As John Witte notes, intricately connected to this development of the bargain theory of contracts based on biblical covenants was the announcement by English courts of a rule of strict liability for contract breach. For Catholic jurists, it was not the failure to keep the subjective agreement that was the heart of the matter but rather the objective injustice of a particular breach of promise. Liability arose due to the fault of one party, creating an injustice. Thus, failures to honor a bargain for a usurious loan or sales at an unjust price were not enforceable even though both parties may have given their subjective consent to the bargain. Parties were free to contract, but only for just contracts supported by *causa*. For Protestant English jurists influenced by Puritan covenant theology, failure to keep one's subjective agreement was a grave failing for which payment must be made. The law could not excuse one from his covenanted bargain even if fulfilling the bargain was unjust to one party. John Witte explains, "The new covenant theology also provided the cardinal ethical principle of Puritanism that each person was free to choose his act, but once having chosen, was bound to perform that act, regardless of the consequences."[47] For Catholic jurists of prior centuries, those consequences were relevant to determine if breach of bargain was morally wrongful. They had developed a list of excuses for failing to honor a bargain that would relieve the promisor of liability.[48] For English courts influenced by Puritan covenant theology, since covenant keeping was enjoined by the Bible, "not even state authority could lawfully relieve one's obligation to perform."[49] This theology, according to Berman, "led to strict liability for breach of contract."[50] John Witte argues that the Protestant development of the radical freedom to contract for almost any bargain, supported by the

---

45. Berman, "The Religious Sources of General Contract Law," 117.
46. Ibid., 118.
47. Witte, "Blest Be the Ties That Bind," 595.
48. See Berman, "The Religious Sources of General Contract Law," 110 for a list.
49. Pryor and Hoshauer, 316.
50. Berman, *Law and Revolution*, 265.

analogy of biblical covenants, greatly influenced this turn toward strict liability for promises supported by bargained for exchange. The theological principles of individual interpretation and the exercise of subjective conscience to decide what is just reinforced this strict liability for subjectively made bargains.

For Catholics, the analysis of whether a breach of promise was actionable was more nuanced. The surrounding circumstances of the promise must be examined to determine if keeping the promise was morally and legally obligatory. The obligation rested on the cause of the promise or the justness of the transaction. Puritans read the biblical notion of covenant to mean that one was free to covenant but strictly liable once the covenant was made. John Selden, a prominent legal scholar of the seventeenth century, explained the absolute strict liability for bargained promises thus:

> We must look to the contract; if that be rightly made, we must stand to it; if we once grant [that] we may recede from contracts upon any inconveniency that may afterwards happen, we shall have no bargain kept.... [H]ow to make our contracts is left to ourselves; and as we agree upon the conveyance of this house, or this land, so it must be. If you offer me a hundred pounds for my glove, I tell you what my glove is—a plain glove—pretend no virtue in it—the glove is my own—I profess not to sell gloves, and we agree for an hundred pounds—I do not know why I may not with a safe conscience take it.[51]

The fact that this exchange was at an unjust price would be irrelevant.

As Harold Berman has noted, English courts shifted the foundation of contractual liability from wrongful breach of promise to mere breach of bargain. "The promisee was entitled to compensation for nonperformance with the terms of the bargain itself; excuses for nonperformance were to be confined, generally speaking, to those provided for within those terms."[52] As a result of this grounding in the bargain itself, English courts began to close defenses—based on the justice of the situation—to breach of contract actions that previously relieved parties who failed to perform to the letter of their bargain. As Professor Berman notes, the courts "established that a bargained exchange was binding and actionable on breach, regardless of the absence of fault."[53]

51. John Selden, "Seldeniana, or the Table Talk of John Selden, Esq." (1789), quoted in Berman, "The Religious Sources of General Contract Law," 118–19.

52. Berman, "The Religious Sources of General Contract Law," 117.

53. Harold J. Berman, "Law and Belief in Three Revolutions," *Valparaiso University Law Review*, 18 (1984): 569–629, 603.

Professor Berman highlights the case of *Paradine v. Jane* (Kings Bench 1647) as the epitome of this change in contract law.[54] In this case, a tenant for land defends a suit by the landlord for unpaid rent by arguing that he was driven off the land due to hostilities in connection with the English Civil War. He argues it would be unjust to force him to fulfill his promise to pay rent when prevented from using the land. Argument before the English Court acknowledges that the rule of strict liability it is about to announce is a break with natural law and the law previously applied by civil and ecclesiastical courts:

> Also by the law of reason it seems the defendant in our case ought not to be charged with the rent, because he could not enjoy that that was let to him, and it was no fault of his own that he could not, and the civil-law, and canon-law, and moral authors do confirm this ... and that law is the law of nature as well as of nations.[55]

The court rejects this Catholic understanding of law in favor of strict liability thus:

> [B]ut when the party by his own contract creates a duty or charge upon himself, he is bound to make it good, if he may, notwithstanding any accident by inevitable necessity, because he might have provided against it by his contract. And therefore if the lessee covenant to repair a house, though it be burnt by lightning, or thrown down by enemies, yet he ought to repair it. Dyer 33. a. 40 e. 3. 6. h. Now the rent is a duty created by the parties upon the reservation, and had there been a covenant to pay it, there had been no question but the lessee must have made it good, notwithstanding the interruption by enemies, for the law would not protect him beyond his own agreement. . . .[56]

Although in more recent times American and English courts have tempered the purity of strict liability as announced in *Paradine v. Jane*, these rules (relating to mistake, frustration of purpose, or unconscionability) are still seen as exceptions to the rule. The starting point is still the inviolability of the bargain and strict liability for freely made covenants. Even in mistake and changed circumstances cases, courts explain the excusing of performance in terms of an agreement by the parties (tacitly or implicitly) as to which party bears the risk of the unforeseen circumstance.[57] Thus, at least verbal homage is still paid to the parties' subjective bargain.

---

54. See Berman, *Law and Revolution,* 281.
55. *Paradine v Jane,* 82 E.R. 519.
56. Ibid., 897–98.
57. See *Restatement (Second) of Contracts* §§ 152–154.

Protestant theology has had its influence on the way we understand and enforce agreements. Even Pryor and Hoshauer, who tend to argue that scholars like Witte and Berman overstate the influence of Protestant doctrine, acknowledge that these doctrines have influenced contract law. "[D]evelopments in this field of law [contracts] were informed by this distinctively English tradition of Protestant Christianity. And when these long-standing approaches to life and the law eventually exploded in Puritanism and the English Revolution, they helped channel developments in the law of contracts."[58] Professor Berman summarizes these changes thus:

> In subsequent centuries, many of the basic principles of the canon law of contract were adopted by secular law and eventually came to be justified on the basis of the will-theory and party autonomy. It is important to know, however, that originally they were based on a sin-theory and a theory of equity. Our contract law did not start from the proposition that every individual has a moral right to dispose of his property by means of making promises, and that in the interest of justice a promise should be legally enforced unless it offends reason or public policy. Our contract law started, on the contrary, from the theory that a promise created an obligation to God, and that for the salvation of souls God instituted the ecclesiastical and secular courts with the task, in part, of enforcing contractual obligations to the extent that such obligations are just.[59]

Property

Many of the same theological principles at work in the transformation of contract law influenced the development of post-Reformation property law. The rejection of the role of works, combined with the elevation of the individual moral sense at the expense of the social community, all joined together to transform property law from a law of personal relationships to a mere economic ordering based on contract.

Pre-Reformation property law was centered on human relationships. Property law prescribed the duties and corresponding rights of persons with respect to things.[60] Property law was not clearly distinguished from contract or other law of obligations to people.[61] Land was not

---

58. Pryor and Hoshauer, 299.

59. Berman, "The Religious Sources of General Contract Law," at 112.

60. See Brian M. McCall, *To Build the City of God: Living as Catholics in a Secular Age* (Kettering, Ohio: Angelico Press, 2014), 119–25.

61. See Berman, *Law and Revolution,* at 167.

"owned" but "held" pursuant to relationships in which "rights of possession, rights of use, and rights of disposal were linked with the landholder's duties to superiors, and privileges over subordinates, in the feudal chain."[62] These duties to people above and below one's station placed restrictions on the rights coupled with interests in property. Approximately between one fourth and one third of all land in Europe was held by church officeholders on behalf of the Church, and their rights with respect to disposal, ownership, and use were restricted by canon law to ensure that the land was used for the good of the Church.[63] Use and disposition of property were restricted by these relationships because material changes in the *status quo* with respect to property required the consent of the feudal overlord.[64]

Further, Catholic jurisprudence drew significant distinctions between rights of ownership and use of property. The towering jurist Gratian included texts in his *Decretum* that firmly established the right of acquisition and disposition of private property but qualified this right by the common ownership of all things.[65] Although the natural law provides for the private ownership of things, the ownership and use of things are two different concepts. St Thomas makes clear that although under the natural law it is lawful for people to own and possess things as their own, a man ought to use "external things not as his own, but as common."[66] Although law recognized the rights of private property, these rights came with duties that required one to use private property not exclusively for his own personal interest but for the common good.

The Protestant ideas discussed previously undermined this conception of property. Pryor and Hoshauer note that Reformation England elevated "contract to its principal place as the means of social organization"[67] and observed that changes in this period "marked the beginning of the shift from status to contract. . . . Just as contract (in the form of leases) had replaced feudal tenure in the countryside, so, too, contract became the principal tool of control in the newly industrialized urban centers."[68] Longstanding relationships with respect to things were replaced by individually bargained for contracts.

By shifting property law away from status to contract, property became disassociated from personal relationships (status) and became

---

62. Ibid., at 167.
63. Ibid.
64. Ibid., at 332.
65. Gratian, *Decretum* d. 1, c. 7, §3.
66. *Summa Theologica*, II–II, q. 66, art. 2.
67. Pryor and Hoshauer, 305.
68. Ibid., 306–08.

rooted in disembodied documents that gave rise to strict liability. Property law shifted from being based on relationships of persons *with respect to things* to relationship of persons *with things*. Property rights were more appropriately described as a right in a thing (*in rem*) as opposed to a right to a thing (*ad rem*). The difference in language, although subtle, is significant. *Ad rem* implies a relationship with a person, giving rise to a right to the thing; whereas *in rem* locates the legal relationship in the object. As one was entitled to the full benefit of his bargain in contract, one was entitled to the free use of the thing in which he had rights. Thus, limitations on the disposition and ownership of property began to be seen as infringements on autonomous individuals with respect to "their" property rather than being naturally inherent in the very nature of property.

In England, this transformation of legal theory was reflected in specific changes to property law. In the Puritan period, English law abolished all feudal tenures and made land freehold.[69] Rather than holding property pursuant to a feudal relationship, property was now held free of any relationship. This change abolished the necessity of obtaining consent from the feudal landlord before disposing of land or transforming its use.[70] Thus, individual owners were free to use their innate moral sense to do with property as they saw fit pursuant to their private judgment. If they misused their property to harm the common good of their neighbors or deplete a resource from future generations, that was not the concern of the earthly kingdom and this work had no effect upon eternal salvation.

The abandonment of the common use of property reinvigorated the enclosure movement, which had been forestalled by pre-Reformation legal restrictions on the use of property.[71] A common right of use to unenclosed pastures was a practice consistent with the Catholic understanding of property. The owner of estates held them as private property but was bound to respect the ancient rights of the people living on the land to use the common areas. His private ownership was subject to this common use. Yet, once property was detached from these status relationships, the law was unable to justify restricting the erection of enclosures to keep the people off the land in which the owner held freehold rights. The Puritan Commonwealth of the English Civil War finally abolished the last remaining legal restraints on enclosure.[72] Just

---

69. See Berman, *Law and Revolution*, 331–32.
70. See Ibid., 332.
71. See Fanfani, 185.
72. Berman, *Law and Revolution*, 331–33.

as contract law developed into strict liability for voluntary covenants, property law shifted to strictly individual rights of dominion over things rather than being interwoven into complex social relationships.

Conclusion

It should not be surprising that theological novelties as significant as those involved in the Reformation would have far reaching consequences. Although we can still trace our current legal system back to the pre-Reformation legal system, the underlying jurisprudential assumptions and even particular rules of law reflect the influence of Protestant teaching on salvation by faith alone, the two kingdoms, individual interpretation of scripture, and the exaltation of the individual moral sense of conscience. These ideas, although preserving in Protestant countries the overall procedural and terminological structures of the prior legal order, fundamentally transformed the understanding of laws governing economic activity. Amintore Fanfani concludes his study of Catholicism, Protestantism, and capitalism by arguing that although Protestantism did not invent individualist capitalism (for the spirit of it had been attempting to assert itself throughout human history), its doctrines did work to remove the ancient obstacles to its widespread adoption. He concludes, "[W]e may say that the religious revolution was able to produce results of most universal consequence where it first took possession of the state. In no European country did this come about more swiftly than in Catholic England...."[73] Therefore, it is not surprising that in England and her legal heir, America, the effects of Protestantism on law are the most pronounced.

73. Fanfani, 184.

9

STEM and the Reformation

Astronomy, Metallurgy, and Economics

Fr. Brian Mužas

Introduction

THERE IS A DEBATE in the United States concerning the minimum wage. Those who favor increasing the federal minimum wage argue that its current value is too little on which to live; that boosting the minimum wage will boost job creation and economic growth; that the falling value of the minimum wage is a primary cause of wage inequality between low- and middle-class workers; and that most Americans, including conservatives, support increasing the minimum wage. Those opposed argue that many businesses are unable to pay their workers more, and if asked to do so will lay people off, reduce hiring, or even close down; that increases would make it more difficult for unskilled or inexperienced workers to find jobs or become upwardly mobile; and that blanket federal action which does not account for regional cost-of-living variations could hurt low-income communities.[1]

Upon digging a bit deeper into the foundations of the arguments advanced by both sides, however, it is striking how one side emphasizes the inherent value of labor while the other side stresses how much labor is valued. I suggest that this more fundamental difference can be connected to the different worldviews found in medieval Catholicism and Reformation Protestantism, frameworks of reality that persist today. I suggest further that the minimum wage debate is but one example of how the Reformation continues to affect contemporary life. In this

---

1. A well-sourced primer on the history of the minimum wage is "Background of the Issue: 'Should the Federal Minimum Wage Be Increased?'" which can be found on-line at http://minimum-wage.procon.org/view.resource.php?resourceID=006456. When accessed on 22 June 2016, it had last been updated on 31 March 2016.

chapter I will explore the more general question of science and the Reformation by exploring the three historical examples of STEM (Science, Technology, Engineering, and Math) subjects. In terms of STEM content, the three cases I will discuss are astronomy, metallurgy, and economics. In terms of the Reformation's legacy, these three cases will provide examples of Lutheran, Anglican, and Calvinist influence.

There are competing narratives about the relationship between the development of Christianity and the occurrence of the Scientific Revolution in the West. Indeed, some argue that Protestantism provided the groundwork for the rise of the Scientific Revolution. While I will treat such approaches in more detail below, I bracket this debate by focusing instead on epistemic communities, both ecclesial and scientific, which I will define below.

This chapter is an exploration, not a hypothesis test. In this spirit, after a brief survey of prior work, I will provide an introduction to the concept of STEM subjects following the definitions of the US National Science Foundation (NSF). Next I will provide the definition, and explain the relevance, of epistemic communities. Then, after briefly explaining the rationale behind their selection, I will examine three case studies that illustrate the influence of Lutheranism on astronomy, Anglicanism on metallurgy, and Calvinism on economics in the context of epistemic communities. The chapter will end with observations and conclusions.

Prior Work

There are at least three streams of literature with which one must contend in order to explore coherently the relationship between STEM and the Reformation. These literatures include: first of all, those which treat Christianity (or particular branches of Christianity) as a source of science or the Scientific Revolution; secondly, those which treat Christianity (or a particular branch of Christianity, or even religion in general) as antithetical to science and the Scientific Revolution; and, thirdly, those which attempt dispassionately to trace the interaction of Christianity (or branches of Christianity) with science or the Scientific Revolution. Sometimes these streams overlap (as, for example, when a work treats one branch of Christianity as congenial to science but another as antithetical to science).

Considering the first stream of literature, some authors draw parallels between the Reformation and the scientific enterprise that resulted in, or is labeled as, the Scientific Revolution. Although to reduce the mention of such authors to single lines does not do justice to their research and argumentation, a common thread in their work can be represented fairly by the following quotation from David Wootton: "And so, before the Scientific Revolution was a revolution, it was a reformation."[2] According to this line of reasoning, human understanding of nature was clarified and deepened by recourse to principles advanced by the Reformation.

Some authors make bolder, or at least more explicit and specific, claims. One author, E.L. Hebden Taylor, concludes, "It is thus no accident that first the scientific and then the industrial revolutions arose in the homelands of Calvinist rather than Roman Catholic Christianity. Without the religious revolution of the Reformation the scientific and industrial revolutions would never have been possible." The preceding idea shows a confluence of the first and second streams: one branch of Christianity is hospitable to science while another branch is not. Hebden Taylor even goes so far as to assert, "Alone of all modern interpretations of Christianity, Calvinism can still provide us today with an integration of religion and science in the ultimate Christian theistic environment of all created reality."[3] Such branches of the literature are often impassioned and adamant.

Although a considerable part of the first two branches of the literature is polemical, much of what has been written is more balanced. Indeed, according to this third stream of literature, "historical study does not reveal science and Christianity locked in deadly combat; nor does it disclose an interaction of unfailing support and mutual compatibility. The relationship between science and Christianity proves to be much more intricate and interesting than these traditional alternatives allow."[4]

Nevertheless, all of the preceding discussions stand and fall on what the terms "science" and "religion" mean. This point is not an idle one. The meanings of these words are historically conditioned, and the above literatures depend on a recent understanding, a paradigm perhaps three centuries old. *Scientia* and *religio*, once understood as interior virtues (the one, an intellectual habit; the other, a moral habit), came, over time, to be understood as exteriorized bodies of knowledge.

Peter Harrison explains that, in the early modern period, the philosophical exercises and bodies of knowledge employed in the inculcation of the interior virtues of *scientia* and *religio* came to stand in for the

2. David Wootton, *The Invention of Science: A New History of the Scientific Revolution* (New York: Harper, 2015), 34.

3. E.L. Hebden Taylor, "The Reformation and the Development of Modern Science," *Churchman* 82, no. 2 (1968): 87–103.

4. David C. Lindberg and Ronald L. Numbers, eds. *When Science and Christianity Meet* (Chicago: The University of Chicago Press, 2003), 5.

things themselves in their entirety. The content of catechisms that had once been understood as techniques for instilling an interior piety now came to be thought of as encapsulating the essence of some objective thing—religion. Religion was vested in creeds rather than in the hearts of the faithful. In a related process, the label "*scientia*," which had traditionally referred to both a mental disposition and a formal body of knowledge, came to be associated with the latter alone, eventually giving rise to the objective thing—science. While there had once been a close correspondence between science considered to be a virtue and science understood in terms of demonstrable knowledge, from this period onward, science was increasingly thought of as a body of systematic knowledge or a method that existed quite independent of the dispositions of its practitioners.[5]

As a result of this development, which came after the time period of Reformers like Luther and Calvin, it seems wise to bypass or leapfrog much of the prior literature by adopting a standpoint calculated to avoid as much confusion as possible. Indeed, David B. Wilson argues, "Understanding the [Galileo] episode historically requires loosening constraints too easily imposed by the words science and religion."[6] I take Wilson's requirement seriously and apply it to other historical cases. As a result, rather than focus on the Scientific Revolution, this chapter examines some consequences of the Reformation through the lenses of STEM and epistemic communities. It is toward these terms that our attention now turns.

What is STEM?

STEM stands for Science, Technology, Engineering, and Math. The US National Science Foundation uses a broad definition of STEM that encompasses subjects including "psychology and the social sciences (e.g., political science, economics) as well as the so-called core sciences and engineering (e.g., physics, chemistry, mathematics)."[7]

---

5. Peter Harrison, *The Territories of Science and Religion* (Chicago: The University of Chicago Press, 2015), 84. For the argument "that the phrase 'Galileo's religion *versus* the Church's science' is as meaningful (or meaningless) as the usual designation: 'Galileo's science *versus* the Church's religion,'" see David B. Wilson, "Galileo's Religion *versus* the Church's Science? Rethinking the History of Science and Religion," *Physics in Perspective* 1, no. 1 (1999): 65–84.

6. Wilson, 82.

7. Heather B. Gonzalelz and Jeffrey J. Kuenzi, "Science, Technology, Engineering, and Mathematics (STEM) Education: A Primer," Congressional Research Service R42642 (August 1, 2012): 2.

This chapter follows NSF practice. In particular, recognized fields of study include physics and astronomy, materials research (including metallic materials), and social sciences (including economics but excluding business administration).[8] Thus, the three cases treated in this chapter fall under STEM.

STEM is a useful concept in this investigation. All human civilizations and cultures have knowledge of the natural world and understandings of how quantities and magnitudes are related. These civilizations and cultures apply this knowledge and understanding in practical fashion to life, society, and the natural and built environments. The preceding two statements could be reframed as follows: All human civilizations and cultures have scientific and mathematical knowledge, and they engineer technology to leverage these insights. Thus, people in every time and place can be said to have had access to STEM. We can thus use STEM as a conceptual tool to avoid the potentially problematic assumptions built into the concept of a Scientific Revolution.

What is an Epistemic Community?

In the study of international relations, the term *epistemic community* is used to refer to a worldwide network of technical or scientific professionals or experts whose expertise can affect policy decisions. The seminal definition of this term, however, is more inclusive: "a network of professionals with recognized expertise and competence in a particular domain and an authoritative claim to policy-relevant knowledge within that domain or issue-area." Moreover, an epistemic community is characterized by (1) *a shared set of normative and principled beliefs*, which provide a value-based rationale for the social action of community members; (2) *shared causal beliefs*, which are derived from their analysis of practices leading or contributing to a central set of problems in their domain and which then serve as the basis for elucidating the multiple linkages between possible policy actions and desired outcomes; (3) *shared notions of validity*—that is, inter-subjective, internally-defined criteria for weighing and validating knowledge in the domain of their expertise; and (4) *a common policy enterprise*—that is, a set of common practices associated with a set of problems to which their professional

---

8. National Science Foundation, "Graduate Research Fellowship Program (GRFP)," nsf15597 (August 4, 2015). When accessed from http://www.nsf.gov/publications/pub_su mm.jsp?ods_key=nsf15597&org=NSF on June 22, 2016, this document was available through three links in HTML, PDF, and TXT format, respectively.

competence is directed, presumably out of the conviction that human welfare will be enhanced as a consequence.[9]

The concept of an epistemic community is useful for the present investigation because, as will be illustrated, both ecclesial and scientific networks often conform to the above definition and exhibit many of the listed characteristics. Thus, it is important to bear in mind that epistemic communities can be identified by shared causal and principled beliefs, a consensual knowledge base, and a common policy enterprise.[10]

Characteristics of the Case Studies in this Investigation

The cases related below are meant to be exemplifications; consequently, I selected cases with as much variety as possible. One aspect of variability is the branch of Reformation Christianity that comes to the fore: the cases respectively emphasize Lutheran, Anglican, and Calvinist Christianity. Another source of variation is that of time period. In terms of the principal Protestant influences, the selected cases date from as early as the sixteenth century to as late as the eighteenth century. Some relevant Catholic roots date from even earlier periods.

STEM, following NSF practice, is broadly defined. As a result, great variability is available regarding subject matter. The disciplines treated in this chapter range from astronomy (a pure science) to metallurgy (an applied or engineering science) and economics (a social science). The type of epistemic community involvement provides further diversity. The first case indicates how one epistemic community can affect another. The second case traces the destruction of an epistemic community and assesses the after-effects. The final case illustrates how different epistemic communities, with different beliefs and commitments, can, in parallel, give rise to different theoretical frameworks and conclusions.

The reader ought to bear in mind that this chapter presents a phenomenological examination. I do not intend to carry out within it a rigorous hypothesis test. However, this investigation could inform a test of the "null hypothesis" that there is no difference between a Catholic and a Protestant milieu concerning scientific inquiry.

---

9. Peter M. Haas, "Introduction: Epistemic Communities and International Policy Coordination," *International Organization* 46, no. 1 (Winter 1992): 3. Emphasis added.

10. Emanuel Adler and Peter M. Haas, "Conclusion: Epistemic Communities, World Order, and the Creation of a Reflective Research Program," *International Organization* 46, no. 1 (Winter 1992): 367–90.

Astronomy: Lutheranism,
Copernican Cosmology, and the Catholic Response

The story of Galileo and the Roman Catholic Church is often told more or less as follows: Galileo Galilei was born in Pisa, Italy on February 15, 1564. A pioneering observer of nature, Galileo constructed a telescope and supported the heliocentric theory of Nicolaus Copernicus, a theory which placed the sun, rather than planet Earth, at the center of the solar system. This theory challenged biblical cosmology and Roman Catholic teaching authority, so Galileo was twice accused of heresy by the Roman Catholic Church for his beliefs. Convicted of heretical heliocentrism by the Inquisition, Galileo was placed under house arrest until he died in Arcetri, Italy, on January 8, 1642. Today, of course, it is well know that Earth and the other planets of the solar system orbit the sun. The moral of the story is that the Catholic Church abhors science, refuses to abandon outdated teachings, and is not infallible.[11]

The conventional story, even when presented in greater depth than this, often misses a number of important points. Let us first consider Nicolaus Copernicus (1473–1543) himself. Without a doubt, Copernicus was a Polish canon. Despite some modern authors who identify him as a priest, however, there is no evidence that Copernicus was ordained. His scientific ability was recognized in professional and ecclesial circles. Encouraged by church and academic colleagues, Copernicus wrote *De revolutionibus orbium coelestuim* (*On the Revolutions of the Celestial Spheres*) which was published the year he died (even though he had formulated the theory earlier). Although indebted to the geocentric, or earth-centered, approaches of Aristotle and Ptolemy, Copernicus proposed a heliocentric, or sun-centered, model of the solar system. His model simplified the calculation of the positions of heavenly bodies in the sky. Copernicus himself saw his forerunners in Heraclides of Pontus, an ancient Greek heliocentrist,[12] as well as Aristarchus of Samos.[13] More immediately, however, he was indebted not only to a "sophisti-

---

11. This thumbnail sketch used as a springboard the article "Galileo Biography," written by the editors of the Biography.com website published by A&E Television Networks. Although no publication date is listed, the article was accessed at http://www.bio graphy.com/people/galileo-9305220 on June 29, 2016. Biography.com attempts to provide disinterested articles; some of the more polemical language is adapted from less dispassionate sources. References to full biographies of Galileo are provided in a footnote later in this section.

12. Peter Harrison, *The Bible, Protestantism, and the Rise of Natural Science* (Cambridge: Cambridge University Press, 1998), 83.

13. Copernicus cited Aristarchus in an unpublished but surviving manuscript of *De revolutionibus*. The reference is not present in the published manuscript. See Owen

cated . . . medieval tradition" but to an epistemic community: a "small, but active and growing, community of competent astronomers."[14]

No controversy was occasioned by the publication of Copernicus' book. From the standpoint of Roman Catholicism, even at the Council of Trent (1545–1563) neither Copernicus' heliocentric theory nor calendar reform (which ultimately would use tables computed from Copernicus' calculations) were discussed.[15] Serious Catholic critique of Copernican cosmology did not begin until the Galileo controversy.

The literature on Protestant critiques of Copernicus is confused and thus hard to describe in general terms. Nevertheless, the Copernican theory certainly did conflict with some Protestant theology of the time, as can be seen in quotations from John Calvin. In his *Commentaries on the First Book of Moses Called Genesis*, Calvin wrote, "We indeed are not ignorant that the circuit of the heavens is finite, and that the earth, like a little globe, is placed in the centre." In his *Commentary on the Book of Psalms*, Calvin wrote of Psalm 93:1:

> The heavens revolve daily, and, immense as is their fabric and inconceivable the rapidity of their revolutions, we experience no concussion—no disturbance in the harmony of their motion. The sun, through varying its course every diurnal revolution, returns annually to the same point. The planets, in all their wanderings, maintain their respective positions. How could the earth hang suspended in the air were it not upheld by God's hand? By what means could it maintain itself unmoved, while the heavens above are in constant rapid motion, did not its Divine Maker fix and establish it?[16]

These quotations from Calvin illustrate an apparent conflict between his ideas and the ideas of Copernicus.

The literature on Martin Luther is more questionable. Although none of Luther's extensive writings treat Copernicus directly or indirectly, Luther is said to have remarked indirectly about Copernicus over dinner:

> So it goes now. Whoever wants to be clever must agree with nothing others esteem. He must do something of his own. This is what that fel-

Gingerich, "Did Copernicus Owe a Debt to Aristarchus?" *Journal for the History of Astronomy* 16, no. 1 (February 1985): 37–42.

14. David C. Lindberg, *The Beginnings of Western Science: The European Scientific Tradition in Philosophical, Religious, and Institutional Context, Prehistory to AD 1450*, 2nd ed. (Chicago: The University of Chicago Press, 2007), 267.

15. Robert S. Westman, *The Copernican Question: Prognostication, Skepticism, and Celestial Order* (Los Angeles: University of California Press, 2011), 194.

16. Quoted in Edward Rosen, "Calvin's Attitude toward Copernicus," *Journal of the History of Ideas* 21, no. 3 (July–September 1960): 431–41.

low does who wishes to turn the whole of astronomy upside down. Even in these things that are thrown into disorder I believe the Holy Scriptures, for Joshua commanded the sun to stand still and not the earth.[17]

Another source reports Luther used the word "fool" rather than the word "fellow" to mean Copernicus. These offhand remarks, alluding to the Battle of Gibeon in the Book of Joshua, were allegedly made four years before the publication of *De revolutionibus*.[18]

Philip Melanchthon, systematic theologian and collaborator with Martin Luther, provides a more interesting and nuanced case. For example, "It has been pointed out ... that Melanchthon promoted a reading of Copernicus in such a way that Copernicus' predictions about the angular position of a planet were accepted but his cosmological claims ignored."[19] Scholars have offered different explanations for this observation. The most convincing account I have encountered is that of Sachiko Kusukawa, who argues:

> Copernicus' heliocentric claims could not have had a meaningful place in Melanchthon's system of philosophy.... [T]he goal of Melanchthon's philosophy was man.... Hence in order for Melanchthon's natural philosophy to be what it was intended to be, the earth, man's habitation, *had* to be the centre of the physical universe, i.e., the centre of God's Creation.... Copernicus' heliocentric claims were a far cry from what Melanchthon intended to achieve in his natural philosophy.... [W]hich cosmological system to choose was not the foremost question.... That is why Melanchthon brushed aside Copernicus' cosmological claim.[20]

The above is not to say that Copernicus was inconsequential to Melanchthon. On the contrary, "Copernicus was important for Melanchthon because of his contribution to natural philosophical astrology. [His] calculative improvements implied better accuracy in predicting planetary positions, a crucial point for astrology."[21] From the conventional wisdom of the present, such an approach may seem puzzling, "but for Melanchthon, he read and used Copernicus in the particular

---

17. Donald H. Kobe, "Copernicus and Martin Luther: An Encounter between Science and Religion," *American Journal of Physics* 66, no. 3 (March 1998): 190–96.

18. Ibid.

19. Sachiko Kusukawa, *The Transformation of Natural Philosophy: The Case of Philip Melanchthon* (Cambridge: Cambridge University Press, 1995), 171.

20. Ibid., 172.

21. Ibid., 172–73.

way that he did, because Copernicus was useful for his natural philosophical astrology."[22]

A few points should be noted. One point is that not all Protestantism falls neatly into a pro-Copernican or anti-Copernican camp. A second point is that Melanchthon's appropriation of the computational convenience of the Copernican system is reminiscent of the Catholic response prior to Galileo (a completely different question situated in the context of a pronounced Protestant critique that I will outline below). As a result of such points, it becomes clear that there was room for Lutheran and Catholic agreement on Copernicus and on a heliocentric solar system.

Of course, there is a problem with identifying a "Lutheran" approach to the natural world. Charlotte Methuen states, "Not everyone who was a Lutheran in the sense of being a follower or an associate of Luther would have been identified as Lutheran in the later, confessional sense. This is particularly true of Melanchthon...."[23] However, we can avoid this problem by using instead the category of epistemic community. Although "[m]odern scholars are ambiguous in their assessment of the authenticity of Melanchthon's 'Lutheran' faith," nevertheless there was a "large overlap of interests and concerns of Luther and of Melanchthon, most significant of which was the pursuit of Reform in order to establish the teaching of justification by faith alone,"[24] known as *sola fides*. This indication of overlapping interests, concerns, and commitments flags the existence of an epistemic community in this instance. Roman Catholicism can also be seen as an epistemic community, as indicated by its understanding of itself: through the marks (e.g., catholicity or universality), attributes (e.g., authority), and Great Commission (an enterprise of international scope) of the Church.[25]

From *sola fides* we move to *sola scriptura*, the Protestant claim that sacred scripture is the supreme authority in all matters of doctrine and practice. (Other authorities exist in this Protestant view, but they are subordinate to, and corrected by, the Word of God as preserved in written form in the Bible.) This Protestant claim, and the critiques of Roman

---

22. Ibid., 173.

23. Charlotte Methuen, *Science and Theology in the Reformation: Studies in Theological Interpretation and Astronomical Observation in Sixteenth-Century Germany* (London: T&T Clark, 2008), 110.

24. Kusukawa, 4 and 5.

25. Straightforward and brief explanations of the marks and attributes of the Church can be found in the *Baltimore Catechism*. On July 3, 2016, the 1891 version of the *Baltimore Catechisms Nos. 1, 2,* and 3 could be found online at http://www.boston-catholic-journal.com/baltimore_catechism.pdf. The marks and attributes are treated in Q.126–135 and Q.517–573. For the Great Commission, see the Gospel of Matthew 28:18–20.

Catholicism which flowed from it, tinted the lenses through which the Catholic Church viewed the Galileo affair as well as those through which the Church viewed its own response to Galileo. This influence can be understood by thinking about the Lutheran movement as an epistemic community. Following Kusukawa, let us think about how Melanchthon's natural philosophy was a *Lutheran* one to the extent that his use of authors and his aim in writing natural philosophy textbooks can be accounted for through his Lutheran conviction:

> Melanchthon saw in natural philosophy a potent response to issues which he believed to be seriously jeopardizing Luther's cause; he reinterpreted classical and contemporary authors along Lutheran principles; and he made natural philosophy an integral part of a pedagogy which was aimed at establishing and consolidating Luther's message. This understanding of natural philosophy ... formed a unity at Wittenberg in achieving a single goal: the knowledge of the Providence of God in this world. It is precisely for this same reason—to know the Providence of God—and not because he wanted to be "progressive," that Melanchthon also adopted the findings ... of Copernicus in the particular way that he did.[26]

By the time Galileo sought to change doctrine on the basis of his hypothesis, the Catholic Church was extremely sensitive to the charge that Catholicism was anti-scriptural. The Catholic Church reacted to Galileo, at least in part, due to this sensitivity. Thus, the brief sketch of the Galileo controversy given at the beginning of this section is incomplete and misleading at best.[27] Galileo wanted doctrine to change on the basis of an unproven hypothesis, and the Catholic Church would brook no such thing.[28]

---

26. Ibid., 4.

27. For more detail, two notable Galileo biographies from the past decade are J.L. Heilbron, *Galileo* (New York: Oxford University Press, 2010) and David Wootton, *Galileo: Watcher of the Skies* (New Haven: Yale University Press, 2010). Heilbron's approach is more finely detailed while Wootton's is more speculative regarding Galileo's motives. Wootten thinks Galileo to be a closet unbeliever while Heilbron highlights Galileo's scientific missteps. Both authors criticize Galileo for needlessly alienating his Jesuit colleagues. (Treatment of the Jesuit order as an epistemic community is beyond the scope of this chapter.) While Wootton's account seems more likely to appeal to the general reader, Heilbron's richer scientific detail make it the more comprehensive treatment.

28. Indeed, according to Einstein's relativity theory (and even in classical relativity, often called "Galilean" relativity in Galileo's honor), there are no preferred reference systems. Thus, it is simply a matter of convenience to take the sun as the center of the solar system. See, for example, Owen Gingerich, "Astronomy," *The Encounter Between Christianity and Science*, Richard H. Bube, ed. (Grand Rapids: William B. Eerdmans, 1968), 109–33.

Although his focus is to analyze the supposed conflict between religion and science, the context of the Copernican and Galilean controversies is summarized well by Peter Harrison who writes:

> For a start, the Catholic Church endorsed the scientific consensus of the period, which, on the basis of the available evidence, held that the earth was stationary in the middle of the cosmos. To this extent it might be better to characterize the episode as a conflict *within* science (or, more strictly, within astronomy and natural philosophy) rather than between science and religion. Second, the first use of the Galileo affair for propaganda purposes was by Protestants seeking to discredit Catholics, so that it was initially given a role in conflicts *within* religion. Related to this is the fact that the Copernican hypothesis had first been postulated some eighty years before the trial of Galileo, and hence the context of the Protestant Reformation is a key to understanding why the papacy took steps at this particular time. Finally, even if it could be constructed as a science-religion conflict, the condemnation of Galileo was not typical of the Catholic Church's attitude toward the study of nature, since at the time the Church was the single most prominent supporter of astronomical research.[29]

Without intending to do so, however, Harrison drives home the point that Lutherans, and more generally Protestants, indeed gave rise to epistemic communities committed to particular enterprises and narratives, for:

> these are myths not only because they are historically dubious, but also because they fulfill a traditional function of myth—that of validating a particular point of view of reality and a set of social practices. This accounts for the persistence of these myths in spite of the best efforts of historians of science.[30]

Thus, our understanding of the history of Copernicus and Galileo can be aided by considering Protestantism and Catholicism as two mutually competing and mutually influencing epistemic communities.

---

29. Harrison (2015), 172–73.

30. Ibid., 173. Harrison thus lends support to Joseph Cardinal Ratzinger who, in a speech in 1990, quoted philosopher Paul Feyerabend, a noted agnostic and skeptic, as writing, "The Church at the time of Galileo was much more faithful to reason than Galileo himself, and also took into consideration the ethical and social consequences of Galileo's doctrine. Its verdict against Galileo was rational and just, and revisionism can be legitimized solely for motives of political opportunism." Joseph Ratzinger, "The Crisis of Faith in Science," in *A Turning Point in Europe: The Church and Modernity in the Europe of Upheavals* (Rome: Paoline Editions, 1992), 76–79. A translation by the *National Catholic Reporter* was posted on January 14, 2008 at http://ncronline.org/news/ratzingers-1990-remarks-galileo. This translation was accessed June 22, 2016.

Metallurgy: Henry VIII and Monasteries

Henry VIII began the process of transforming Catholic England into a Protestant country. Although the precise narrative of this complex history is contested in the literature, it is agreed that Henry remained an observant Catholic (and even received the title of "Defender of the Faith" from Pope Leo X) until 1527 when he appealed to Pope Clement VII for an annulment of his marriage to Catherine of Aragon (a marriage for which Pope Julius II had to grant a dispensation in the first place since Catherine had previously been married to Henry's late brother Arthur). The conventional narrative is that the pope's refusal to grant an annulment triggered Henry's rejection of the papal supremacy that he had previously defended.[31]

Be that as it may, it was Henry who pressed both the bishops and Parliament to create the structure of the Church of England between 1532 and 1537 by means of a number of statutes dealing with the relationship between king and pope. These included: the Statute in Restraint of Appeals, which made introducing papal bulls into England punishable by death; the Supplication against the Ordinaries and the Submission of the Clergy, which asserted royal supremacy over the Church; the Ecclesiastical Appointments Act, which required clergy to elect bishops nominated by the Crown; and the Act of Supremacy, which asserted that the king was the earthly head of the Church of England (backed up by the Treasons Act which made it a capital offence to refuse the Oath of Supremacy, which acknowledged the king as such).

The above actions were supplemented by a series of legal and administrative measures from 1536 to 1541 to disband Catholic monasteries and other, similar houses of religious life. One of the monasteries thus suppressed was Rievaulx Abbey in Yorkshire, a Cistercian house closed in December of 1538.

The Cistercian monks are well described as an epistemic community. An international network of religious, their order stressed manual labor and self-sufficiency. They can be considered professionals—and not just of the religious type—because their expertise and competence in relevant technical knowledge was recognized throughout medieval Chris-

---

31. For different accounts of the narrative, see Gregory Johnson, "Competing Narratives: Recent Historiography of the English Reformation under Henry VIII," St. Louis University (Fall 1997), available online at http://gregscouch.homestead.com/files/Henry8.html, accessed June 25, 2016. See also G. R. Elton, *Reform and Reformation: England, 1509–1558* (Cambridge: Harvard University Press, 1977). For a political argument that Henry might have rejected papal supremacy even had he not required an annulment, see A. F. Pollard, *Henry VIII* (London: Longmans, Green & Company, 1919), 230ff.

tendom. Furthermore, Cistercian monks were notable for their values and enterprising endeavors.

The Cistercians, well known for their agricultural prowess, were also technologically savvy, not least of all in metallurgy. According to Jean Gimpel:

> Every monastery had a model factory, often as large as the church and only several feet away, and waterpower drove the machinery of the various industries located on its floor. . . . It has been suggested that the forge at Fontenay operated with a water-powered trip-hammer as early as the twelfth century. This seems plausible since the Cistercians were always on the lookout for new techniques to increase the efficiency of their monasteries.[32]

One such increase in efficiency was the development of a precursor to the modern blast furnace for smelting iron ore. Laskill, a satellite of Rievaulx Abbey, was the site of a medieval blast furnace—to this author's knowledge, the only one yet identified in Great Britain, and one of the most efficient blast furnaces of its time. We know this fact because the site today is "dominated by a prominent mount of slag,"[33] the by-product of refining iron ore. The characteristics of the slag point to advanced technology. Slag from typical, less-efficient furnaces of the time, contain a substantial concentration of iron, but the slag found at Laskill is low in iron content.

High-iron slag indicates a relatively ineffective production process: the considerable iron content of the slag indicates an inefficient process since much iron has not been extracted from the ore. In contrast, low-iron slag indicated a highly effective production process: the paucity of iron in the slag indicates that the process was much more successful at extracting iron from raw ore. Indeed, the low iron content in the slag points to the conclusion that Laskill's furnace produced cast iron with efficiency similar to that of a modern blast furnace.

The dissolution of the monasteries resulting from the English Reformation was disastrous for the English Cistercians, who, along with other religious orders, lost assets and land. At Rievaulx Abbey, the monks may have been on the verge of building furnaces for the production of cast iron, but Laskill's furnace did not survive Henry's dissolu-

---

32. Jean Gimpel, *The Medieval Machine: The Industrial Revolution of the Middle Ages* (New York: Holt, Rinehart and Winston, 1976), 67. This work was first published in French under the title *La revolution industrielle du Moyen Age*.

33. R. W. Vernon, G. McDonnell, and A. Schmidt, "An Integrated Geophysical and Analytical Appraisal of Early Iron-Working: Three Case Studies," *Journal of the Historical Metallurgy Society* 32, no. 2 (1998): 75.

tion in the late 1530s. Indeed, the type of blast furnace pioneered at Laskill did not spread outside Rievaulx; an agreement in 1541 with the Earl of Rutland refers only to less-sophisticated bloomeries.[34]

Henry's dissolution had an impact far beyond the English Cistercians, however. Consider the Cistercians from an epistemic community perspective. If the Cistercians were an epistemic community with advanced furnace technology, one would expect them to spread the technology for the sake of the common good. In fact, according to Bradford University archaeo-metallurgist Gerry McDonnell, "One of the key things is that the Cistercians had a regular meeting of abbots every year and they had the means of sharing technological advances across Europe." As is to be expected of an epistemic community, a network is present. McDonnell continues, "They effectively had a stranglehold on iron." The Cistercians thus had the expertise and competence expected of an epistemic community. Finally, McDonnel states, "They had the potential to move to blast furnaces that produced nothing but cast iron. They were poised to do it on a large scale." Hence, the Cistercians had the societal relevance expected of an epistemic community. However, McDonnell noted, "The break-up of the monasteries broke up this network of technology transfer," and so "by breaking up the virtual monopoly, Henry VIII effectively broke up that [large-scale] potential."[35]

The English Reformation thus destroyed an epistemic community—and with it, a network of technology transfer. The cost of this breakup is hard to know. However, some historians believe that the suppression of the English monasteries may have stamped out an industrial revolution. In the assessment of McDonnell, "Without the Reformation, it is possible that the seeds of industrial Britain could have been sown in the tranquil cloisters of North Yorkshire."[36] Although this chapter is not a rigorous hypothesis test, such a conclusion nevertheless poses a serious challenge to the argument of Hebden Taylor that the Reformation was a necessary condition for the Industrial Revolution.

Economics: Calvinism and the Theory of Value

Hebden Taylor's treatment of Calvinism and the development of the Industrial Revolution permits a convenient segue to Calvinism and the

34. H.R. Schubert, *History of the British Iron and Steel Industry from c. 450 BC to AD 1775* (London: Routledge, 1957), 395–397.

35. David Derbyshire, "Henry 'stamped out Industrial Revolution,'" *The Daily Telegraph*, Friday, June 21, 2002.

36. Ibid.

development of different schools of economic thought. In particular, Catholic and Calvinist economists came to think about value in different ways depending upon how subjective and objective factors were taken into account.

The first school of thought, a subjective theory of value, is indebted to thirteenth-century Franciscan Pierre de Jean Olivi. Olivi contended that three factors determine economic value: scarcity (*raritas*), usefulness (*virtuositas*), and desiredness (*complacibilitas*).[37] The effect of scarcity, or supply, is clear: the more rare the good, the more valuable the good (and *vice versa*). Olivi's contribution to value theory stems from the crucial insight that utility should be divided into usefulness and desirability, one objective criterion and one subjective—and it is the subjective component that determines price.[38] Thus, Olivi proposed a subjective value theory based on subjective utility. Bernadine of Siena followed Olivi's approach 150 years later. Others continued and refined this approach as well. In the 1500s Luis Saravía de la Calle wrote:

> Those who measure the just price by the labour, costs, and risk incurred by the person who deals in the merchandise or produces it, or by the cost of transport or the expense of traveling ... or by what he has to pay the factors for their industry, risk, and labour, are greatly in error.... For the just price arises from the abundance or scarcity of goods, merchants, and money ... and not from costs, labour, and risk.... Why should a bale of linen brought overland from Brittany at great expense be worth more than one which is transported cheaply by sea?... Why should a book written out by hand be worth more than one which is printed, when the latter is better though it costs less to produce? ... The just price is found not by counting the cost but by the common estimation.[39]

Jesuits, including Juan de Lugo, concurred with their predecessors. De Lugo argued:

> Price fluctuates not because of the intrinsic and substantial perfection of the articles ... but on account of their utility in respect to human need, and then only on account of estimation.... And we must take into account not only the estimation of prudent men but also of the

37. Murray N. Rothbard, *Economic Thought before Adam Smith: An Austrian Perspective on the History of Economic Thought*, Vol. 1 (Brookfield, VT: Edward Elgar Publishing Company, 1995), 60.

38. Ibid., 60–61.

39. Murray N. Rothbard, "New Light on the Prehistory of the Austrian School," in *The Foundations of Modern Austrian Economics*, ed. Edwin G. Dolan (Kansas City: Sheed & Ward, 1976), 55.

imprudent, if they are sufficiently numerous in a place. Communal estimation, even when foolish, raises the natural price of goods, since price is derived from estimation. The natural price is raised by abundance of buyers and money, and lowered by contrary factors.[40]

Like Luis Saravía de la Calle, Juan de Lugo emphasizes the importance of common estimation. Nevertheless, it is important to recognize that subjective value theory has nothing to do with moral relativism; rather, it has to do with human choice and its implications. Sound economic theory must take into account the values that underlie human acts—values that, incidentally, need not necessarily be endorsed. The issue is one of understanding and not necessarily one of approbation.

In contrast to the above economists, Adam Smith, John Locke, and others developed a labor theory of value rather than a subjective theory of value. Indeed, this school of thought shows little to no interest in the school of thought elaborated above. Why might this be?

Max Weber argued that Calvin and his followers made work the center of social theology.[41] Emil Kauder argues that this centrality means:

All work in [such a Calvinist] society is invested with divine approval. Any social philosopher or economist exposed to Calvinism will be tempted to give labor an exalted position in his social or economic treatise, and no better way of extolling labor can be found than by combining work with value theory, traditionally the very basis of an economic system. Thus value becomes labor value, which is not merely a scientific device for measuring exchange rates but also the spiritual tie combining Divine Will with economic everyday life.[42]

Kauder concludes, "Locke and Adam Smith did not clearly see the relation between their theory of labor value and Calvin's glorification of work, although traces of it can be found in their writings."[43]

As noted above, epistemic communities are characterized by a set of shared causal beliefs as principles as well as a shared knowledge base and policy enterprise. One can find two such communities in the Catholic thinkers above and in the classical economists like Locke and Smith.

---

40. Alejandro A. Chaufen, *Faith and Liberty: The Economic Thought of the Late Scholastics* (Lanham, MD: Lexington, 2003), 84–85.

41. Max Weber, *The Protestant Ethic and the Spirit of Capitalism*, trans. Talcott Parsons (London: Routledge Classics, 2001).

42. Emil Kauder, *A History of Marginal Utility Theory* (Princeton: Princeton University Press, 1965), 5.

43. Ibid. Kauder quotes Locke's *Second Treatise on Civil Government* 31 and 33: "God . . . commanded man also to improve the world which God has given men for their own benefit."

For Locke and Smith in particular, their approach is especially connected to norms: Locke is particularly concerned with just acquisition, and Smith is best understood if *The Theory of Moral Sentiments* is taken as a whole, together with *An Inquiry into the Nature and Causes of the Wealth of Nations*.[44] Many of these norms, then, bear Calvinist fingerprints. For example, Smith, a Deist, was sympathetic to Presbyterianism (a form of Calvinism) throughout his life, so his Calvinist sympathies cohere well with an emphasis on a labor theory of value.[45]

Of course, it is natural to assess the two contrasting approaches to value in order to evaluate their respective merits. One way to do so is to compare how both approaches treat the so-called value paradox. This paradox comes about as follows: Consider a good that is essential to life like water or bread. Classical economists like Smith would say that such a good has high use value and thus would expect such a good to command a high price. In contrast, gold and jewels are not essential to support life; so classical economists would say that such goods have low use value and thus should command low prices. However, just the opposite is observed: water and bread are cheap while gold and jewels are expensive. Eighteenth- and nineteenth-century classical economists proposed a solution based on a dichotomous separation between use value and exchange value. This distinction perhaps strikes one as artificial.

Olivi, however, proposed a more elegant solution in the sense that his answer arises organically from his first principles. Consider the following. Goods like water and bread, although necessary, are also abundant and available. As a result, such goods command low market prices. In contrast, gold and jewels are much less common and less available. Hence, such goods command high market prices. When it comes to determining price, utility (usefulness and desiredness) is not absolute;

---

44. Locke is often misunderstood. He did not *per se* stress the labor theory of value. Locke's attention focused on just acquisition of un-owned goods. From Locke's state-of-nature perspective, few if any goods belong to individual owners as private property. In the state of nature, then, a person may claim a tract of land or a good by mixing labor with it, for example by clearing or plowing a field or by harvesting fruit from a tree. However, once goods are claimed by initial owners, the owners are free to do with their goods as they will: They have a moral and legal claim to the good and, since the good is now privately owned, there is no further need to apply labor to retain it. Hence, goods are legitimately private if they have been acquired by purchase or from the state of nature. In contrast to Locke, Smith does stress a labor theory of value. However, his approach to economics has to do with limiting human self-interest. For this reason *Wealth of Nations* presents competition as a limiting factor while *Theory of Moral Sentiments* explores psychology as a limiting factor.

45. Kauder, 6.

rather, it is relative to supply.[46] In sum, for Olivi and like-minded economists, the market is an arena in which prices for goods are formed out of the interaction of individuals with differing subjective utilities and valuations of the good. Just market prices, then, are not determined by referring to the objective qualities of the good, but by the interaction of subjective preferences on the market.[47]

Concerning Smith and Locke, there does not seem to be a smoking gun providing a definitive link between their thought and that of Calvin. Even Kauder concedes this point. Nevertheless, especially given Weber's arguments, the gun seems warm to the touch, and observing epistemic communal connections between Calvinism and the milieu of Locke and Smith makes the gun seem even warmer.

Observations and Conclusions

Writing about scholarly assessments of Melanchthon, Kusukawa perceives a problem that affects broader segments of scholarship:

> It is a problem . . . that has arisen for historians of science who have tried to understand the sixteenth century in terms of the "Scientific Revolution"—a movement which broke away from the Aristotelian qualitative explanation of natural phenomena to pursue the mathematical, quantitative explanation of natural change, and culminated in the triumph of experiment and observation over the occult, the superstitious and the religious. In other words, they have tried to tease out of the past some elements of "modern science," the end product of this "Revolution," thus dissociating those elements from the "non-modern," superstition and religion. Because it is a search for what modern historians themselves regard as respectable science or modernity, their history has been and forever will be about a past trapped in a strange mixture of "modernity" and "non-modernity."[48]

The three cases above have been explored using the concepts of STEM and epistemic communities to gain insight into the influence of the Reformation in a way that is different from prior authors. The framework of STEM has allowed this investigation to cover a broader range of topics than would otherwise have been possible; to bring into comparison similarities within or across differences, and to avoid potential and actual pitfalls present in the conceptual frameworks of prior literatures. Moreover, attention paid to epistemic communities illustrates how these

46. Rothbard, 61.
47. Ibid.
48. Kusukawa, 2.

communities can affect one another by their existence and interaction (as with the Catholic Church's response to Galileo being conditioned by Protestant criticism), can be crushed with demonstrable effect (as in the case of the Cistercian order), and can yield markedly different analyses and conclusions (as in the contrast between economic theories of value).

None of the facts presented in this chapter are new. However, it is hoped that new insights have been offered and that further insights will be inspired by this investigation. The concepts of STEM and epistemic communities allow us to assemble existing knowledge in a new way. Novel reassembly of existing knowledge permits us to question, refine, or re-conceptualize conventional understandings. For instance, different STEM disciplines and different branches of Protestantism invite new comparisons and contrasts. The different roles of epistemic communities in the past prompt questions about how such communities can influence us in the present and future. Moreover, fresh approaches avoid conceptual ruts and polemical problems found in some earlier writings. Calling to mind the example of the minimum wage debate with which this chapter began, we can appreciate anew how valuable reconceptualization is. For understandings—and misunderstandings— have real-world effects even in the present day.

10

Negative Liberty, Protestantism, and the War on Nature

Msgr. Ignacio Barreiro-Carámbula

Negative Liberty, Positive
Liberty, and Historical Consciousness

WHAT I WOULD LIKE to demonstrate in this study is the unnatural "nature" of what has been labeled "negative liberty." Unlike a positive conception of liberty—which accepts the reality of creation by the supremely good God and the obligation of human beings to use their God-given freedom to cooperate voluntarily with His designs—negative liberty rejects or is indifferent to questions regarding the nature of things and their purpose. It is an empty concept, a "freedom" from the restraints imposed by fundamental realities, a "liberty" arbitrarily to create and recreate our own selves and the world around us in a way that is horribly destructive to both.

St Paul compares in an eloquent way the situation of man when he is dominated by false freedoms with the situation of man when he has accepted the Redemption offered by Christ:

> For when you were slaves of sin, you were free from righteousness. But what profit did you get then from the things of which you are now ashamed? For the end of those things is death. But now that you have been freed from sin and have become slaves of God, the benefit that you have leads to sanctification, and its end is eternal life.[1]

He then underlines the extraordinary purposefulness of the Redemption offered by Christ, indicating that in becoming "free from slavery to

---

1. Rom. 6:20–22.

corruption" men will "share in the glorious freedom of the children of God."[2]

The entire path to true freedom illustrates the fact that man is not created to live in isolation, but needs the assistance of society and social authority on every level of his existence. From his very birth, the Lord places a man in a natural social context in which he receives some of the gifts that he needs to grow to perfection. To begin with, he comes to life and grows in a family. But the family is an imperfect society and itself needs the support of an organized local community. Through this, man is also introduced to political society, which exists in a variety of modes from the local community upwards. At the same time, the family and the different social forces from the village through the various levels of political society must be guided by the constant teaching of the Church through her legitimate authorities. Through the concomitant action of family, other natural communities, and the Church the individual receives language, culture, a sense of belonging to a structured society, and a spiritual community of which he is a legitimate member. All these elements create a certain sense of security that is part of the Creator's plan for the mature growth of each individual and his freedom to promote it.

Negative liberty seeks to destroy this purposeful and socially guided development of positive liberty. A rational understanding of the absurdity of such absolute, negative freedom must be grounded on the perennial philosophy that accepts the objective reality of the external world in which we exist.[3] The Catholic Faith vigorously supports the acceptance of that rationally grounded perennial philosophy and authoritatively identifies the errors flowing from failing to do so. But I think that it is especially important, given the path and the means by which the unnatural concept of a negative liberty has both gained and defends its dominant position in the modern world, for us to examine this topic here with reference to the need for a serious study of history.

In speaking of individual freedom, we must always be concerned for the real person in his concrete historical reality: not the abstract "citizen" of liberalism. A civilization is the incarnation of a social history, a reality "surrounded by so great a cloud of witnesses."[4] The real person has deep roots in given societies and in given cultures. As Leo Strauss pointed out, every great age of humanity grew out of a particular rootedness in the

---

2. Rom. 8:21.
3. Frank Sheed, *Theology and Sanity* (San Francisco: Ignatius Press, 1993), 22.
4. Heb. 12:1.

soil.[5] The soil that we have in mind is far richer than that contemplated by the Chicago professor. It is the soil of a Roman Empire nourished by all sorts of positive elements, in which the saving message of Christ was incarnated in many different ways through its conversion to Catholicism.

To be "rooted in the soil" means to be anchored in what is concrete and permanent, in what can be touched and experienced—and provide a bridge to something that is everlasting. A man who is not rooted in the soil suffers the most extreme form of homelessness and alienation and tends to be moved by constant and shallow passing experiences that in the end leave him more anguished and empty than when rooted.[6] Being rooted in tradition prevents us from being imprisoned solely within contemporary presentations of what is, and is not, real. This happens because rootedness in historical experience provides us with the interpretative tools we need to discern what is real from what, in the end, is unreal. The virtue of prudence is grounded in historical and personal experience and leads us in a wise way to make proper provisions for the future.[7]

It should be clear that for historical knowledge to have an impact it has to be part of the lived experience of the community, and not just a memory of past events that lack connection with contemporary life. A society that is isolated from its previous stages of existence suffers a massive social amnesia, and loss of historical knowledge gravely injures human conscience.[8] A society that is deprived of living memory will most likely fall into collective anomia, and as a consequence sink into chaos.

Believers must take another factor into account. Faith is rooted in sacred history, the stories of the Bible, and the traditions of the Jewish

5. Leo Strauss, "Philosophy as Rigorous Science and Political Philosophy," in *Studies in Platonic Political Philosophy,* Introduction by Thomas L. Pangle (Chicago: University of Chicago Press, 1983), 33.

6. A perceptive analysis of this contemporary social plight is given by Ricardo Yepes Stork, in *Las Claves del Consumismo* (Madrid: Palabra, 1989) and also by Enrique Rojas, *El Hombre Light: Una Vida sin Valores* (Madrid: Temas de Hoy, 1992). We also have to consider that "[m]any of the victims of modern media saturation may simply glance at their experiences without being willing or able to go very far towards understanding or interpreting them." Joseph O'Collins, S.J., *Retrieving Fundamental Theology: The Three Styles of Contemporary Theology* (London: Geoffrey Chapman, 1993), 115. This statement that was made well more than twenty years ago is very much true today when the media saturation is far worse due to the prevalence of the web and different forms of electronic communication.

7. St Thomas Aquinas, *S.T.,* II-II, q.47, a.1.

8. George William Rutler, *The Seven Wonders of the World: Meditations on the Last Words of Christ* (San Francisco: Ignatius Press, 1993), 120.

people and of the Church. Therefore, if we deny the relevance of history, faith becomes impossible.[9] As Joseph Ratzinger explains in his study of *The Theology of History in St Bonaventure*, "Scripture points to the future; but only he who has understood the past can grasp the interpretation of the future because the whole of history develops in one unbroken line of meaning in which that which is to come may be grasped in the present on the basis of the past."[10] Later, Ratzinger concludes this section by underlining that "[i]n this way, the exegesis of Scripture becomes a theology of history; the clarification of the past leads to prophecy concerning the future."[11] We should also keep in mind that Jesus, as both the bearer of the message and the message Himself, united in His own person history and revelation. Faith is rooted in the constant remembrance with gratitude of the historical actions of God for the benefit of His creatures. He is the Lord of history who by continuous acts of merciful grace revives in the human memory awareness of what He has done from the beginning of time as an assurance of what He will do for us in the future. [12]

Some people dismiss the value of history with the claim that the past is too complex, too susceptible to ideological distortions, and too anachronistic to use as a tool to sort out our contemporary problems. Here we should note that we are not arguing for the use of history to *solve* contemporary problems *but to understand the roots of those problems*, so as to find a better way to deal with them in accordance with the constant nature of man. History serves to provide a better understanding of human nature, teaching us how human beings possessing that same unchanging nature have acted under different circumstances. It preserves the inherited wisdom of the community where man was brought up and where he lives,[13] providing a key to how we can interpret new events and even the ability to determine if they are truly new at all. St Thomas in the *Exposition super Job ad litteram* shows the value of

---

9. Robert Royal, *A Deeper Vision: The Catholic Intellectual Tradition in the Twentieth Century* (San Francisco: Ignatius Press, 2015), 27. Royal adds that "[w]hatever uncertainties, gaps and conflicts of interpretation may exist with respect to biblical history and significant events in Catholic history, without some effort to hold on to the golden thread of tradition and the action of Divine Providence in history amid the various twists and turns of the labyrinth, there is simply no maintaining the Catholic faith."

10. Joseph Ratzinger, *The Theology of History in St Bonaventure* (Chicago: Franciscan Herald Press, 1971), 8.

11. Ibid., 9.

12. Rutler, *The Seven Wonders of the World: Meditations on the last Words of Christ*, 121.

13. Dermont A. Lane, *The Experience of God* (Dublin: Veritas, 1981), 7.

history as a means of receiving the wisdom of past generations, which can then be applied to the interpretation of contemporary events. The Angelic Doctor notes that in particular cases experience has maximum significance as a proof, and, when it is of long duration, an infallible significance. He underlines the value of having recourse to the accumulated wisdom of past generations, underscoring the shortness of life of the individual person.[14] This allows us to see the value of tradition that empowers us to think, because it provides us with a valid and universal frame of reference.

According to St Thomas, the fact that human knowledge is influenced by history does not condemn man to historicity.[15] For him, man clearly goes beyond the horizon of time. Man is undeniably rooted in the temporal realm, yet the true homeland of man is beyond time; and while the sensitive part of the soul is subject to time, the spiritual part of the soul, considered in and of itself, is above time.[16] For St Thomas, man is capable of abstract thinking, of moving from the sensible data that he experiences to universal concepts. In consequence, man is capable in some way of freeing himself from being determined by concrete temporal circumstances.[17] The Common Doctor clearly states that "[t]he intellect is above time taken as the measure of the motion of corporal realities."[18] And this happens because "the human soul, being so lofty, is not a form immersed in physical matter or wholly swallowed up by it. So nothing prevents it from having some non-bodily activity."[19] This means that man with his intelligence is capable of moving beyond time and history, and as a consequence, he is able to be aware how the historical circumstances in which he lives can create limitations or distortions to his knowledge.

An essential characteristic of modernity is its prodigious contempt for history. This is built upon its utopian conviction that we have reached a point in the historical evolution of mankind that makes the consideration of the past unnecessary. That negation of history is achieved in two ways.

One of these is the insistence upon the changing character of human nature through the ages. If each historical period were to produce substantial changes in the nature of man, we would be placed today in a dif-

---

14. St Thomas Aquinas, *In Iob*, c.8, nn. 8, nn. 127–161.

15. Battista Mondin, *Storia/Storicità*, in *Dizionario Enciclopedico del Pensiero di Santo Tommaso D'Aquino* (Bologna: ESD, 1991), 38.

16. St Thomas Aquinas, *S.T.*, I–II, q. 53, a.3., ad. 3.

17. Ibid., I, q. 16, a.7, ad. 2.

18. Ibid., I, q. 85, a.4, ad. 1.

19. Ibid., I. q. 76, a.1, ad. 4.

ferent hermeneutical circle from the man of the past. This would preclude a serious understanding of previously existing societies. It would also prevent us from receiving any benefit from the accumulated wisdom of past generations, thus making any historical study an exercise in futility. At the same time, it would also render impossible any appreciation of the historical experience of cultures foreign to our own, and, in fact, any knowledge of these cultures whatsoever. After all, we can only contemplate such appreciation of another culture if we share the same basic nature and inclinations of those men that have lived or who are now living under the different circumstances they offer. We can only make comparisons regarding them if we predicate the same permanent transcendental aspirations of mankind and the same rational apparatus.

It is understandable that change in and of itself has left an impression on modern man. Since the Renaissance, man has undergone a speeding up of the process of change, and after the beginning of the twentieth century this process has accelerated remarkably.[20] Such change is not to be rejected out of hand. It should be evident that scientific progress in accordance with nature should always be encouraged and supported. What must be rejected, however, is change that leads to a separation of the universe and men from the nature that God has given them, and from God's revelation as well. This negative change has been caused to a significant extent by ideological forces that are either alien or hostile to the existence of permanent values; and these same forces will have us believe that the process of change that leads us away from the nature that God has given to man and the universe is irreversible.

As a consequence of such ideas, we see too much stress placed on the positive value of the "new." To combat this tendency, we need to stress the elements of continuity in the human condition and man's permanent thirst for the same universal values while he is pummeled by the same, perennial anguishes wherever he is and in whatever historical period he might happen to live. We must stress the fact that accidental realities may change, but the substance of the human condition always remains the same.

A second means of negating history is the ongoing effort of "dumbing down" society that is fomented by totalitarian or secular humanist gov-

---

20. As it is shown by Alvin Toffler in his two well-known works: *Future Shock* (New York: Bantam, 1971) and *The Third Wave* (New York: Bantam, 1981). These two works document without doubt the factuality of this process of accelerated change but it would be difficult to agree with the normative-ideological interpretations that Toffler provides of this process.

ernments. Such dumbing down is effective because "those who are ignorant of the past can be more easily fooled and controlled in the present by power-hungry ideologues, or by their own worse impulses."[21] Profiting from this ignorance, proponents of different ideologies offer a distorted or selective representation of historical facts to justify themselves. A clear case of this immoral distortion of history can be seen in the Black Legend regarding Spain.[22] Having dispensed with a distorted past, these ideologues then move forward, naively presuming that an adequate social and technological engineering of society will appropriately end all human anguish. All negative traits, among which are included religious tendencies, will be removed and positive ones fostered through a eugenics program under a different name: that of well-planned genetic engineering.

A serious knowledge of history is necessary to demonstrate the falsity of the myth of constant progress. A progress that is divorced from God and the nature that He has given us is really a regression. Any serious study of recent history demonstrates that even if the population of most of the industrialized countries has acquired a significant improvement in its material standard of living, the twentieth century was one of the bloodiest in recorded history. At the same time, any serious Christian would agree that most western countries have suffered an appalling moral decay in the last hundred years. An examination of the historical record shows that the growing dominance of the concept of negative liberty is at the root of this decay.

Negative Liberty, the Protestant Reformation, and its Consequences

History begins with the act of Creation; an act that modern theology for most practical purposes denies or abandons.[23] The history of the radical definition of freedom begins with the promise of the enemy of mankind: "You will be like God."[24] Subsequent history is then full of examples of what Dostoevsky sees as Lucifer-like "rebels against Creation,"[25] all of

---

21. Carlos M.N. Eire, *Reformations: The Early Modern World, 1450–1650* (New Haven: Yale University Press, 2016), viii.

22. Ignacio Barreiro-Carámbula, *La Leggenda nera contro la Spagna* (Civitella del Tronto: Quaderni degli Incontri Tradizionalisti, 2015).

23. Joseph Ratzinger, *'In the Beginning…' A Catholic Understanding of the Story of Creation and the Fall* (Grand Rapids: Wm. B. Eerdmans Publishing Co., 1995), x.

24. Gn. 3:5.

25. Richard Pevear, Introduction to Fyodor Dostoevsky, *The Idiot* (New York: Everyman's Library, 2002), xxii.

them fighting a futile war against God, nature, and the true, positive freedom of man. This negative freedom that entered into the world with the sin of our first parents grew with the accumulation of actual sin. Here we have to understand that at the very center of sin we find the refusal of human beings to accept their condition as creatures and the natural limitations that go with that condition. Human persons in their rebellion refuse to be dependent on a creating, sustaining, and providential God. "They consider their dependence on God's creative love to be an imposition from without."[26] St Paul shows in a prophetic way how freedom can be ill used and abused in his letter to the Galatians: "For you were called for freedom, brothers. But do not use this freedom as an opportunity for the flesh; rather, serve one another through love."[27]

We have to see the unnatural rebellion of man in the context of the history of the Church and of human redemption. Regrettably this is also the "the history of the frustration of God's purposes."[28] But there is always hope in the midst of frustration. After all, we first learn of the promise of the redemption of God to Adam and Eve immediately after the Fall. Our hope is grounded in the *gesta Dei*, which we have experienced in the course of history and which provide us with a reference point for interpreting current events. When we study different periods in the life of mankind where God's plan and human nature have been respected, we can use what we learn as a fundamental guideline for renewal in the present time. We have to look with the eyes of faith even to recent times, searching whatever bears witness to God's intervention in human affairs. And this examination of history should lead us to see the truth that, just as the teaching of Christ remains always the same, human nature does not change during the course of history.

Still, the consequence of our parents' first sin is a struggle that mankind undertakes bound by many fetters. His first bondage is to sin, whose ravages are combatted with the assistance of grace, the teaching of the Church, and the good example of fellow Christians. His second bondage is to the concupiscence that remains part our fallen nature even after the reception of baptism and of the other sacraments. A third bondage is to the specific temptation to accept the gnostic argument that "knowledge" alone or, worse still, the "knowledge" whose secrets only a select minority are permitted to learn, is the pathway out of this

---

26. Ratzinger, '*In the Beginning…*', 70.

27. Gl. 5:13.

28. H.J.A. Sire, *Phoenix from the Ashes: The Making, Unmaking and Restoration of Catholic Tradition* (Kettering, Ohio: Angelico Press, 2015), 1.

valley of tears. And, finally, man suffers from a bondage to ignorance, which some may see as a valid reaction against false knowledge, but which should never be praised as such. A virtuous man may be ignorant, but ignorance is not a virtue. It should be obvious that if a man loves God knowing a little about Him, he should love God more from knowing more about Him; for every new thing known about God is a new reason for loving Him.[29]

Due to all these fetters, God's plan for the world and human nature in its proper sense have not always been respected. The Renaissance, with clear roots in classical antiquity, exalted the human person in an abusive way, trying to break his dependence upon the Church, Christendom, and all the forms of social guidance; in other words, trying to break his reliance on an objective, external norm of conduct necessary for understanding how to use freedom properly and thereby gain perfection. But Protestantism delivered a much more effective blow in this regard.

It is important to avoid calling the Protestant Revolution the "Reformation," because this designation implies that something corrupt was reformed and improved.[30] Far from being objective, this terminology explicitly supports the Protestant position. What we actually see in this revolutionary movement is, on the one hand, a very negative view of the nature of man and of his ability to use his freedom properly. On the other hand, simultaneously, and in a rather contradictory way, we see an erroneous view of the right of the faithful to cut off bonds with the Church and freely examine scriptures, thereby opening the door to different forms of destructive individualism.

Through this revolution, the whole institutional system of the Church was denied its guiding role. From the Protestant perspective, man could be said to have been "liberated" from the Church: "The institutions that were actually supposed to support and save people appeared to be a burden: they were no longer obligatory, which meant they no longer had significance for redemption. Redemption is liberation, being liberated from supra-individual institutions."[31] But, once again, simultaneously and in a quite contradictory way, after exalting the ability of man on his own to find the truth in the Bible, Protestantism taught that the individual was so corrupted by original sin that he was not capable

29. Sheed, *Theology and Sanity,* 29.
30. Eire, *Reformations,* ix.
31. Joseph Ratzinger, *Truth and Tolerance: Christian Belief and World Religions* (San Francisco: Ignatius Press, 2004), 237.

of cooperation with his salvation at all.[32] The clear conclusion must be that the real freedom of the individual possessing a corrupt human nature is very much vitiated.

Martin Luther reached the conclusion that there was something drastically wrong with human existence, that human nature was totally corrupted, due to his own profound and personal experience that human evil tendencies could not be conquered. He also concluded that human reason was totally incapable of understanding the word and the work of God.[33] He claimed that "[o]riginal sin has ruined us to such an extent that even in the godly who are led by the Spirit, it causes abundance of trouble by striving against good."[34]

It is difficult to determine to what extent Luther's personal struggle with evil and sin were influenced by his particular psychological constitution.[35] Confronted with a deeply troubled conscience, Luther suffered awful bouts of despair, with elements of doubt, panic, desolation, and rage, all rolled into one abysmal, downward experience leading into hell itself, making him think that God had abandoned him forever and that God's promises were false.[36]

Whatever the impact of his psychological state, it is clear that his experience of the overpowering character of man's sinfulness brought him to conclude that the anguished conscience was at the base of Christianity.[37] In consequence, in his Commentary on the *Miserere* Luther argued that, as far as he was concerned, the only proper subject for theology was, on the one hand, man as guilty of sin and condemned, and, on the other, God the justifier and savior of the sinner. This meant that whatever was asked or discussed in theology outside these parameters was error and poison.[38] He underlined his conviction that the freedom of the will was a total fiction, and he grounded this opinion on his peculiar interpretation

---

32. Guillermo Jorge Cambiasso, "La estrategia de Satanás," *Gladius* 87 (2013): 55.

33. Widow, *La Libertad y sus servidumbres,* 228–29.

34. Martin Luther, *Bondage of the Will,* in *Martin Luther, Selections from His Writings,* ed. John Dillenberger, (New York: Anchor Books, 1962), 203.

35. Ricardo Garcia-Villoslada, *Martin Lutero, Vol. I, El fraile hambriento de Dios* (Madrid: BAC, Segunda Edición, 1976), 267; Erik Erikson, *Young Man Luther: A Study in Psychoanalysis and History* (New York: Norton, 1958), 125; Heribert Somlinski, "La Personalità di Martin Lutero: Teologia Come Destino, in Martin Lutero," in *Atti del convegno internazionale nel quinto centenario della nascita* (Roma: L'Agostinina, 1984), 75.

36. Eire, *Reformations,* 141.

37. Roger Haight, S.J., *The Experience and Language of Grace* (New York: Paulist Press, 1979), 84.

38. Ibid., 87; Ramon Garcia de Haro, *Historia teológica del modernismo* (Pamplona: EUNSA, 1972), 205.

of scripture and what he considered to be the teaching of history and personal experiences.[39]

Luther taught that "free will without God's grace is not free at all, but is the permanent prisoner and bond slave of evil, since it cannot turn itself to good."[40] He overturned the position of St Thomas Aquinas in accordance with which grace perfects nature, affirming instead that grace neither perfects nature, nor presupposes nature, but that it suppresses nature because nature is totally corrupt.[41] As Catholics, we must insist that this is wrong. Freedom does not entirely disappear as a consequence of the sin of our first parents. Such a disappearance would entail a radical alteration of human nature.

John Calvin shared the basic negative view of Luther on the human condition after the Fall.[42] Luther's catechism of 1529 was his principal and long recognized source.[43] He underlined the Lutheran position that human nature after the Fall was "a seed-bed of sin," adding that "nature is not only devoid of goodness, but so prolific in all kinds of evil, that it can never be idle. Those who term it concupiscence use a word not very inappropriate provided it were added ... that everything which is in man, from the intellect to the will, from the soul even to the flesh, is defiled by concupiscence."[44] Calvin stressed that man's fallen condition had stripped him of "sound intelligence" and moral integrity, and this corruption extended to the intellect as well as to the will.[45] Calvin considered that after the Fall "even if God wills his fatherly favor to us in many ways, yet we cannot, contemplating the universe, infer that he is the Father."[46] This means that after the Fall natural knowledge is powerless to lead man to salvation. But it also destroys the possibility of knowledge of all of objective reality.

Leo XIII describes how this Protestant Revolution stimulated a pas-

---

39. *Assertio omnium articolorum M. Lutheri per bulam Leonis X novissimam damnatorum*, WA, Vol. 7, as quoted in Widow, 225.

40. Martin Luther, *Bondage of the Will*, in Dillenberger, 187.

41. Roberto de Mattei, *A sinistra di Lutero: sette e movimenti religiosi nell'Europa del'500* (Roma: Città Nuova, 1999), 107.

42. José Antonio Sayes, *Antropología del hombre caído: El Pecado Original* (Madrid: B.A.C., 1991), 181.

43. Bruce Gordon, *John Calvin's Institutes of the Christian Religion* (Princeton: Princeton University Press, 2016), 25.

44. John Calvin, *Institutes of the Christian Religion* (Grand Rapids, Michigan: Eerdmans, 1970), II, 2, 8.

45. Ibid., II, 3.

46. Ibid., II, 6.1.

sion for innovation that gradually grew into a practical force for rejecting all objective reality:

> But that harmful and deplorable passion for innovation which was
> aroused in the sixteenth century threw first of all into confusion the
> Christian religion, and next, by natural sequence, invaded the pre-
> cincts of philosophy, whence it spread amongst all classes of society.
> From this source, as from a fountain-head, burst forth all those later
> tenets of unbridled license which, in the midst of the terrible upheavals
> of the last century, were wildly conceived and boldly proclaimed as the
> principles and foundation of that new conception of law which was
> not merely previously unknown, but was at variance on many points
> with not only the Christian, but even the natural law.[47]

Protestant disrespect for the supernatural order of things also worked
progressively to break down the proper natural order of society and promote the fiction that man is an autonomous individual, without any
roots grounded in his family, regional and national traditions, and in his
Creator. Its combination of this "liberation" with an insistence on man's
radical depravity is perhaps not as contradictory as it at first seems, for
stripping the person of all his natural bonds is part of the devil's program for mankind. This plan of radical isolation of the human person
will be fully realized in hell, where the bonds of the family, of society,
and especially the bonds with God will be fully destroyed.[48]

The liberal and radical secularism of the French Revolution, along
with the Marxist secularism of the Russian Revolution, can be seen as
practical applications and further developments of the Protestant
vision, as supporters of the ideas behind them have themselves often
indicated. For "among the secularists and materialists some took comfort—as many still do—in finding the precursors among reformers and
dissidents of the early modern age."[49]

The next step in this process leading directly to hell, one that the
United Nations Declaration on Human Rights is used to justify, has been
the effort to establish an absolute negative liberty that wishes to free
society from the "tyranny of nature" in general. In this stage of destruction, any and all natural precepts must be viewed as obstacles to "liberty"

---

47. Leo XIII, *Immortale Dei* (November 1, 1885), n. 23
48. Sire, *Phoenix from the Ashes*, 169.
49. Eire, *Reformations*, 757. Michael Massing, in his book review of Eire's work points
out, "The most lasting legacy of the period, Eire argues, was the fragmentation of Christianity and the space this created for secularism, skepticism and unbelief." On this I
am obviously in agreement with Eire, but then Massing adds, "This is a plausible conclusion for Europe, but has little to say about the place the Reformation's present-day

and the "rights" flowing from it and, as such, must be removed.[50] All logical heirs of the Enlightenment must commit themselves to this liberation. To admit the sovereignty of God and the prime duty of obeying His law would destroy the fundamental liberal principle that human will should never be restricted and should always be paramount.[51] The world must be viewed as

> self-explanatory, without any need for recourse to God, who thus becomes superfluous and an encumbrance. This sort of secularism, in order to recognize the power of man, therefore ends up by doing without God and even by denying Him. New forms of atheism seem to flow from it: a man centered atheism, no longer abstract and metaphysical but pragmatic, systematic and militant. As a consequence of this atheistic secularism, we are daily faced, under the most diverse forms, with a consumer society, that promotes the pursuit of pleasure set up as the supreme value, a desire for power and domination, and discrimination of every kind: the inhuman tendencies of this "humanism."[52]

Negative Liberty, Consensus Politics, and Verbal/Social Engineering

The reality of individual freedom brings with it the possibility of social conflict. Social peace in a society guided by objective natural law respects the individual mind and soul, giving human persons "a window through which one can see outward to that common truth that founds and sustains us all, and so makes possible through the common recognition of truth the community of wants and responsibilities."[53] When the objective order of things is abandoned, and negative liberty rules supreme, secular societies must recreate truths guaranteeing "social peace" by

---

effects are strongest: America." Here I beg to differ with Massing. The roots of secularism, skepticism, and unbelief in America can also be traced to the Protestant Revolution because Europe and America share the same cultural history. Perhaps it has taken more time in the United States for secularism, skepticism, and unbelief to be a significant part of the social reality of America, but they are clearly manifested today and they have the same roots as those elements in Europe. See Michael Massing, "Reinventing God," *The New York Times Book Review* (August 14, 2016), 19.

50. Gabrielle Kuby, *The Global Sexual Revolution: Destruction of Freedom in the Name of Freedom*, Foreword by Robert Spaemann (Kettering, Ohio: LifeSite-Angelico Press, 2015), 8.

51. Sire, 163.

52. Paul VI, *Evangelii Nuntiando*, n.55.

53. Joseph Ratzinger, *On Conscience* (San Francisco: Ignatius Press, 2007), 16. Addresses at The National Catholic Bioethics Center in Philadelphia.

means of the working out of a "consensus" through the democratic pro-cess.[54] Confidence in the ability to recreate order is fed by the sense of power over nature owing to the scientific and technological progress of the past two centuries, which has given man the idea that he can be the omnipotent creator and legislator for his world. This is true even though the ideological plans to which the sense of power gives birth "tend also to be abstract and unembarrassed by the need for empirical indicators of their major assumptions."[55] This danger can be seen in the unbridled subjectivism of many U.S. Supreme Court decisions preceding and fol-lowing the 1973 decision in Roe v. Wade which legalized abortion. As the court consistently repudiated challenges to this decision over the years, it adopted ever more sweeping articulations of radical subjectivism, which reached its apotheosis in Planned Parenthood v. Casey, in the infamous "mystery" passage written by Justice Anthony Kennedy: "At the heart of liberty is the right to define one's own concept of existence, of meaning, of the universe, and of the mystery of human life."[56]

But this has no relation to anything permanent and actually repre-sents a victory for the strength of number over universal reason. Even the basic concepts that are overemphasized as fundamental in secular-ized society—concepts such as liberty and equality—are understood differently by different secularists. And the apparent truth that is achieved is always subject to change. Sad to say, the relativism that has become the dominant ideology in our times has even entered into the Church, as Cardinal Ratzinger noted and condemned in his homily for the Mass "Pro Eligendo Romano Pontifice" of April 18, 2005.[57]

Moreover, the supposedly "democratic" consensus achieved does not even represent the victory of number, but rather the victory of factions armed with various ideologies and ready to impose their will as the dog-mas of a new kind of religion.[58] What is, at best, never more than a conventional consensus becomes a manipulated consensus reflecting the desire of a minority of strong men. Freedom may be the banner, but the real priority is the imposition of the system by the controlling fac-tion. This is why all the modern revolutions promising an advance of

54. St John Paul II, *Fides et Ratio*, n. 56.

55. Jane J. Kirkpatrick, *Dictatorships and Double Standards: Rationalism and Reason in Politics* (New York: Simon and Schuster, 1982), 10.

56. John M. Haas, "Foreword," in Joseph Cardinal Ratzinger, *On Conscience*, 5.

57. http://www.vatican.va/gpII/documents/homily-pro-eligendo-pontifice_2005041 8_en.html.

58. Pedro Daniel Martínez Perea, "Política y vida virtuosa en Santo Tomas de Aquino," *Gladius* 92:25.

"negative liberty," from that in France onwards, have actually resulted in the creation of bloody dictatorships.[59]

It is important to stress that this totalitarian tendency is visible not only in Jacobin or Marxist societies, but also in committedly liberal ones.[60] In the writings of August Comte, a liberal French writer who was particularly influential in Brazil and Uruguay in the second half of the nineteenth century, we see this same temptation at work. He maintained that the only valid road to knowledge was through scientific investigation, which would not only supplant religion but all kinds of metaphysical speculation.[61] In coherence with his view, as well as his conviction of the thoroughly scientific nature of his system, he proposed the abolition of freedom of thought and conscience, an open assault on the individual's sacred duty to form his conscience properly and then act in accordance with it.[62]

The work of the Protestant Revolution and the negative liberty that it did so much to stimulate is carried on today by the proponents of our hedonist, consumerist society, wherein sexual issues play a central role in the attack upon objective truth, the social organs teaching it, and the integrity of human nature as such. Parenthetically, in this regard, we must remember the common sense comment of St Thomas Aquinas: "Blindness of the mind is the first daughter of lust."[63] Whatever the specific weight of sexual hedonism in promoting our overall problems today, the world we live in is indeed guided by the notion that the value of human life can be measured by how much pleasure a person can experience, and the concomitant idea that pain is an evil to be avoided at all costs. On the one hand, this has opened the door to the permissibility and even the encouragement of suicide, assisted suicide, and involuntary euthanasia.[64] On the other, it has led to the sexual aberrations promoted by the homosexual lobby, as well as the proponents of "gender theory" and of transhumanism, all of which will be addressed below.

Proponents of these various hedonist liberties demonstrate the perennial revolutionary willingness to use dictatorial force to achieve goals. Not long ago artistic freedom and freedom of speech in the secu-

59. Tomas Casares, "Plenitud del derecho," en *La justicia y el derecho* (Buenos Aires: Abeledo-Perrot, Third Edition, 1974), 214.

60. Michael Schooyans, *La dérive totalitaire du libéralisme* (Paris: Mame, 1999).

61. Richard Weikart, *The Death of Humanity—and the Case for Life* (Washington, DC: Regnery Faith, 2016), 31.

62. Estanislao Cantero Núñez, *Augusto Comte, revolucionario a su pesar: El control social contra la liberta y el derecho* (Madrid: Marcial Pons, 2016), 46.

63. St Thomas Aquinas, S.T., II–II, q. 153, a. 5, ad. 1.

64. Weikart, op. cit., 157.

lar humanist culture took precedence over every moral value, but we now see countries that consider the proclamation of the constant teachings of the Church on homosexuality to be a form of hate speech that must be punished by law. The different LGBT organizations are working aggressively to expand those punishments to verbal attacks on many other kinds of moral aberrations. They call hate speech any speech that expresses disagreements with their ideas. And it is necessary to underline the fact that abortion decisions giving the mother the right to kill her child involve attributing "to human freedom a perverse and evil significance: that of an absolute power over others and against others."[65]

Still, a more effective coercive method than force, whose limitations historians can readily identify, is the use of systematic manipulative propaganda, with verbal engineering as its main tool. This type of psychological warfare involves an effort to change the way reality is perceived by changing the way it is depicted. Words that traditionally have a positive meaning have other meanings attached to these. The underlying idea is that people will accept the new meaning as also being positive because they are accustomed to its customary good use. When successful, it convinces people that they have arrived at a change of belief of their own volition. They cannot discern that the old meaning has served as a Trojan horse introducing a new meaning that they otherwise would have rejected.

The objective of this verbal engineering is behavioral change in individuals, but also in society at large; hence, the use of the term "social engineering." This social engineering has been passed off since the time of the Enlightenment as "progress," but it represents no such thing. It is profoundly immoral because it is a planned deception. It is a clear violation of the most basic human dignity, because the persons against whom this procedure is directed are no longer treated as human beings, but as objects to be dominated and controlled, all for the sake of the general social engineering project. Moreover, it is an unjust assault not just on individuals, but also on entire peoples. These are led to accept a manipulated social consensus; one based on the introduction of non-organic and unnatural revolutionary changes into a given society, profoundly at odds with its real tradition, understood as a living historical continuity shaping life and culture.

The new, deceptive, socially engineered society then works as a kind of anti-social "social force" acting upon recalcitrant individuals who cling to outmoded beliefs. This is due to the quite natural truth that

---

65. St John Paul II, *Evangelium Vitae*, n. 20.

men are obviously influenced by the society in which they live. Verbally changed concepts are enshrined in the positive laws that regulate the way people act, and these laws exercise an educative influence over them. Normally, people act on the presumption that laws have been vetted and passed by wise men and, therefore, if something is legal it must be just and good. This is why it is part of the prophetic role of the Church to denounce as evil many positive laws in different countries that are contrary to the law of God.

Oligarchies controlling the socially engineered society work hard to impose thought patterns and to destroy the ability of the majority to exercise critical judgment on the basis of objective principles. Thus, they deprive most of the members of society of the use of their organs of thought. Through manipulation, the superficial and "light" man of consumer societies, incapable of deep thought, is reduced to dependence upon and acceptance of the prevailing "consensus" presented by the strong powers that dominate society.[66] Objective reality itself cannot be changed and attempting to do so can only lead to disaster. Nevertheless, it is clear that the manipulation of words and concepts in ways that appeal to the temptations for which our wounded nature has a special predilection—what George Orwell in 1984 already recognized and called "newspeak"[67]—can and have worked to confuse people's perception of what is and is not true and changed their behavior, thereby bringing about the disaster that a war against nature always ensures.

Such planned deception is as old as the Fall of our first parents. The seduction of Adam and Eve by the serpent could well be described in terms of verbal and social engineering. The Sophists with whom Plato engaged a lifelong battle were masters in this type of deception.[68] Luther and the Protestants engaged in it with great success by calling their teaching "Gospel Christianity." Due to the influence of the media and the liberal teaching establishment, along with the increasing power of the modern state, verbal and social engineering has become much more pervasive in our time.

Once again, "negative liberty" is the primary basis for verbal and social engineering. Once the need for such liberty—promoted by a bad education, the constant pressure of the media, positive law, and the erosion of the influence of those natural intermediate societies like the

---

66. Ratzinger, *On Conscience*, 17, 21.

67. George Orwell, 1984 (New York: New American Library Times Mirror, 1981), 246.

68. Joseph Pieper, *Abuse of Language: Abuse of Power* (San Francisco: Ignatius Press, 1992), 7.

family and the village that have worked to protect the human person from ideological deformation in the past and engender in him a good dose of common sense—is accepted as an absolute, the population loses its ability to exercise critical judgment. The word "discrimination" itself having been stripped of its traditional solid meaning, a people cannot "discriminate" between the good and the bad. Any force demanding consideration of truths that enable a man properly to discriminate is accused of being intolerant or pharisaical, with the Church at the top of the list. The Church, rather than teaching, is thereby condemned to a liberty enhancing "dialogue"; a dialogue stripped of its classical and Christian role as a logical tool for arriving at the truth and effecting conversion, and reduced to being a means for putting all opinions on the same level. This primary focus on dialogue has the obvious goal of establishing some sort of world syncretistic religion that will itself be an instrument of the liberal establishment. Due to the power of verbal and social engineering, this secularization, as Cardinal Raymond Burke has recently indicated, has had a great success inside the Church as well.[69]

Once acceptance of absolute negative liberty is achieved, each new liberty can be used to ensure another. We can examine the interconnect- edness of the use of "liberty" starting with the theme of marriage. The indissolubility of marriage has been considered an affront to human lib- erty since the time of the Enlightenment. But opposition to this "tyran- nical" demand for a life-long commitment was then used, to take but one example, as the grounds for the Mexican Constitution of 1917 to forbid monastic orders.[70] From here, one could move on to lament the tyranny of forcing a woman to have a child or a person to stay alive against his will, as would be the case if abortion, suicide, and euthanasia were not permitted. Ultimately, as the promoters of this last evil regu- larly indicate, the question is one of providing the liberating choice empowering people to control their own bodies.

A type of verbal engineering—what might be called the semantics of oppression—involves attributing subhuman traits to the innocent victims of the liberated strong men, or even denying their humanity altogether. We can see an example of this approach in the promotion of

69. Raymond Leo Cardinal Burke, *Hope for the World* (San Francisco: Ignatius Press, 2016), 28.

70. Mexican Constitution of 1917, art. 5. "El Estado no puede permitir que se lleve a efecto ningún contrato, pacto o convenio que tenga por objeto el menoscabo, la pérdida o el irrevocable sacrificio de la libertad de la persona, ya sea por causa de trabajo, de educación o de voto religioso. La ley, en consecuencia, no permite el establecimiento de órdenes monásticas, cualquiera que sea la denominación u objeto con que pretendan erigirse."

abortion and euthanasia. To justify early abortions some have coined the invalid, non-scientific term "pre-embryo" for the newly conceived human being less than fourteen days old. This makes it seem that before the fourteenth day the embryo is not human, but a being that is merely moving towards becoming human. As this pre-embryo, in their opinion, is not yet human it can be manipulated in any way that societies seem fit and even be destroyed in the course of research. The words "kill" or "destroy" are never used with respect to an abortion or the place where it occurs. One speaks, instead, of a "voluntary termination of pregnancy," done at a "reproductive health center."

Verbal engineering has been very effective in promoting the sexual revolution, as the use of the term "gay" alone indicates. How could one not have a positive image of persons engaging in homosexual acts when they are regularly described by a word that traditionally meant someone with a cheerful and happy disposition? How could the apparent consensus (verbally constructed) regarding the meaning of the word "equality" not impress upon a population the need to give to "gays" the obvious right to contract the same kind of marriages as heterosexuals? But by this point in time the verbal engineers supporting the growth of negative liberty had a new and still more revolutionary tool at their disposal: gender theory. This is one of the strongest manifestations of negative liberty in our times, because in accordance with this ideology man is free to choose his sexual identity.

Gender ideology has its intellectual origins in the rejection of objective truth.[71] The case can be made that Lutheran and Calvinist theology regarding the total corruption of man after the Fall leads to an inclination to expect any aberration in sexual behavior. Certainly, the Enlightenment and liberal emphasis on liberty and equality prepared the way for justifying sexual aberrations as well. Still, before the 1950s the word "gender" was mostly used with respect to grammar; regarding it as a synonym for "sex" was not common at all. However, in 1950s John Money, a psychiatrist at John Hopkins Hospital in Baltimore and early proponent of "gender reassignment" surgery, proposed the distinction between biological sex and socio-cultural gender. In the 1960s he opened the first clinic for sex change operations, the Gender Identity Clinic.[72] In the decades that followed, we have seen the development of the ideology of "gender theory," sometimes also called "gender mainstreaming," which posits that there is a multiplicity of "genders"; not just the two "sexes" of

---

71. Ettiene Roze, *Verita e splendore della differenza sessuale* (Siena: Cantagalli, 2014), 37.
72. Kuby, *The Global Sexual Revolution*, 33.

male and female. With its roots in the previous revolutionary process, this ideological assault on gender identity destroys every standard of ethical sexual behavior.[73]

We can see a regrettable application of the gender ideology in a recent decision by the Supreme Court of Mexico. In a unanimous vote on January 26, 2016, a plenary assembly of all eleven ministers of the Supreme Court ruled that Article 258 of the civil code of the state of Jalisco was unconstitutional, seeking to nullify it because it declares that "[m]arriage is an institution of public character and social interest, by means of which a man and a woman decide to share a state of life in search of their personal fulfillment and the foundation of a family." The Supreme Court's ruling came in response to a complaint by the National Commission on Human Rights (CNDH) which promoted a legal action on the grounds that the law was violating the constitutional guarantee of the "free development of personality" as a right of each citizen, as well as its promise of freedom from "discrimination" due to "sexual preference," a provision that was added to the Mexican Constitution in 2011.[74] This decision follows a previous ruling of the Mexican Supreme Court of June 12, 2015 that imposed same sex marriage in that country.[75] The idea that there is a right to the "free development of personality" with regard to sexual identity is a direct consequence of gender ideology.

Transhumanism is another example of negative liberty developing the revolutionary onslaught against God and the created order. Its objective is to liberate the human race from its biological constraints. Transhumanists promote the idea that humanity can wrest its biological destiny from what they consider to be evolution's blind process of random variation and adaptation and move it to its next stage as a species. It works hand in hand with the idea of genetically engineering children so as substantially to improve their intellectual and physical capabilities. Transhumanism, like many other ideological constructs, is not a united movement. But all transhumanists do believe that the human condition is burdened with ignorance, violence, sickness, and death, and that these limitations can be overcome through technology. The ethics of transhumanism is utilitarian. The aspirations of transhumanists are morally unacceptable: eugenics, body modification (or mutilation), mind-

---

73. Ibid., 8.

74. Matthew Hoffman, "Mexican Supreme Court rules state law upholding man-woman marriage is unconstitutional," https://www.lifesitenews.com/news/mexican-supreme-court-rules-state-law-upholding-man-woman-marriage-is-uncon.

75. Sofia Vasquez-Mellado, "Mexican Supreme Court legalizes gay 'marriage' nationwide," https://www.lifesitenews.com/news/mexican-supreme-court-legalizes-gay-marriage-nationwide

uploading, genetic engineering, hostility towards disability, chemical control of emotions, and a host of other projects.[76]

Mental Health and Recovery of the Real

Mental health can be defined as the ability of the person to perceive, receive, reflect upon, and act upon the real.[77] To act in accordance with the law inscribed in our nature leads to mental health. That is why the exercise of negative liberty and commitment to the different philosophies and ideologies denying the existence of an objective reality lead to alienation, varieties of mental illness, and eventually in some extreme cases to insanity—as history well shows us.[78] When a man acts against the natural law that is inscribed in his conscience, he experiences some degree of guilt. The feeling of guilt, the capacity to recognize guilt, is part of the essential spiritual character of a man. His feeling of guilt disturbs his false calm and might be called the complaint of conscience against a self-satisfied existence.[79] Contemporary society tries to silence the complaints of human nature through all sorts of means, intellectual and sensual. Still, the gradual path to mental illness of a man exercising a negative liberty cannot be halted.

The individualism and relativism of the modern practitioner of negative liberty can make him incapable of any committed and systematic effort. Many contemporary youth consider their search for self-actualization some sort of creative process and not the encounter with an objective reality that is our pre-existing condition for action. These persons formulate a philosophy of truth as a personal project that is ongoing and provisional, subject to alteration and modification as life continues, with elements being added and removed according to one's shifting taste and need. With nothing definite, their moral principles do not translate into fixed and binding moral obligations.[80] They are

---

76. Cf. Michael Cook, "Is transhumanism really the world's most dangerous idea?" http://www.mercatornet.com/articles/view/is-transhumanism-really-the-worlds-most-dangerous-idea/18394.

77. G.C. Dilsaver, *Imago Dei® Psychotherapy: A Catholic Conceptualization* (Ave Maria, FL: Sapientia Press of Ave Maria University, 2009), 24.

78. As case in point is Stalin as described by Nikita Khrushchev in *Khrushchev Remembers:* with an Introduction Commentary and Notes by Edward Crankshaw (Boston: Little, Brown and Company, 1970), 306ff. At the same time this memoir of the former Soviet leader provides evidence of his complicity in many of Stalin's crimes.

79. Ratzinger, *On Conscience*, 18.

80. Rev. Donald Haggerty, *The Contemplative Hunger* (San Francisco: Ignatius Press, 2016), 44.

inclined to a hedonistic, "fence-sitting" life style, favoring a permanent paralysis of productive action. This is one of the many reasons why contemporary youth are afraid of entering into marriage or having children and can accept the validity of any kind of sexual relationship. It is no surprise that the temporal punishment for a liberty that leads to hell is barrenness.

But perhaps all of these evils stemming from negative liberty can be turned into an indirect road to God. If the independent man imitates Lucifer in trying "to be like God,"[81] the departure from the truth that "first lulls man into a false security and then abandons him in the trackless waste,"[82] may indicate the workings of the God who continues to love him and leads him to see before it is too late that he is headed for the precipice. The short duration of the initial exhilaration in his newly found absolute freedom and his plunge into the void of nothingness may be a foretaste of the wrath of God preceding His saving justice.[83] The experience of the exercise of negative liberty and its ill effects of the person with at least some Christian roots can lead him to meditate on his sad condition apart from Christ. An atomized and unjustly leveled society is so deeply unnatural that the human person may well feel a longing to belong to a natural society once again. If the Church were to begin again to preach the importance of natural society, she would thus find many persons ready to receive her message. But to do so she would have to reject her own subservience to the secular worldview.

Our hope is grounded on the fact of God's primacy and absolute lordship over history and the world.[84] As a consequence, we hope to see His intervention in history for the salvation of souls and the common good of society. At the same time, it is true that "the ways of His providence are often unknown to us. Only at the end, when our partial knowledge ceases, when we see God 'face to face,' will we fully know the ways by which—even through the dramas of evil and sin—God has guided His creation to that definitive Sabbath rest for which He created heaven and earth."[85] Our experience of the oppressive nature of a society that is dominated by the use of negative liberty should increase our longing for the establishment of a society that would help us to live virtuously. The idea of becoming a new man in a new society has New Testament roots and it is a legitimate goal of Christianity. But what is more

81. Gn. 3:5.
82. Ratzinger, *On Conscience*, 22.
83. Rms. 2:21ff; 3:19–21.
84. *CCC*, 304.
85. *CCC*, 314.

important is to live in a society that would assist us to enjoy God forever after living virtuously here on Earth.[86] We must do our best to rebuild this—and that involves freeing us from the Protestant temptation and the negative liberty that it has done so much to stimulate.

86. St Thomas Aquinas, *De regimine principum,* Lib. 1, cap. 15.

11

Multiple Anti-Semitisms in Luther, Lutheranism, and Bergoglio

Fr. John Hunwicke

UNTIL THE GLOOM of the Enlightenment put an end to such freedoms and frivolities, the Oxford academic year concluded with the "University Act": a three-day celebration in the University Church, transformed for these purposes into a theatre, in which, among other things, a speaker called *Terrae Filius* declaimed a scurrilous satire against the great and the good.

But in June 1581, the assembled academics were surprised to find some newly bound copies of a small book smuggled into and awaiting them within the theatre, self-described as a *munusculum* and entitled *Rationes Decem*.

In the exuberant spirit of *Terrae Filius*, it described Zwingli as *Helvetus gladiator*; Calvin (in a reference to his alleged branding for homosexuality) as a *stigmaticus perfuga*; and the great Martin Luther himself (the subject this year of our papal-sponsored celebratory joys) as *Fraterculus*. The author (a former officer of the university but by then the under-cover Jesuit missionary we now call St Edmund Campion) asked —his question was a rhetorical one—whether there could really have been no Christian truth in the world *donec Lutherus constuprasset Boram*. It is recorded that the Act proceeded in complete silence as the huddled dons, oblivious of rhetoric emanating from the podium, avidly perused this secretly printed *tour de force.*[1]

---

1. Most sources may easily be found on the Internet. The *Rationes Decem* is given there in facsimile; Zwingli and Calvin appear on page 22, in the *Tertia Ratio*; in a passage

241

Campion's picture of the entire edifice of "Reformation" thought waiting, trembling, to be born, until the tiny Augustinian felt his libidinous urge *constuprare Boram* is, indeed, a fitting object of mirthful contemplation. (Was the Muse of all Lutheran and Protestant Truth, the former Sister Catherine Bora, in the mind of the *Fraterculus* when he penned a description of "an evil, stubborn shrew who clamorously contradicts her husband and insists on having the last word although she knows she is in the wrong"?)[2]

St Edmund Campion, as I shall show, was not the last Catholic to be driven to laughter and satire by the inherent absurdities of the events and the intellectual follies that we group together as "The Reformation." Perhaps I may hazard an impertinent suggestion that these absurdities are structurally inherent within and not accidental to Reformation theology in general and Luther's contribution to it in particular. But first I wish to emphasize that Luther's anti-Semitism is not a mere detail which can be acknowledged, apologized for, and then set aside so that we may turn our attention to some "real" and important "message" of his teaching on which "we can all agree." Luther's anti-Semitism was the engine room in the stern of his disreputable boat. He gave his considered views towards the end of his life in his *On the Jews and Their Lies* of 1543—from which, incidentally, the parenthesis above is taken: Luther's "shrew" in fact represents Judaism.[3]

It is with no apologies that I shall remind the reader of the contents of that generously expansive work. After all, in the lengthy 2013 Vatican-Lutheran document, *From Conflict to Communion*, Luther's views on the Jews got all of two lines in paragraph 229: "On this occasion, Lutherans will also remember the vicious and degrading statements that Martin Luther made against the Jews. They are ashamed of them and deeply deplore them." On this showing, I may well be the only writer this year to spill these particular beans. So here are some tiny snatches from Luther's extensive text:

> I shall give you my sincere advice. First, to set fire to their synagogues or schools and to bury and cover with dirt whatever will not burn, so that no man will ever see a stone or cinder of them. . . . Second, I advise that their houses also be razed and destroyed. . . . Third, I advise

---

closely resembling the style of Classical declaimed rhetoric, [Catherine] Bora ["...until Luther had defiled Bora"] functions as the terminal bathos which gets the laugh at the end of the *Septima Ratio* on page 58.

2. See note 3, below.

3. *On the Jews and their Lies* is quoted from an Internet translation. See http://www.preteristarchive.com/Books/1543_luther_jews.html

that all their prayer books and Talmudic writings, in which such idolatry, lies, cursing, and blasphemy are taught, be taken from them.... Fourth, I advise that their rabbis be forbidden to teach henceforth on pain of loss of life and limb.... Fifth, I advise that safe-conduct on the highways be abolished completely for the Jews....[4]

The Middle Ages were not devoid of anti-Semitic incidents and even structures. But the passages I have dipped into above—unattractive as they are (I make no apologies for condensing pages of offensive ranting into a few short lines)—are something quite different. Luther himself acknowledged this at the beginning of Chapter XI of *On the Jews and their Lies*. He wrote:

Whatever we tolerated in the past unknowingly—and I myself was unaware of it—will be pardoned by God. But if we, *now that we are informed*, were to protect and shield such a house for the Jews, existing right before our very nose, in which they lie about, blaspheme, curse, vilify, and defame Christ ... it would be the same as if we were doing all this and even worse ourselves....

His own distinctive brand of anti-Semitism appears thus to have been not a pardonable hangover from medieval Catholicism but the fruit of a lifetime spent meditating upon his own distinctive theological "insights." How so?

The *Fraterculus* came to believe that the errors of the Jews and of the papists were precisely the same and to resist each with equal venom. In each case, they sought salvation through works rather than through faith. Inevitably, his hatred of both groups increased *pari passu* throughout his life. In the same work of 1543 he wrote:

If I had not experience with my papists, it would have seemed incredible to me that the earth should harbor such base people [as the Jews] who knowingly fly in the face of open and manifest truth, that is, God himself. For I never expected to encounter such hardened minds in any human breast, but only in that of the devil. However, *I am no longer amazed by either the Turks' or the Jews' blindness, obduracy, and malice, since I have to witness the same thing in the most holy fathers of the church, in pope, cardinals, and bishops.*

In other words, Luther extended the enmities of anti-Semitism; the papists were spiritually Jews, a new field in which to exercise his hatreds.

And it can hardly be new to analyze this fury as the result of Luther's personal experiences of failing to obey the rule of his order and the

---

4. Ibid.

chaste celibacy enjoined by his Church: in other words, his own sexual incontinence, his *libido constuprandi*. He drew comfort from his own understanding of the Epistle of St Paul to the Galatians, upon which he wrote three commentaries:

> Therefore, when I see a person who is bruised enough already being oppressed with the law, terrified with sin, and thirsting for comfort, it is time for me to remove the law and active righteousness from his sight and set before him, by the Gospel, the Christian and passive righteousness. This excludes Moses with his Law and offers the promise made in Christ, who came for the afflicted and for sinners.[5]

The Protestant construct of justification by faith alone proved to be less simple and univocal than its first protagonists imagined, and an entire industry of competing scholasticisms was to create systems of ever-proliferating complexity in the attempt to make it fit all the biblical data. In 1848, an acute and analytical mind that had experienced controversy among Protestant Scholastics in Oxford wrote a characteristic account (Henry Chadwick called Newman "as supreme a master of irony and satire as any in our literature") of those struggles to understand an idea that had seemed so plain to Luther. Blessed John Henry Newman's semi-autobiographical novel, *Loss and Gain*, in its Chapter XVII, presents a picture that deserves a careful analysis by someone competent to disentangle the threads. I offer a brief taste of the Evangelical Tea Party:

> "Oh, faith is certainly a holy feeling," said No. 1. "No, it is spiritual, but not holy," said No. 2; "it is a mere act, the apprehension of Christ's merits." "It is seated in the affections," said No. 3; "faith is a feeling of the heart; it is trust, it is a belief that Christ is *my* Saviour; all this is distinct from holiness. Holiness introduces self-righteousness. Faith is peace and joy, but it is not holiness...." "Pardon me, Reding," said Freeborn, "it is as my friend says, an *apprehension*. An apprehension is a seizing; there is no more holiness in justifying faith than in the hand's seizing a substance which comes its way. This is Luther's great doctrine in his 'Commentary' on the Galatians. It is nothing in itself—it is a mere instrument; this is what he teaches when he so vehemently resists the notion of justifying faith being accompanied by love." "I cannot assent to that doctrine," said No. 1; "it may be true in a certain sense, but it throws stumbling blocks in the way of seekers. Luther could not have meant what you say, I am convinced. Justifying faith is always accompanied by love." "That is what I thought," said Charles. "That is

---

5. 1535, from the section headed, "The Argument of the Epistle to the Galatians."

the Romish doctrine all over," said No. 2; "it is the doctrine of Bull and Taylor." "As Luther calls it *"venenum infernale,"*" said Freeborn. "It is just what the Puseyites preach at present," said No. 3. "On the contrary," said No. 1, "it is the doctrine of Melanchthon. Look here," he continued, taking his pocket-book out of his pocket, "I have got his words down, as Shuffleton quoted them in the Divinity-School the other day. '*Fides significat fiduciam; in fiducia inest dilectio; ergo dilectione sumus justi.*'" Three of the party cried "Impossible," the paper was handed round in solemn silence. "Calvin said the same," said No.1 triumphantly. "I think," said No. 4, in a slow, smooth, sustained voice, which contrasted with the animation which had suddenly inspired the conversation, "that the con-tro-ver-sy, ahem, may easily be arranged. It is a question of words. . . ."

Newman eventually concluded his chapter:

Now they got into a fresh discussion among themselves; and as it seemed as interminable as it was uninteresting, Reding took the opportunity to wish his host a good night, and to slip away. He had never had much leaning towards the Evangelical doctrine; and Freeborn and his friends, who knew what they were holding much better than the run of their party, satisfied him that he had not much to gain by inquiring into that doctrine further. So they will vanish in consequence from our pages.

These themes, however, failed to vanish from Protestant discourse. In 1944 the great Anglo-papal controversialist Dom Gregory Dix put a cat among Evangelical pigeons; he was suspected of having his tongue in his cheek when he summarized the Evangelical dogmas thus:

[E]ven a man's apparently good works are in themselves in the eyes of God damnably sinful. Nothing that a man can do in itself ever has the least value in the eyes of God, on this theory. Man has therefore only one hope of salvation. God the Father sent His only Son to become Man and be crucified outside the gates of Jerusalem in the first century AD; thus He offered the one, true, perfect, sufficient and complete sacrifice to atone for all human sin. To the end of time anyone, however sinful, who believes and fully accepts that fact, and trusts altogether and only in the merit of that sacrifice, is forthwith "justified" in the sight of God. He needs nothing more, can do nothing more, than be conscious of that feeling of confidence, for it is all that stands between him and the damnation his own inescapable sinfulness entails. That is the famous doctrine of "justification by faith alone," which in the eyes of all Protestants was the very essence of Protestantism. . . .[6]

6. Gregory Dix, *The Question of Anglican Orders* (London: Dacre Press, 1944), 19–20.

But, as late as 1988, in *ARCIC: An Open Letter to the Anglican Episcopate*, a large worldwide group of Anglican Evangelicals criticized an Anglican-Roman Catholic accord on justification by protesting that "no actual definition of faith is given. We miss the Reformers' emphasis that *fides est fiducia*. . . ."

In the twentieth century, justification (and, consequently, our estimate of Jews and Judaism) was to be given a new twist in Germanic scholarship before the terms of the debate were radically changed. Ernst Käsemann (1906–1998) believed that "[i]n and with Israel [Paul] strikes at the hidden Jew in all of us." According to Günther Bornkamm (1905–1990), "For Paul, the Jew represents mankind in general . . . the man is indeed not somewhere outside, among unbelievers; he is hidden within each Christian."[7]

Thus, they achieved the reappropriation by redefinition of the anti-Semitism of their primeval *Fraterculus*. But in the writings of E.P. Sanders (born 1937), the traditional Jew of Protestantism who attempts to earn salvation by works—who might be incarnate in a particular and particularly offensive race or might be lurking in the heart of any human—was laid to rest. Pauline scholarship has not been immobile since Sanders, an academic of Methodist origins, launched the new perspective on Paul by eventually succeeding in getting his *Paul and Palestinian Judaism* published in 1977. But it has not reverted to the simplicities of Luther's construct.

For Sanders, "covenantal nomism" means that a Jew is a member of the People of God because of the covenant with Abraham, and he stays in it by keeping the Torah. This is set against the participationist eschatology of St Paul: one enters the community of salvation by becoming one with Christ Jesus and one stays in it by remaining pure and blameless and not entering into unions which are destructive of the union with Christ. Hence, the Law, the Torah, is no longer the evil bugbear of Lutheranism which deludes men into believing they can earn their own salvation by succeeding in obeying it; a destructive tyrant which weighs upon the helpless individual and drives him to misery with its unattainable demand for observance.

In Catholic circles, the late twentieth-century revolution in Pauline studies had a much smaller effect than one might have expected. Since the burden of the new look on St Paul constituted a substantial if not

---

7. E. Käsemann, "Paul and Israel," in *New Testament Questions of Today* (Philadelphia: Fortress Press, 1969), 142; G Bornkamm, "The Letter to the Romans as Paul's last Will and Testament," in Karl P. Donfried, ed. *The Romans Debate*, 28–29, reprinted from *Australian Biblical Review* 11 (1963), 2–14.

total dissolution of the fundamental structures of Reformation soteriology, a simple man might have expected the papists to show some signs of gratified triumphalism. Instead, there has been a painstaking and deferential appetite to engage ecumenically with and to appease Lutheran dogmatists on their own terms. But it is in the pontificate of Pope Francis, Jorge Bergoglio, that the comical aspects of this have descended into the purest farce.

The media machine, which is encouraged to purvey a neatly specialized image of Bergoglio, has told us that he has a particular friend who is an Argentinian rabbi and, since the last conclave, has been known to travel with him. The pope has performed the now customary ritual visits to synagogues, and in his apostolic exhortation *Evangelii gaudium* he appeared to teach that the covenant with the Jews was still fully valid.

But despite such a surprisingly positive estimate, this pope is capable of writing passages to which the *Fraterculus* would have been happy to append his *imprimatur*. Consider this, from near the end of the *Misericordiae Vultus*, the "Bull of Indiction" proclaiming his Year of Mercy:

> Before [St Paul] met Christ on the road to Damascus, he dedicated his whole life to fulfilling in every way the Righteousness of the *Torah* [Lex]. But, converted to Christ, he so radically [*prorsus*] changed his mind that he wrote in his Letter to the Galatians: "We have believed in Christ Jesus, so that we are made righteous out of Faith in Christ and not out of works prescribed by the *Torah*." Paul turns totally upside down the basic idea of Righteousness [rationem iustitiae omnino evertit]. He puts in the first place, not now the Torah, but Faith. *Keeping the Torah does not save, but Faith in Jesus Christ*, who through His death and resurrection brings His salvation through the Mercy which makes righteous.

And he cites Philippians 3:6 and Galatians 2:16, in both of which St Paul is concerned to emphasize strongly that salvation is not by means of Judaism and its identity markers.[8] And on January 1, 2016 Bergoglio referred disparagingly to "the Torah with its quibbles [*cavilli*]."

It is as if the pope speaks two different and unrelated languages. When he is concerned to speak graciously and ecumenically to Jews, we are made aware that God's covenant with that people is irrevocable. But when he is attacking a particular mindset which, in his view, is found especially among those clergy of his own Church whom he judges an obstacle to his own plans, he speaks with the voice of *Fraterculus Marti-*

---

8. In my own English translation of a paragraph from *Misericordiae Vultus*, I might be criticized for rendering "Lex" as "Torah." But the entire context is so exclusively referential to the Torah that any misunderstanding is the pope's fault and not mine.

nus and exhibits no evidence of knowing that many Pauline scholars since the Sanders revolution no longer consider the anti-Semitic strictures of the Reformation period to be any better than inaccurate and slanderous. (One might wonder about the breadth of reading of those who do his drafting and those who revise on his behalf.)

Another example of this that many have noticed is his obsession with "pharisees" and its relevance to a question which the German bishops have clearly convinced him is of prime importance: the status of those formerly married and now civilly "remarried" after divorce:

> Criticizing the "pharisees" is recurrent in Pope Francis' words. In numerous discourses between 2013 and 2015 he has spoken of the "sickness of the Pharisees" (November 7, 2013), "who rebuke Jesus for not respecting the Sabbath" (April 1, 2014); of "the temptation of self-sufficiency and of clericalism, that codification of the faith in rules and regulations, as the scribes, the Pharisees, the doctors of the Law did at the time of Jesus" (September 19, 2014). The reference to the Pharisees is evident, ultimately, in the pope's concluding discourse of October 24, 2015, at the end of the XIV Ordinary Synod on the Family. In effect, he says, who are the "closed hearts, which frequently hide even behind the Church's teachings or good intentions, in order to sit in the chair of Moses and judge, sometimes with superiority and superficiality, difficult cases and wounded families," if not "the Pharisees who were making religion ... a never-ending chain of commandments"? (June 26, 2014)[9]

Yet, on the question of divorce, it is the man from Nazareth who cites precisely the scriptural mandate and who, without any magisterial use of inverted commas, calls "remarried" divorcees "adulterers." In fact, it is the Pharisees, who for Bergoglio hand down their narrow-minded, insensitive, and imperious judgments from the "chair of Moses," who advocate the admissibility of divorce! And is the pope not aware that the synagogue-based and family-based Judaism that was devised to fill the vacuum left by the destruction of the Temple and its sacrificial *cultus* was the product of such groups as ... the Pharisees? Rather arbitrarily, he responds with sentiments of warm approbation to the sight of a rabbi, while the thought of one of his own clergy obediently adhering to the teachings of Christ and the discipline of the Church elicits from him scorn and intemperate abuse. His mind appears to be free from any prejudices against self-contradiction.

---

9. I borrow here Roberto de Mattei's summary given on the *Rorate* blog on November 11, 2015.

Bergoglio's attitude of elaborate sympathy towards rabbinic Judaism, which, perhaps a little tritely, I have attributed to Germanic influence, has an interesting history that could bear a closer examination than we have space for. But perhaps a few seldom-regarded pieces of information may be of interest.

It is commonly either implied or explicitly asserted, with that mendacity which comes so easily to those who mediate "the council" to the gullible, that *Nostra aetate* asserted the salvific validity of the Jewish covenant, condemned "supersessionism," and prohibited any sort of "mission" to the Jewish people. None of these claims is true. Indeed, at the beginning of the next decade, the newly composed *Liturgia Horarum* (its authorization is dated April 11, 1971) showed no evidence of the assertions erroneously attributed to the conciliar documents. Many of its patristic readings express or assume supersessionism. I take at random from Volume I the *lectio* from Faustus of Riez, appointed for January 12:

> Recedit lex, gratia succedit: umbra removetur, veritas repraesentatur: carnalia spiritalibus comparantur: in novum testamentum observatio vetusta transfertur: sicut beatus Apostolus dicit: Vetera transierunt, et ecce facta sunt nova.

But perhaps the sharpest focus will be provided for us by the question of whether prayer should be offered for the conversion of the Jews, since this is what has recently become, for liberals, a centrally defining issue. We shall have to search through the intercessory prayers, the *preces*, which were new compositions confected for this form of the Divine Office, and therefore cannot be regarded as unreflective continuations of formulae inherited from the *Breviarium Romanum*. And we shall not have to search for long. Again in Volume I, Lauds for January 2 gives us: "*Christe, quem ab angelis glorificatum et a pastoribus annuntiatum, Simeon et Anna confessi sunt et praedicaverunt—te rogamus ut Evangelium tuum a populo promissionis recipiatur.*" And at Vespers on Easter Sunday itself (and repeated on other days during Eastertide): "*Israel in te Christum spei suae agnoscat—et omnis terra cognitione tuae gloriae repleatur.*"

Something, however, appears to have happened during the 1970s, at least in the land scarred by guilty memories of the Holocaust. The German version of this Office Book, in 1978, did not render the second of these formulae at all; the first it "translated" by means of "*Christus, von den Engeln besungen, von den Hirten kundgemacht, von Simeon und Anna gepriesen—gib, dass wir deine Frohe Botschaft annehmen* (Sung by the angels, made known by the shepherds, praised by Simeon and Anna; grant that we may accept your joyful message)." *Traduttore*, indeed: *traditore*. Perhaps this is why, when the German hierarchy began a campaign against the Prayer for the Jews which Pope Benedict XVI had so recently composed for use in the Extraordinary Form of the Roman Rite on Good Friday, it did not occur to them to seek also a revision of the *Liturgia Horarum,* with the *editio typica* (the authentic Latin text) of which they will probably have been unfamiliar. Since, by contrast, the English translations in use translate the Latin accurately, the English bishops, who decided to follow the lead of the Germans at their 2015 meeting, would seem to have less defense against an accusation of spectacular hypocrisy.

In December 2015, the Vatican's Commission for Religious Relations with Jews released a document, *The Gifts and Calling of God are Irrevocable,* exploring "the unresolved theological questions at the heart of Christian-Jewish dialogue." This text described itself as "not a magisterial document or doctrinal teaching of the Catholic Church." It also admitted that:

> the conciliar text is not infrequently over-interpreted, and things are read into it which it does not in fact contain. An important example of over-interpretation would be the following: that the covenant that God made with His people Israel perdures and is never invalidated. *Although this statement is true, it cannot be explicitly read into* Nostra aetate. (my italics)

Faced, on the other hand, with the plain words of the New Testament scriptures, it confesses that, "It is the belief of the Church that Christ is the Saviour for all. There cannot be two ways of salvation, therefore, since Christ is also the Redeemer of the Jews in addition to the Gentiles." It deals with the contradiction here by explaining, "That the Jews are participants in God's salvation is theologically unquestionable, but how that can be possible without confessing Christ explicitly is and remains an unfathomable divine mystery."[10]

Rarely can a religious organization have painted itself so embarrassingly into a very awkward corner. The extremely fathomable answer to

---

10. The 2015 Vatican document "The Gifts and Calling of God are Irrevocable" cites the Pauline *topos* of the wild olive branches grafted into the true olive without showing much interest in the allegorical detail of the true olive branches which were "broken off" and, in the now-time, remain broken off (Rom. 11:17 sqq.). It dates to 1980 the invention, by St John Paul II, of the idea that "the Old Covenant had never been revoked by God." It has never been at all clear what was meant by this. It is alluded to "magisterially" in the Catechism of the Catholic Church, paragraphs 121–22, which are not concerned with the status of the Jewish people but with the abiding authenticity of the books of the Old Testament. "Valorem servant permanentem, quia Foedus Vetus nunquam est retractatum. *Etenim* Veteris Testamenti Oeconomia ad hoc potissimum disposita erat, ut Christi universorum Redemptoris . . . Adventum praepararet. . . ."

this "divine mystery" can be found quite simply by returning to the essential grammar of biblical intertextuality found explicitly in the New Testament writers themselves; in the early and later patristic writers; in the Scholastics; and throughout the liturgy. It has long been called "typology."[11]

The Old Testament deals with types, shadows. The New Testament of the Redemption worked in Christ replies with antitypes; with realities. The latter necessarily supersede the former. There is no need now for the *tamid* lamb to be sacrificed daily in the temple, for Christ is the sacrificed Lamb of God, prefigured in the sacrifices of Abel and of Abraham, who takes away the sins of all. It is fetishism to be preoccupied with a shadow when the truth is here. *Et antiquum documentum novo cedat ritui. In hac mensa novi Regis, novum Pascha novae legis, Phase vetus terminat. Vetustatem novitas, umbram fugat veritas, noctem lux eliminat.* The Lord Himself assured us that He is—in His own Body—the New Temple of which the old was but a type. What could be clearer than that?

We should not fall into the *old* Germanic error—Luther's error—of saying that Jewry is erroneous because it attempts to earn salvation, and of then extending that attack to Catholics, who thus become "proxy Jews," exposed in the same pillory to the same abuse and humiliation. Neither should we fall into the anti-Semitism of discerning some failing in the Jewish temperament that inclines Jews to do religion all the wrong way. Nor the neo-anti-Semitism of detecting and attempting to exorcise a "hidden Jew" in each of us. *There is nothing wrong with Judaism—except that it has been superseded.* It no longer functions as a marker of where God's salvific action is to be found. Its observances are no longer, objectively, signs of obedience to God. And we should not fall into the *new* Germanic error of attempting to atone for the Holocaust by assuring potentially suspicious partners in dialogue that we view the Judaic dispensation as still efficacious for Jews, so that no mission or even prayer for that people is either necessary or even permitted.

There is nothing wrong with Judaism—except that it has been superseded. There is nothing wrong in circumcising your male children so as to set upon them the visible mark and "type" of God's covenant— except that *He* has now said, "Go and teach all nations and *baptize*." There is nothing wrong with the precepts of the Torah, which Bergoglio so offensively called *cavilli*, except that God, the Incarnate Torah, has

---

11. F. Kermode, *The Classic: Literary Images of Permanence and Change* (New York: Viking Press, 1975), 89–90. The almost total disappearance of typology from current Catholic discourse is clearly the reason for the Church's complete *aporia* when it comes to saying anything useful or even clear about Judaism or, indeed, the scriptures.

now said, "You have heard that it was said of old . . . but *I* say unto you." There is nothing wrong in paying a Temple tax to enable the daily sacrifice of the *tamid* lambs . . . except that God, the Lamb of God, has given a new table of sacrifice and has emphatically said, "*Touto poieite*"—*This is what you are now to do.*[12]

So Papa Bergoglio is leading us in celebrating the Reformation launched by *Fraterculus Martinus*. This celebration is riddled with contradictions and irreconcilabilities. Bergoglio implicitly invites us to reassess Luther without addressing the root cause of Luther's rebellion against the Church—namely, that Luther hated Catholicism because he saw it as precisely the same error which St Paul attacked in his polemics against Jews and Judaizing Christians. This identification was not tangential to the Reformation project, but central. Bergoglio entangles himself in contradiction by inviting us to an irenic approach towards Judaism while incessantly attacking the Pharisees, apparently ignorant of what modern Judaism owes to the sects that survived the cataclysm of AD 70. He adopts the classical Lutheran critique of Judaism without realizing that this has lost the confidence of modern non-Catholic Pauline scholarship. While seeking the esteem of the Jewish community, he attacks his fellow Catholics, especially clergy, for allegedly having the same failings of character as those hitherto associated with Judaism. In sum, he repeatedly lacerates the Torah while affirming the Jewish community that lives in and by the Torah. Jews might well wonder whether, with a friend like that, they have any room left to accommodate enemies.

We shall not recover our identity as Christians and Catholics by celebrating Luther, with his anti-Semitism, his bile, and his conviction that Judaic error and popish error are identical. We shall find no solution to the crisis of faith at the heart of the Catholic Church by the farce of constructing a Luther from whom his hatreds have been anachronistically airbrushed away through a ludicrous ritual of "apology." Nor will there be any help for us in affirming a "Christianity" which boasts of living harmoniously alongside its "elder brother." We will not recover a sense of integrity by proclaiming noisily that our God calls us to spread our Gospel to every corner of the world, bringing the Good News to the very margins of society, while breaking off when necessary to murmur quietly behind our hands, "Of course, I don't include the Jews in that; I guarantee we won't bring it as far as Tel Aviv." The full malice, the full menace, of Luther's error, far from having evaporated in five centuries,

---

12. Parts of this paper owe much to the stimulus of a short article by Rabbi Jacob Neusner, "Money Changers in the Temple: The Mishnah's Explanation," *New Testament Studies* 35 (1989): 287–90.

is even now making its worst attack yet on the Catholic Faith, in this pontificate of Jorge Bergoglio.

"Tradition" is not one option among many others, so that it can put in a deferential request to be allowed toleration in a Church that permits a thousand contrary blossoms to flourish. It is fitting that its enemies should so hate Tradition, because it is the caustic solvent which radically subverts both Luther's manic anti-Semitism, as well as the error on the other side of the coin, which in effect and *practically* implies the notion of two simultaneous salvific covenants.

For the "traditionalist" Catholic, there is no "problem" about Judaism; we express every day of our lives our knowledge that we are the children of Abraham and heirs of the ancient prophets and priests in covenants which have never been renounced but *have* been fulfilled. Each morning, a Catholic priest stands in motionless humility and proclaims that he has been brought by God's light and truth to the foot of His Holy Mountain; and that he will go in unto God's altar. Then, like Abraham ascending Mount Moriah and the Incarnate Word going up to the hill of Calvary, he climbs the steps to the place where the old sacrifices are all fulfilled, and enters, not once a year, but every day, the Holy of Holies. Perhaps he remembers the words of Newman:

> You, who day by day offer up the Immaculate Lamb of God, you who hold in your hands the Incarnate Word under the visible tokens which He has ordained, you who again and again drain the chalice of the Great Victim; who is to make you fear? What is to startle you? What to seduce you? Who is to stop you?[13]

---

13. J. H. Newman, *The Second Spring*, a sermon preached on July 13, 1852 in St Mary's College Oscott, during the First Provincial Synod of Westminster, near the end. See http://newmanreader.org/works/occasions/sermon10.html.

12

Sweden and the Five Hundred Year Reformation *Anamnesis*

A Catholic Perspective

Clemens Cavallin

To Remember the Reformation

ACCORDING TO *Collins Concise Dictionary,* "commemoration" means, "to honour or keep alive the memory of."[1] It is weaker than the wording "Reformation Jubilee," which generated 393,000 hits on Google, compared with merely 262,000 for "Reformation Commemoration."[2] According to the same dictionary, the meaning of "jubilee" is "a time or season for rejoicing."

For a Swedish Catholic, there is, however, little to rejoice about when considering the consequences of the Reformation; instead, the memories that naturally come to mind are those of several centuries of persecution, repression, and marginalization.[3] If the rejoicing of a jubilee is completely alien for a Swedish Catholic looking back to the Reformation, it is also difficult for him to accept the weaker meaning of "honoring" the Reformation, as implied by the notion of commemoration as well. For the Reformation in Sweden was not especially honorable.

The second part of the meaning of commemoration, "to keep alive the memory of," is more suitable, but this in the form of a tragic

---

1. Patrick Hanks, ed. *Collins Concise Dictionary Plus* (London and Glasgow: Collins, 1989), s.v. "commemoration."

2. Author's translation. The search was done 2016.05.28.

3. A good example of this mode of remembrance is Magnus Nyman's overview of the Reformation and Swedish Catholicism during the sixteenth and the seventeenth centuries in his book *Förlorarnas historia* [The History of the Losers]. He writes, "This

remembering: we grieve over what we have lost. In the village where I live, for example, there is a beautiful white stone church from the twelfth century. It was thus Catholic for five hundred years before the Reformation, but has since then been a Lutheran church. Instead, I have to travel by car for half an hour to attend Mass in the Catholic church, which is a former Protestant Free Church chapel from the 1960s.[4] All the priests are Polish, and so, it seems, is half the parish.

The Swedish Catholic memory of the Reformation and its consequences is, then, one of rupture, of a loss of connection between, on the one hand, the national and local identity, and on the other hand, Catholicism—the universal Church. Every time I see my village church on the hilltop overlooking a little lake, I remember what could have been, what actually once was natural, but which now is looked upon often with suspicion, or at least seen as something strange.

It is important to emphasize that for a Swedish Catholic the living memory made present by a consideration of the Reformation is that of the Middle Ages. The imagination then stretches out to reach behind the period of five hundred years, to what preceded them, and tries to reconnect with it. For this purpose, the old traces, the material remains of the medieval period are vital, especially churches and convents; perhaps the ruins even more than the buildings taken over and modified by the Lutheran Church. They speak to us as living memories, or perhaps more correctly as dormant or repressed memories.

When I was a child, we lived on the large island of Gotland, situated in the middle of the Baltic See. Being full of medieval church ruins, it is therefore called the Island of the Hundred Churches. I remember walking into one of them one day, looking up and seeing that some of the vaults of the ceiling still remained, and that around me all of the walls were intact. I instinctively looked for the holy water font into which to dip my fingers, but, of course, I could not find it. The next place my eyes

book has slowly grown as the result of my interest in what took place from 'the perspective of the losers' during the sixteenth century in Sweden. The losers are for me primarily the Swedish Catholics and their customs and a culture that since centuries had so deeply formed Swedish mentality. Through the victories of the Reformation, Sweden was in many ways placed outside the mainstream of European culture, and many of the spiritual values that had been so laboriously built up during the Middle Ages were destroyed. How could this happen? Were the late medieval Church and culture really doomed to destruction?" Magnus Nyman, *Förlorarnas historia* (Uppsala: Katolska bok-förlaget, 1997), 19–20.

4. From 1961 to 1971, it belonged to The Mission Covenant Church of Sweden. http://www.lansstyrelsen.se/vastragotaland/SiteCollectionDocuments/Sv/publikationer/2014/2014-34/bilaga-5-alvsborg-3.pdf.

searched for was where the tabernacle would have been. I saw a cubic hole somewhere in the chancel, and in my imagination, the old stone structure came to life. Once again, it had a beating heart.

It startled me, when I found toward the end of writing this article how central the Eucharist had become to my act of remembering. The divine sacrifice had grown in strength during my reflections, as the organ in Oliver Messiaen's work *Apparition de l'église éternelle*, which slowly, powerfully—and, as it seems, filled with pain—moves to a crescendo. With the Eucharist, my commemoration moved from the theme of human memory and history to that of divine presence and sacrifice. The Greek word *anamnesis* (remembrance), which lies behind the command of Jesus translated into English as "Do this in remembrance of me," both deepened my historical reflections and brought them into the heart of Catholic-Lutheran controversy.[5] The main question became the interconnection between different understandings of human history and of the Eucharist. And the word *anamnesis* proved to play a central role.

The Relevance of Sweden

The particular history of Sweden is, I believe, not only of relevance for us living in this country. The form that Lutheranism took in our land and the form of modernization that emerged when this was relaxed in the twentieth century have wider significance. Sweden is, in a sense, the test case for a more or less complete modernization and marginalization of religious belief. It is a secularist, welfare-state utopia, which, however, is showing signs of stress. Dangerous cracks have appeared in the edifice.

The canonization in June 2016 of Elisabeth Hesselblad (1870–1957), a twentieth-century Swedish convert to Catholicism, points to a competing story—that of the return of the Catholic Church to Sweden. In October of that the same year, this competing story was reinforced by the unprecedented "Joint Ecumenical Commemoration of the Reformation" in Lund, in southern Sweden. The particular significance of the lat-

---

5. For example, Dom Gregory Dix, *The Shape of the Liturgy* (London: Dacre Press), 243–47. For Plato anamnesis was a remembering of what one already knew: the eternal truths. When recapturing a tradition that seemed dead and extinct, but that slumbered under the surface, or that had taken a meandering way outside of the nation, this meaning is appropriate, as in a consideration of the Reformation and the Catholic Church in Sweden. Also, the medical meaning of anamnesis is applicable to this talk. By posing questions to the patient, the doctor probes his or her memory for information on the sickness and its course. In the same way, I am to pose certain questions to our collective memory, to our history, to understand what went wrong, why, and what we can do about it.

ter event was due to the fact that Pope Francis himself participated in it. Together with Lutheran church leaders, he led a "communal liturgy" based on the document, *The Common Prayer*, and signed a joint statement.[6]

The Complete Nature of Lutheranism in Sweden

If one looks at a map of early post-Reformation Western Europe, it is apparent that the Reformation was mainly a northern European phenomenon. Moreover, in countries like England, or what later became Germany, the Catholic Church did not disappear completely. The Nordic countries are special due to the thorough transformation of their societies in the sixteenth and seventeenth centuries made possible by the ideology of Lutheranism.

In Sweden, Lutheranism fused with the early modern state created by Gustav Vasa, who became king in 1523. This fusion and development of the state continued with some twists and turns until the end of the century.[7] With the emergence of the Swedish empire in the seventeenth century, Lutheranism became the state ideology, and it was, consequently, punishable by death to become Catholic from 1617 until 1781, after which time one was merely expelled from the country.[8] Only at foreign embassies, as those of France and Spain, could Catholic chapels and priests exist, protected by diplomatic immunity.[9]

One must, of course, mention on the other hand the extraordinary

6. Liturgical Task Force of the Lutheran-Roman Catholic Commission on Unity, "Common Prayer: From Conflict to Communion Lutheran-Catholic Common Commemoration of the Reformation in 2017" (2016), https://www.lutheranworld.org/sites/default/files/dtpw-lrc-liturgy-2016_en.pdf. Vatican Radio, "Pope and President of LWF sign Joint statement," October 31, 2016, http://en.radiovaticana.va/news/2016/10/31/pope_and_president_of_lwf_sign_joint_statement/1269150.

7. See, Martin Berntson, *Klostren och Reformationen* (Skellefteå: Artos, 2003), for an account focusing on the dissolution of the monasteries.

8. However, in his article, "Myten om enhetskyrkan" [The Myth of the Unitary Church], Martin Berntson, Associate Professor of the History of Christianity, criticizes this picture of a homogenous Sweden and state church. He probes the opposite perspective, that the hard rules and regulations put into place are symptoms of increasing pluralism during the seventeenth and eighteenth centuries. His argument is made in relation to the present teaching of history in Swedish schools and the necessity of confronting the emerging nationalism that sees immigration as a threat, and as a recent phenomenon, destroying an earlier homogenous Swedish Society. Martin Berntson, "Myten om enhetskyrkan: En diskussion om historievetenskapliga perspektiv i religionskunskapsämnet," in "Det historiska perspektivet," ed. Hans Albin Larsson, special issue, *Aktuellt om historia* nos. 2–3 (2015): 133–53.

9. Nyman, *Förlorarnas historia*, 229.

conversion to Catholicism of the Swedish Queen Kristina in 1654, which, however, I cannot treat of at length in this talk. Suffice to say that she was symbolic of a longing for European culture (the classical Catholic synthesis as incarnated in the city of Rome) and dissatisfaction with the austere restraint of the cold and sparsely populated North. She managed to draw Descartes to Stockholm, but he suffered in the cold climate and died of pneumonia after merely a few months. So far, this is the most substantial Swedish contribution to "continental" philosophy.

From 1781 immigrants were allowed to keep their Catholic Faith and build churches, but Swedes were not allowed to become Catholics, or even enter a Catholic Church. It was only by new laws in 1860 and 1873 that the government decriminalized leaving the Church of Sweden if you left it for another acknowledged Christian faith.[10] One important factor in ensuring this change was that Queen Josefina, the wife of the Swedish king, Oscar I, was Catholic. Furthermore, in 1858, six female Catholic converts had been expelled from the country, causing an international uproar.[11] But, anti-Catholicism did not die easily, and in 1910, the liberal and "ecumenical" archbishop of Sweden, Nathan Söderblom, wrote that Jesuitism was the most dangerous enemy of modern civilization, and in 1924, the bishops of the Church of Sweden issued a warning of the papist danger.[12]

In the 1950s, during the discussion of a new law providing more extensive religious freedom, which was introduced as late as 1951, some Social Democrats warned that Catholicism was anti-progressive and reactionary and that it was incompatible with the democratic values of Swedish society.[13] Before the new law, a Catholic could not, for example, be a teacher or a nurse. And it was only in the 1970s that the parliament abolished the restrictions remaining on founding monasteries. In Sweden, the Catholic-phobia of Lutheranism combined with the liberal and socialist view of the Catholic Church as the bastion of the old order and the main adversary of the new emerging modern world.[14]

During the first half of the twentieth century, Sweden developed from a Protestant nation-state with the king as its guarantor to the welfare state of the Social Democratic period, which stretched from 1932 to 1976,

---

10. Per Dahlman, *Kyrka och Stat i 1860 års svenska religionslagstiftning* (Skellefteå: Artos, 2009).

11. Yvonne Maria Werner, *Katolsk manlighet i Skandinavien Katolsk manlighet: Det antimoderna alternativet—katolska missionärer och lekmän i Skandinavien* (Göteborg: Makadam förlag, 2014), 46.

12. Yvonne Maria Werner, "Den katolska faran" *Scandia* 81: 1 (2015), 48.

13. Yvonne Maria Werner, *Katolsk manlighet i Skandinavien Katolsk manlighet*, 54.

14. Yvonne Maria Werner, "Den katolska faran," 40–61.

when it suffered its first electoral loss. In this era, the idea of a modern society was built upon a strong paternalistic state ruled by the Social Democratic Party (SAP), and was funded by high taxes. The paternalistic state knew what was best for you, and in return provided you with security and a basic level of material well-being. The state had a monopoly in many fields such as television, radio, postal services, health care, education, and railroads.[15] The goal was to a build a brave new society that cut its roots to old traditions and inequalities.[16] During the 1960s, many of the old buildings of Sweden's inner cities were torn down to make place for modernist architecture. Functionalism was the aesthetic ideal. In the twentieth century, the new Swedish state ideology was, then, modernism itself, and through this it created a decisive break with history—with the tradition of Christian civilization. The Lutheran state church, being at the mercy of the government, had to follow suit.

The first electoral loss of the Social Democratic Party in 1976 broke the interdependence of party, unions, and a strong state, but the socialist vision crumbled more decisively in 1989 with the fall of communism in Eastern Europe. The struggle to have more than two (state) television channels was ended in the 1990s, when the government had to admit defeat. When I was a child, no commercials were allowed on television. Besides news, entertainment, and documentaries, we could only see information from the government and its agencies. These small information films on topics such as the necessity of wearing a life jacket and not drinking while driving a boat, or remembering to submit your income tax return form in time were the closest that we came to commercials. When satellite dishes were introduced in the 1980s, a Social Democratic politician, Maj Britt Theorin, argued that private persons should be prohibited from owning such dangerous devices:

> Give the children a chance, for heaven's sake; let them be spared advertising on television. Our party should no longer crouch in the wind of the right and commercialism; we must go on a counter-attack against the exploiters of freedom of speech, whatever seductive guise they appear in.[17]

Severe restrictions were also the method proposed in the late 1980s by the new environmentalist party, all, they said, for the purpose of protecting the children. However, in 1993, the radio monopoly was abol-

---

15. Sven Aspling, *100 år i Sverige: vägen till folkhemmet* (Stockholm: Tiden, 1992).

16. Karl-Olov Arnstberg, *Miljonprogrammet* (Stockholm: Carlsson, 2000).

17. https://sv.wikiquote.org/wiki/Maj_Britt_Theorin. See also, http://data.riksdage n.se/fil/6348FA5E-5E99-4F97-B8BF-EDB9E5B52D3D.

ished.[18] Before that there was a pirate radio station in Sweden broadcasting from a boat in the Baltic Sea, and a Swedish television channel (TV3) based in London.

It is vital for a discussion of religion in Sweden to understand that the country has just emerged from this rather totalitarian state of affairs. And, I would like to add, conscientious objection in health care is not recognized, nor is, for example, homeschooling.[19]

Even since the state church system in several respects was dismantled in the year 2000, the political parties have kept a tight grip on the Church of Sweden. The members of the church assembly, together with those of local and regional assemblies, are appointed through general elections. In these, the political parties have their special groups. The Social Democrats are the largest force in the church assembly, but the former Communist Party is also represented as well as the new nationalist party, The Sweden Democrats.

The church is, therefore, thoroughly politicized and, furthermore, dependent upon the state for its financing. A Social Democratic politician recently even publicly admitted that she was not a believer, but that the church stood for good values, and therefore she was entering church politics as a candidate.[20]

This development has not been without criticism. An example of individual high profile protest is when Eva Hamberg, a professor of theology, priest in the Church of Sweden, and member of its highest teaching committee left the church and her assignments in 2013. She said that she deemed it no longer possible to be a member due to the level of internal secularization within the church. The last straw was the public questioning of candidates for the office of archbishop, something that is part of the regular election procedure. Antje Jackelén, who that year became the first female archbishop, could not answer clearly whether Jesus or Mohammed provided the best image of God, and, Hamberg noticed, even considered that the virgin birth was metaphorical.[21]

However, no strong organized opposition to modernization in the name of tradition seems possible, for, in a sense, the Swedish tradition *is*

18. Still today, if you own a television set you have to pay a special fee that goes to SVT, the state television.

19. Anna Heino et al., "Conscientious objection and induced abortion in Europe" *European Journal of Contraception & Reproductive Health Care* 18, no. 4 (2013): 232.

20. Magnus Jarefors, "Margareta Winberg (S) på väg in i politiken igen," *Östersundsposten*, June 7, 2013, www.op.se/jamtland/ostersund/margareta-winberg-s-pa-vag-in-i-politiken-igen.

21. Richard Ringqvist, "Ledande teolog går ur Svenska kyrkan," Dagen, October 10, 2013, www.dagen.se/ledande-teolog-gar-ur-svenska-kyrkan-1.106846.

modernization. At the same time, the Church of Sweden is losing members in what looks like an inevitable decline. The percentage of Swedes considering themselves members is falling precipitously. In 1972, 95.2% of the population thought of itself as members of the church. By 2015, that number had gone down to 63.2%.[22] And of those only approximately 3% went to Sunday service every week.[23]

I would like to emphasize that the function of Lutheranism in Sweden as state ideology did not abruptly end when ushering in the creation of a modern liberal secular state. The two ideals of a strong state (Lutheranism and the welfare state) walked together during the twentieth century. The Social Democrats have been adamant regarding not letting go of the control of the Lutheran Church, as the kings had been before them. This very close connection between state, modernization, and religion (that is, ideology) colored the form of modernity and secularity emerging in Sweden (The Swedish Model) and is an important factor to be considered when discussing the legacy of Luther, given that it was in the Nordic countries that Lutheranism was most completely put into practice.

Swedish Modernism

Building on the ideological and social system enabled by Lutheranism, a particular form of modernism (modernist consciousness) emerged in Sweden during the twentieth century, which in a global overview seems extreme. This comes out clearly in the chart of the "World Value Survey 2015," which has two axes: "traditional vs. secular-rational values," and "survival vs. self-expression values."[24] "Secular-rational values" reflect preferences opposite to "traditional values." Societies possessing these values place less emphasis on religion, traditional family values, and authority. Divorce, abortion, euthanasia, and suicide are seen by them as relatively acceptable.[25] "Self-expression values" give high priority to environmental protection, growing tolerance of foreigners, gays and lesbians, gender equality, and rising demands for participation in decision-making in economic and political life.[26]

---

22. "Svenska kyrkans medlemsutveckling år 1972-2014" www.svenskakyrkan.se/default.aspx?id=1470789.

23. Jan Strid, "Tro, religion och kyrkobesök i Göteborg," in *En region för alla? Medborgare, människor och medier i Västsverige*, eds. Annika Bergström & Jonas Ohlsson (Göteborg: Göteborgs Universitet SOM-institutet, 2013), 219.

24. www.worldvaluessurvey.org/images/Cultural_map_WVS6_2015.jpg.

25. www.worldvaluessurvey.org/WVSContents.jsp.

26. Ibid.

The countries most influenced by Lutheranism are all present in the upper right corner with Sweden as the most extreme case, combining the level of secular rationality of Japan with the self-expression value of Canada. The level of importance given to religion by Swedes, also a part of the World Value Survey, is not encouraging—that is, if you are sincere believer. For example, 78% of people below twenty-nine years of age considered religion as either not at all important (51%) or not very important (27%).[27] Only 6.2% considered religion very important. One can understand the culture shock experienced when coming from North Africa, in the lower left corner, to Sweden. The ideological distance is immense.

Canonization of Elisabeth Hesselblad

My *anamnesis* up to this point has indicated how complete the break with Catholicism became after a few generations, and how in the twentieth century, Lutheranism, as managed by the state church, became infused with the modernist ideology underlying the Social Democratic welfare state.

The direction of my argument is that what Sweden is, other parts of the Western World might become. Sweden is on a trajectory of modernization that many other nations and countries seem determined to travel. The end point is a more or less complete break with the idea of tradition. This was initiated by the Reformation and perfected by secular ideologies during the twentieth century.

However, with the return of the Catholic Church in the late nineteenth century a discourse of resistance that had Archimedean points outside of the Swedish nation state was introduced. Instead of the revolutionary principle inherent in Protestantism, it rested on the idea of an unbroken tradition and on the papal Magisterium standing outside and above secular governments. It was, as I have said, looked upon with suspicion, as it was, by its very nature, subversive to the closed Swedish society.[28] I believe that the Swedish situation points to processes, some necessary, some possible, and some impossible, when not only the Catholic tradition has been decisively broken, but the very idea of tradition.

In Sweden, the Catholic tradition had to be reintroduced. But what,

---

27. "F00001433-WV6_Results_Sweden_2011_v_2016_01_01.pdf"www.worldvalues-survey.org/WVSDocumentationWV6.jsp.

28. Of course, Catholicism can also become a kind of national ideology, but such variants of Gallicanism always live in a fundamental contradiction with the universal nature of the Catholic Church, and its Petrine office.

then, would one make of "Swedish" Catholicism, as these streams of tradition had flowed through the history of other nations, and were distinctively colored by other cultures and languages? In Sweden, a scenario of nationalist Catholicism is unrealistic, and this Swedish situation is more instructive for the future of the Catholic Church than the dying national churches of, let us say, Italy, France, or Ireland. In these countries, one can dream of a return to a unified national culture and with it a rebirth of Catholicism. To become a true Italian would then also mean becoming, once again, a true Catholic. Presently, when becoming a member of the Catholic Church, a Swede enters into a multi-ethnic mélange of languages and cultures.

However, in the beginning of the twentieth century, this was not so, and the Catholic Church was still very small. In 1940, there were just 5,200 Catholics in Sweden.[29] Of these, half were born in Sweden, while in 1995 those born in Sweden made up less than 10% of all Catholics.[30]

One of the Swedish converts to Catholicism in the early twentieth century was Elisabeth Hesselblad, who was canonized June 5, 2016. Her life story illustrates in an illuminating way how the Swedish, the universal, and the international combine. Due to the poverty of her family in Sweden, Hesselblad emigrated to the United States in 1888 and trained and worked as a nurse. Meeting many Catholics, she became interested in the Faith, and in 1902 she was received into the Catholic Church. At the same time, she became sick with what she thought was a fatal illness: a bleeding ulcer. Therefore, she did not finish her studies to become a doctor, but travelled to Rome, to die, as she thought, in the holy city. Instead, she experienced a calling to bring back the Brigittine Order to Rome, to the house in Piazza Farnese where St Brigid (1303–1373) had lived. At that time, Carmelite nuns were staying there, and in 1906 she was received into the Carmelite order, but wearing a Brigittine habit. Nevertheless, in 1911, she managed to found a small community of Brigittine nuns in the *Casa di Santa Brigida*. And in 1923, she also established a convent in Sweden, although due to the anti-monastery legislation it had to be designated as a sanatorium.

The mission of St Elisabeth Hesselblad was to work for Christian unity, and that mission was carried out by a particular act of *anamnesis*, both remembering and making alive Swedish Catholic history, establishing a link to the Middle Ages and St Brigid. At the same time, it was

---

29. Gärde, Johan, *Från invandrarkyrka till mångkulturellt samfund: En kyrkosociologisk analys av katolska kyrkan i Sverige från 1970-tal till 1990-tal* (PhD thesis Uppsala University, 1999), 92.

30. Gärde, *Från invandrarkyrka till mångkulturellt samfund*, 97.

international, receiving its inspiration from both the United States and Rome. A telling incident from the saint's life was when she, a priest, and a few Catholics sneaked into the Blue Church, the old church of the Brigittine motherhouse monastery in Vadstena, Sweden, very early in the morning of July 24, 1923, to celebrate a Catholic Mass in secret. It was the first Mass for almost four hundred years in that church, and now with a Brigittine nun present once again. In Hesselblad's own words:

> It was a moving moment in the silent morning hour. The holy words of the priest echoed throughout the spacious church; at that moment, the whole atmosphere changed; the once cold and desolate sanctuary was filled with a richness that no human words can describe.[31]

In this episode, commemoration is central: the honoring and enlivening of the memory of the medieval Catholic Church in Sweden was combined with the *anamnesis* at the heart of the Eucharistic sacrifice. By means of this reconnection over several centuries, anchored in the transcendent axis, the Lutheran period was seen as a gap, a deplorable hiatus, which was closed, and with it, the fabric of tradition restored. In this event, the central role played by the religious orders in Swedish Catholic culture was also highlighted. It was because of this role that it was natural and inevitable for the Reformation in Sweden to abolish the convents, and so necessary for the return and revival of Catholicism that these were reinstated and reinvigorated.[32]

Post-Babel Church

However, the Catholic Church that took shape in Sweden from the 1960s onward was of a different character.[33] With the Second Vatican Council, the Church as an alternative to modernity was weakened. Some intellectual converts, as, for example, also in England, experienced this development as a shock. The alternative to which one had turned instead surprisingly embraced modernity at the height of modernist frenzy in the 1960s, moving closer to Protestantism in many respects in the process. Instead of reconnecting to the dormant heritage of medieval times, one's gaze became directed toward the bright future of the western world.

---

31. Björn Göransson, *Maria Elisabeth Hesselblad: Ett helgon från Sverige* (Ängelholm: Catholica, 2016), 133. Author's translation.

32. See Martin Berntson, *Klostren och Reformation* (Skellefteå: Norma, 2003); Nyman, *Förlorarnas historia*.

33. Hans Hellström, ed., *Stockholms katolska stift 50 år* (Stockholm: Veritas, 2003).

Furthermore, the new practice of celebrating the Mass in the local language had unfortunate consequences in Sweden, for it was at the same time that large groups of Catholic immigrants arrived, and the diocese (there is just one in Sweden) was transformed into an umbrella for this multi-ethnic, multi-cultural and multi-lingual mix of peoples. As Swedish was not their primary language, many of them naturally instead went to, for example, the Polish, Croatian, or Philippine Mass. Presently, there are over eighty different nationalities and eighty percent of the priests are born outside of Sweden.[34] The Swedish Mass therefore cannot function as an anchor to a national identity, nor make the liturgy easy to understand for most of the parishioners. In a way, the Swedish language points toward the Swedish secular society and the Lutheran Church, while the primary languages of most parishioners are connected to Catholic customs and songs.

Latin, on the other hand, could have provided unity among all these languages and cultures. Besides this, it points back to the Middle Ages, the natural anchor of a Swedish Catholic identity, which furthermore provides a healthy cultural distance from the surrounding Swedish society. The latter is important as the parishes right now function primarily as temporary buffers for the cultural shock suffered when arriving in Sweden, and in two or three generations most are lost to the Church. To become Swedish is to become secular.

Lutheran-Catholic
Common Commemoration of the Reformation

On the last day of October 2016, in Lund, in southern Sweden, a unique inauguration of the Reformation commemoration year of 2017 took place, led by Lutheran church leaders and the pope, in an expression of ecumenical good will. The pope's choice of coming to Sweden singled out this country as the focal point for his attempts at making peace with the Reformation and the Protestant world. It also brought together the themes of my *anamnesis* into one event, as during the first half of the twelfth century, Lund was the metropolitan archdiocese not just for Sweden, but also for Norway and Denmark. That the pope came here was, therefore, significant for Swedish Catholics.[35] Still, how are we to understand this event, and what was the intention of the pope? Did he realize the importance of Swedish history, or was he more intent on a

---

34. Gärde, *Från invandrarkyrka till mångkulturellt samfund*, 226.

35. Nowadays, the archbishop of the Church of Sweden resides in Uppsala; and the Catholic bishop in Stockholm.

Lutheran-Catholic convergence in the process of modernization and *aggiornamento?*

On October 31, as part of a day of ecumenical meetings and gestures, there was a common worship service in the cathedral of Lund based on the Catholic-Lutheran "Common Prayer" liturgical guide. This, in its turn, was based on an almost one hundred-page-long joint study document entitled, *From Conflict to Communion: Lutheran-Catholic Common Commemoration of the Reformation in* 2017. I cannot at this time provide a thorough analysis of the contents of the two texts, but it will suffice to point out some tendencies relevant to the theme of this talk.

The first impression is the very positive view of Luther that runs like a red thread throughout *From Conflict to Communion*. Its background assumption is the thesis that more unites than divides Lutherans and Catholics.[36] The year of 2017 is seen as an opportunity to discuss the person and thought of Luther and "to develop perspectives for the remembrance and appropriation of the Reformation today."[37] The text paints a picture of Luther as a religious hero who found the way to a more true form of Catholicism: "The breakthrough for Catholic scholarship came with the thesis that Luther overcame within himself a Catholicism that was not fully Catholic."[38]

The combination of "remembrance and appropriation" nicely brings forth the ideas of honoring and of making present inherent in the notion of commemoration. We are not only to remember in a neutral way the Reformation, but also to appropriate its vital principles, I suppose here in the meaning of taking them to heart to internalize a never-ceasing process of reform.

In the liturgical guide, the *Common Prayer,* the positive image of Luther is even more strongly worded. The section called "Thanksgiving" is intended to express, "our mutual joy for the gifts received and rediscovered in various ways through the renewal and impulses of the Reformation." As part of this section, the pope prayed aloud in Lund:

> O Holy Spirit, help us to rejoice in the gifts that have come to the Church through the Reformation, prepare us to repent for the dividing walls that we, and our forebears, have built, and equip us for common witness and service in the world.[39]

---

36. The Lutheran World Federation & The Pontifical Council for Promoting Christian Unity, *From Conflict to Communion: Lutheran-Catholic Common Commemoration of the Reformation in 2017, Report of the Lutheran-Roman Catholic Commission on Unity* (Leipzig, Bonn: Evangelische Verlagsanstalt, Bonifatius, 2013), §1, §17.

37. *From Conflict to Communion,* §3.

38. Ibid., §21.

39. *Common Prayer,* 12.

For a Swedish Catholic it is difficult to understand what gifts the pope had in mind when reading this prayer, as the Catholic Church was thoroughly destroyed in our country through the Reformation. If this had been the case in the whole of Europe, there would not have been any Catholic Church left in the sixteenth century.

In both the Lutheran and Catholic "reading" part of the Thanksgiving section, it is Luther and his works toward which thanksgiving is expressed. First, the Lutheran reading states that "Lutherans are thankful in their hearts for what Luther and the other reformers made accessible to them"[40] and the Catholic reading concludes by saying that "[t]he ecumenical journey enables Lutherans and Catholics to appreciate together Martin Luther's insight into and spiritual experience of the Gospel of the righteousness of God, which is also God's mercy."[41]

One of the two "presiders," the leader of the Lutheran World Federation, then concluded this section with the following prayer of gratitude for the Reformation:

> Thanks be to you, O God, for the many guiding theological and spiritual insights that we have all received through the Reformation. Thanks be to you for the good transformations and reforms that were set in motion by the Reformation or by struggling with its challenges. Thanks be to you for the proclamation of the Gospel that occurred during the Reformation and that since then has strengthened countless people to live lives of faith in Jesus Christ. Amen.[42]

After expressing repentance and regret for the mutual exaggeration and caricature (and physical and psychological violence) by Lutherans and Catholics in the sixteenth century, participants exchanged a sign of peace. There followed the reading of the Gospel on the true vine (John 15:1–5) and a common sermon delivered by the two presiders. The instruction emphasizes that the sermon should focus on Christ as the center and on the commemoration of the Reformation, which should be a celebration of Jesus Christ, since the reformers saw their main task in pointing to Christ as "the way, the truth, and the life" and calling people to trust in Christ. Christ should be celebrated, as Martin Luther and the other reformers only sought to be "witnesses to Christ." The pope in his part of the sermon very much followed these instructions. Besides the themes of reconciliation and the path to unity, he included a positive presentation of the Lutheran doctrine of justification with its

40. Ibid., 13.
41. Ibid.
42. Ibid.

central principle of grace alone, which the pope interpreted as the fact that "God always takes the initiative."[43]

Then "the five imperatives" were ritually read: to begin always from the perspective of unity; to let ourselves be transformed in the encounter with each other; to seek visible unity; to rediscover the power of the Gospel for our time; and to give witness together of the mercy of God.

Between these readings, children successively lit one of the five large candles standing behind the altar close to a cross from El Salvador painted with bright colors. Lena Sjöstrand, priest in the Lund parish, said that for her the cross describes "the journey of the people of God from the baptismal font to the Eucharistic table, and it is a common symbol for the meeting on October 31."[44] And, quite rightly, at the bottom of the cross is a baptismal font with the vine and grapes, plus a dove and an earth globe. In the center of the cross, Jesus is seated at a table inviting everyone to come and take part in bread, wine, and fish. Surrounding the table is a multitude of people from many different parts of the world, rejoicing but not all directed toward the table. The interpretation of this as an open Eucharistic table of which all Christians, without discrimination, partake is plain and obvious. This is significant, given that the prayer service in the Lund Cathedral did not include a Eucharistic section, but only readings, a profession of faith, and psalms. Still, the ceremony contained this direction toward a projected second part, as a promise of what is to come: the concrete manifestation of full unity is the common Eucharist, open both to Lutherans and Catholics.

In the short talk following the five imperatives, the female Norwegian bishop, Helga Haugland Byfuglien, emphasized the intention to strive toward a common Eucharist. She said that:

> Many members yearn to receive the Eucharist at one table, as the concrete expression of full unity. We long for this wound in the body of Christ to be healed. This is the goal of our ecumenical endeavours. Now we call upon all Catholic and Lutheran parishes and communities to be bold and creative.[45]

That the primary goal of the ecumenical process from the Lutheran part was not doctrinal and organizational unity but intercommunion was

---

43. "Pope's Homily at Ecumenical Prayer Service in Lund," https://zenit.org/articles/popes-homily-at-ecumenical-prayer-service-in-lund, last modified October 31, 2016.

44. Jacob Zetterman, "Hans kors inleder gudstjänsten i Lund," *Dagen*, October 27, 2016, http://www.dagen.se/hans-kors-inleder-gudstjansten-i-lund-1.796644.

45. "Gudstjänst från Lunds domkyrka med påve Franciskus," video at svtplay.se, 1.13.23–1.15.37, www.svtplay.se/video/10848033/gudstjanst-fran-lunds-domkyrka-med-pave-franciskus/gudstjanst-fran-lunds-domkyrka-med-pave-franciskus-31-okt-14-30.

also clearly expressed on the webpage of the Church of Sweden before the event. To the question, "Is there an effort/dream of becoming a united church again?"[46] the answer was as follows:

> What we foremost wish is that the common celebration of the Eucharist will be officially possible. This is especially important for families where members belong to different denominations. The prayer of Jesus that we all may be one is a guide for us. The visible unity (which is not automatically the same as organizational unity) so that the world will believe is our mission and our goal.[47]

This theme was emphasized in the article "Divided Christianity Travels Together toward the Future," by the present archbishop of the Church of Sweden, Antje Jackelén.[48] Her act of commemoration is self-critical and even mentions Luther's anti-Semitism, but it ends by first quoting Pope Francis on the reception of the Eucharist in mixed Catholic-Lutheran marriages:

> The pope recently was asked by a Lutheran woman married with a Catholic how they could receive the Eucharist together instead of separately each in their own church. The pope reminded the woman that we have the same baptism and that the spouses walk a common road. "And you should also teach your children that, irrespective if it is done in a Lutheran or Catholic way," he said. Regarding differences in the view of the Eucharist between Lutherans and Catholics the pope pointed out, "Life is larger than explanations and interpretations! Think always of the baptism. One Faith, one baptism, one Lord, that is what Paul tells us. And draw your conclusions from that. . . . Pray to the Lord and walk the way forward."[49]

46. "Frågor och svar om påvebesöket i Lund," last modified May 11, 2016, www.svenskakyrkan.se/lundsstift/fragor-och-svar-om-pavebesoket-i-lund.

47. Ibid. Author's translation.

48. Antje Jackelén, "Delad kristenhet reser gemensamt mot framtiden," *Svenska dagbladet,* January 24, 2016, http://www.svd.se/delad-kristenhet-reser-gemensamt-mot-framtiden.

49. Ibid. Author's translation. Then the archbishop quotes Cardinal Walter Kasper saying that ecumenism and catholicity are two sides of the same coin: that the complete realization of Catholicism is possible only through ecumenical exchange. In the same spirit, the Cardinal is also to have said that ecumenism does not mean the conversion of one church to another, but the conversion of everyone to Christ. I suppose more detailed insights into the mind of Cardinal Kasper on this issue can be found in his recently released book on Luther (with the subtheme of mercy), *Martin Lutero: Una prospettiva ecumenica* (Brescia: Editrice Queriniana, 2016) which has also appeared in English as *Martin Luther: An Ecumenical Perspective* (Mahwah, NJ: Paulist Press, 2016).

Furthermore, before the arrival of the pope in Sweden, the Catholic bishop, William Kenney, a former auxiliary bishop in Sweden, expressed his wish for an opening up of the possibility of intercommunion:

> If I wanted Francis to cause a pleasant revolution in Lund, he would say Lutherans can, under certain circumstances, without asking all the time, receive the Eucharist. That would be a major gesture. The sort of thing I would like to see is that in a so-called ecumenical marriage, the non-Catholic party can always go to Communion with his or her partner. That would be a major step forward, and it's pastorally very desirable.[50]

So there were prominent Catholic voices supporting the primary goal of the Lutheran part in the ecumenical dialogue: that is, concrete moves toward a common Eucharist. Still, the pope made no sensational announcements or controversial gestures, keeping very close to the script during the two days in Sweden. However, after the talk of Bishop Byfuglien, the pope, together with Bishop Munib Younan, President of the Lutheran World Federation, signed a joint statement that contained a paragraph about the Eucharist, echoing Byfuglien's words:

> Many members of our communities yearn to receive the Eucharist at one table, as the concrete expression of full unity. We experience the pain of those who share their whole lives, but cannot share God's redeeming presence at the eucharistic table. We acknowledge our joint pastoral responsibility to respond to the spiritual thirst and hunger of our people to be one in Christ. We long for this wound in the Body of Christ to be healed. This is the goal of our ecumenical endeavours, which we wish to advance, also by renewing our commitment to theological dialogue.[51]

It is important to note that the verbs used all express feelings. People "yearn," "long for" healing, "feel" pain, thirst, and hunger. To this existential desire a pastoral response is put forward, the goal of the whole ecumenical work. However, no attention is given to the question of the Real Presence in the Eucharist and its spiritual effects. The focus is on the subjective desires and the pastoral responsibility to fulfill them. Consequently, the theological dialogue on the question of the Eucharist is sub-

---

50. Austen Ivereigh, "Pope in Sweden Could Break Ground on Inter-communion, Bishop Says," *Crux*, October 21, 2016, https://cruxnow.com/interviews/2016/10/21/pope-sweden-break-ground-inter-communion-bishop-says.

51. "Joint Statement on the Occasion of the Joint Catholic-Lutheran Commemoration of the Reformation," Vatican Radio, last modified October 31, 2016, http://en.radio-vaticana.va/news/2016/10/31/pope_and_president_of_lwf_sign_joint_statement/1269150.

ordinated to feelings and tasked with finding ways to lessen the dogmatic differences in order to fulfill this desire of Eucharistic unity. It does not, therefore, come as a surprise when, in *From Conflict to Communion*, the Council of Trent is presented as primarily a reaction to *perceived* Protestant errors, and thus not quite authentic. With the Second Vatican Council, the text states, the Church could correct its infelicitous defensive and confessional approach, which was not suitable for an ecumenical conversation where the emphasis is on what unites, not what divides.

This narrative comes to a critical point under the heading "Catholic Concerns Regarding the Eucharist." As regards the doctrine of "Transubstantiation," the text says, "This concept seemed, in the Catholic view, to be the best guarantee for maintaining the real presence of Jesus Christ in the species of bread and wine and for assuring that the full reality of Jesus Christ is present in each of the species."[52] To use the verb "seem" clearly indicates that this has not objective value for Catholics and that other notions could be used for the same purpose and perhaps even with better effect.

Regarding the sacrificial nature of the Eucharist, the theme of conceptual insecurity is continued in that Catholics of the sixteenth century are portrayed as having struggled to express the Eucharist as a sacrifice, but that due to lack of "adequate categories," they had to wait until Vatican II for the concept of commemoration (*anamnesis*). As a result of the loss of an integrative concept of commemoration, Catholics were faced with the difficulty of the lack of adequate categories with which to express the sacrificial character of the Eucharist. Committed to a tradition going back to patristic times, Catholics did not want to abandon the identification of the Eucharist as a real sacrifice even while they struggled to affirm the identity of this Eucharistic sacrifice with the unique sacrifice of Christ. The renewal of sacramental and liturgical theology as articulated in the Second Vatican Council was needed to revitalize the concept of commemoration (*anamnesis*).[53]

In *From Conflict to Communion*, the notion of commemoration, consequently, provides a crucial link between the Eucharist and the Reformation Year of 2017. This interpretive key signals not only the intention of the text to honor the Reformation and the act of keeping its memory alive, but also that this form of remembering points the way to a common understanding of the Eucharist; a development that it says was enabled by the Second Vatican Council.

---

52. *From Conflict to Communion*, §149.

53. Ibid., §151. The basis for passages on the Eucharist is *The 1978 Lutheran-Roman Catholic Final Report on the Eucharist.*

Consequently, under the heading, "Convergence in Understanding Eucharistic Sacrifice," the tool put forward is the very notion of *anamnesis*, which is supposed to unite the different approaches of Catholics and Lutherans in a common understanding of the Eucharist:

> This convergence, however, must be zealously enforced. The liturgical form of the holy meal must, however, exclude everything that could give the impression of repetition or completion of the sacrifice on the cross. If the understanding of the Lord's Supper as a real remembrance is consistently taken seriously, the differences in understanding the eucharistic sacrifice are tolerable for Catholics and Lutherans.[54]

However, such a principle requires interpretation: what is "an impression" if not something existing in the eye of the beholder? Why not simply dissuade from repetition or completion themselves? A focus on appearance and impressions can be used to dilute a Catholic understanding of the sacrificial nature of the Eucharist, and with it the sacrificial role of the priest. That the text also adds the remark that the practice of Eucharistic adoration should not diminish the meal character of the Eucharist indicates a Protestant tendency.

With the last two years of intense emphasis upon mercy and the reception of the Eucharist in mind (including an apparent approval by the pope of intercommunion in precisely the kind of case that the Church of Sweden mentions as especially important), it is not wholly surprising if a similar controversy appears as the concrete result of the visit of the pope to Sweden.[55] I would not be surprised if a joint document on the Eucharist will come to light in the not so distant future, probably as a result of the work of a committee that will have tried to address this yearning for Eucharistic unity and be "bold and creative."

Final Thoughts

As I said in the beginning, I was somewhat surprised that the theme of the Eucharist increased in strength as I worked with this article. In the notion of commemoration, *anamnesis*, the central act of the Eucharist and my historical exploration came together. The perfect symbol of this is the Mass that Elisabeth Hesselblad and her fellow Catholics celebrated

---

54. Ibid., §159.

55. For an indication that something of the sort is intended, see the translation of part of Giancarlo Pani's article in *La Civiltà Catholica,* on Sandro Magister's blog *Chiesa,* July 1, 2016, "Communion For All, Even for Protestants," chiesa.espresso.repubblica.it/ articolo/1351332?eng=y.

in the Blue Church in 1923, re-establishing the link with the medieval Church through both the Eucharist and the physical building of the church. In this way, divine presence and sacrifice enriched the human act of remembrance and provided it with transformative power.

In the documents written for the "Lutheran Catholic Common Commemoration of the Reformation," the notion of *anamnesis* is also used as the connecting link between the historical imagination and the Eucharist. However, in Sweden the danger is that this form of *anamnesis* instead turns into amnesia, as in 2014 when the Uppsala diocese of the Church of Sweden celebrated its 850-year jubilee. In the exhibitions and brochures connected to this jubilee, the organizers presented the Church of Sweden (a name coined in the nineteenth century) as if it had a continuous history back to the ninth century. In protest, twelve Swedish Catholic university professors wrote the article "The Church of Sweden Tries to Monopolize History."[56]

> This view of history is also present on the Church of Sweden's homepage. During the Middle Ages, the Church of Sweden was part of the Roman Catholic Church. Then many of the churches in which we celebrate Mass were built. . . . During the Middle Ages, the Church in Sweden was under the authority of the pope. This was changed during the reformation in the sixteenth century. Then an autonomous Swedish national church took form with an Evangelical-Lutheran confession and the king as the head of the national church.[57]

The continuity thesis of the Church of Sweden and the institutional form of memory it creates stands in tension to that of Swedish Catholics, who see themselves as the exiled Church that has returned. Therefore, for me and, I think, for many "native" Swedish Catholics, the best symbol for the Catholic Church is the medieval church ruins, where the rupture is so obvious—where the Eucharistic sacrifice has not been celebrated since the Middle Ages. In those places, our *anamnesis* becomes almost a physical experience of presence; one can sense the sleeping potential of a rebirth made possible by the sacrifice of the Mass. And perhaps this is the main relevance of the Swedish situation for the worldwide Catholic Church. It speaks of a period after complete rupture, when nothing seems to be left; it speaks about the possibility of

56. Anders Piltz, "Svenska kyrkan försöker ta monopol på historien" September 10, 2014, http://www.dagen.se/debatt/svenska-kyrkan-forsoker-ta-monopol-pa-historien-1.92453

57. Author's translation. "The History of the Church of Sweden" https://www.svenskakyrkan.se/historik, last modified April 24, 2016.

once again celebrating the Eucharistic sacrifice in the old stone ruin, with its Gothic arches and the sky as roof.

To this one could add that Swedish history provides a witness of the danger of being too closely connected to a national identity or a state. It points to the importance of the universal Church and of a *lingua franca*.

Finally, I would like to tell you that when the Catholic Church in the 1980s got permission to build a new church on Gotland within the medieval city walls of its capital, Visby, the archeologists, when doing their obligatory excavation, found a house structure. Amazingly, the position of its walls matched exactly those on the blueprint of the proposed new church, which was then symbolically built on top of the old structure. They also found a head of a Christ figure and some rosary beads. Therefore, half of the church is old and beneath the ground, while the other half is new and above ground.

About the Contributors

Miguel Ayuso

Miguel Ayuso is Professor of Constitutional Law at Comillas Pontifical University (Madrid), President of the International Union of Catholic Lawyers (Rome), President of the Sectorial Group in Political Science of the International Federation of Catholic Universities (Paris), and Editor of *Verbo* (Madrid). Author of many books and articles on political philosophy, law, and Catholic themes in general, he regularly organizes and participates in conferences throughout Europe and the entire Hispanic world.

Msgr. Ignacio Barreiro-Carámbula

Msgr. Ignacio Barreiro-Carámbula was born in Montevideo, Uruguay in 1947. After receiving his legal doctorate, he entered the foreign service of his country. He was for more than five years member of the delegation of Uruguay to the U.N. In 1983 he entered Dunwoodie Seminary in New York, and in 1987 was ordained a priest. In 1991 he started his studies at the University of Holy Cross in Rome. In 1996 he received a doctorate in Systematic Theology. From 1998 to 2015 he was director of the Rome Office of Human Life International (HLI). In this position he traveled many times to the U.S. From 2010 to 2011 he was the interim president of HLI. He has been chaplain and lecturer for the Roman Forum since the early nineties. He was written extensively on theological and historical matters for English and Spanish publications.

Clemens Cavallin

Clemens Cavallin was born in 1969 in Lund, Sweden. In 1995, after finishing his undergraduate work in philosophy, art history, and religious studies—and after five years studying painting at the Art Academy Valand in Gothenburg Sweden, he began his Ph.D. studies in History of Religion. He defended his doctoral thesis in 2002 on Vedic religion and began working at the University of Bergen in Norway in 2003. In 2007 he returned to the University of Gothenburg in Sweden, where he is presently Associate Professor in History of Religions in the Department of Literature, History of Ideas, and Religion. Cavallin's broad research interests include Hinduism, Ritual theory, and Catholic Studies. His thesis, *The Efficacy of Sacrifice* (2002), falls within the first field, more precisely focusing on Vedic sacrifices, while his second book, *Ritualization and Human Interiority* (2013) is within the second field of ritual theory. Within Catholic Studies he has written on the novels of the Canadian Catholic artist and author Michael O'Brien, as well as a biography of his life (2017). He is presently coediting a book on religious studies institutions in India and is working on a project analyzing the life stories of Christians practicing yoga. He is an active artist, painting portraits, and also on commissions from churches.

Christopher A. Ferrara, Esq.

Christopher A. Ferrara is an attorney and founder (1990), President, and Chief Counsel of the American Catholic Lawyers Association, Inc., specializing in First Amendment and civil rights law. He is a featured writer for *The Remnant*, author of hundreds of articles and six books, including the widely acclaimed *The Church and the Libertarian*, a defense of Catholic social teaching, and two books from Angelico Press: *The Great Facade*, a co-authored study of changes in the Church since Vatican II; and *Liberty, the God That Failed*, a brilliant retelling of American history and political life.

Rev. John Hunwicke

Fr John Hunwicke, an Oxford graduate in *Litterae Humaniores* and Theology, spent 43 years in the priesthood of the Church of England, during which time he served three curacies and was a parish priest. For 28 years he was a chaplain and Head of Theology at Lancing College, where he mainly taught Latin and Greek language and literature, and later a Senior Research Fellow at Pusey House in Oxford (an academic center and library in the Anglo-Catholic tradition). He joined the Ordinariate of our Lady of Walsingham at its inception in 2011, and now from his retirement gives lectures and conferences when invited to do so. His blog is called *Father Hunwicke's Mutual Enrichment.*

Brian McCall

Having received his B.A. from Yale University and his Masters at King's College, University of London, Professor McCall obtained his law degree from the University of Pennsylvania, after which he joined the international law firm of Dechert LLP, where he focused on cross-border mergers and acquisitions, and corporate finance transactions. In 1999 he transferred to the firm's London office and in 2004 was elected a partner of the firm. There he worked on many ground-breaking transactions. Professor McCall is now Associate Dean for Academic Affairs, Associate Director of the Law Center at the University of Oklahoma, Director of Legal Assistant Education, and Orpha and Maurice Merrill Professor in Law. He is the author of many articles and books, including *The Church and the Usurers: Unprofitable Lending for the Modern Economy* (Sapientia Press of Ave Maria University 2013) and *To Build the City of God* (Angelico Press, 2014).

Sebastian Morello

Sebastian Morello is a formator and lecturer at the Centre for Catholic Formation in the Archdiocese of Southwark. A convert to Catholicism, Sebastian has studied scripture, philosophy and theology in India, Italy, and England. He is a frequent speaker at Catholic conferences and events and is heavily involved in initiatives to encourage liberal arts education in London.

Rev. Richard A. Munkelt

Rev. Richard A. Munkelt, a convert to Catholicism, is a priest working in the New York metropolitan area, where he celebrates the Traditional Latin Mass. Angelico Press has published two works with extensive introductions by Fr. Munkelt: *Compendium of Theology* by St. Thomas Aquinas and *The Political and Social Ideas of St. Augustine*. Fr. Munkelt holds a doctorate in philosophy, has taught at Fairfield University and other colleges, and is a chaplain of the Roman Forum. He is currently writing a book on the social crisis of late modernity.

Rev. Brian Muzás

Rev. Muzás is Assistant Professor of Diplomacy and International Relations at the School of Diplomacy and International Relations of Seton Hall University. Having completed a B.S.E. in mechanical and aerospace engineering at Princeton University in 1996 and an M.S. in aeronautics at the California Institute of Technology in 1998, he then entered seminary. After receiving an M.Div. in pastoral ministry, an M.A. in systematic theology, and two John Paul II Medals for academic accomplishment at Seton Hall University, Father Muzás was ordained a Catholic priest in

2003, and in 2007 assigned to the priest community at Seton Hall University, where he served for a year as a full-time adjunct in the School of Diplomacy and International Relations. Despite such well-rounded activities, it was a Harrington Fellowship that ultimately allowed Father Muzás to pursue scholarship at University of Texas in Austin that drew on all aspects of his background. He graduated with his Ph.D. in Public Policy in 2013. Father Muzás' research interests include international security, defense systems, and ethics, and he is currently exploring how religious cultural heritage has influenced nuclear decisions in the past in order to better understand similar issues today.

John C. Rao

John C. Rao obtained his doctorate in Modern European History from Oxford University in 1977. He worked in 1978–1979 as Eastern Director of the Intercollegiate Studies Institute in Bryn Mawr, PA, and is now Associate Professor of European History at St. John's University in New York City, where he has taught since 1979. Dr. Rao is also director of the Roman Forum, a Catholic cultural organization (www.romanforum.org) founded by the late Professor Dietrich von Hildebrand in 1968. He writes for numerous French, German, Spanish, and Italian journals. Many of his writings can be found online (jcrao.freeshell.org). Perhaps the most important of his works are *Americanism and the Collapse of the Church in the United States* (Roman Forum Press, 1995), *Black Legends and the Light of the World* (Remnant Press, 2012), and *Removing the Blindfold* (The Angelus Press, 2014), a discussion of Catholics rediscovering their own heritage in the post-French revolutionary era.

Thomas Heinrich Stark

Thomas Stark is Ordinarius at the Philosophisch-Theologische Hochschule, St. Pölten, Austria, and Professor for Philosophical Anthropology and Metaphysics at the Philosophisch-Theologische Hochschule Benedikt XVI in Heiligenkreuz Austria. After obtaining degrees and diplomas in philosophy and theology in the course of the 1980s, he earned his doctorate from the University of Eichstätt in 1995. Interdisciplinary in his wide interests and writings, his chief fields of study are philosophical anthropology, the philosophy of religion and culture, and general spiritual and cultural history. Stark has been closely involved in the Cusanuswerk and the John Henry Newman Instituts für Christliche Weltanschauung. He also spent some years in the banking industry before being able to dedicate himself entirely to his vocation as philosopher, teacher, and writer.

62483534R00175

Made in the USA
Lexington, KY
08 April 2017